SLOW TRAVEL

North Devon & Exmoor

Local, characterful guides to Britain's special places

Hilary Bradt

EDITION 1

Bradt Travel Guides Ltd, UK
The Globe Pequot Press Inc, USA

North Devon & Exmoor

From fishing villages to lonely moorland, from the South West Coast Path to bridleways, this is a landscape that invites Slow travel. For visitors there's the extra bonus of cliff railways and steam trains, not to mention the ubiquitous cream tea. The region has it all.

1 Clovelly Harbour. 2 Pony-trekking on Exmoor. 3 The cliff railway between Lynton and Lynmouth. 4 A classic cream tea. 5 Walking the South West Coast Path.

1

RURAL LIFE

The region's landscape is just as inviting in winter as summer, especially for walkers who will have the place to themselves. It's a tough time for farmers, who look forward to agricultural shows later in the year. The villages have a timeless quality: thatched cottages and tearooms, and medieval bridges across the many rivers are as much part of the scene as coast and moor. The region's festivals, dating back many centuries, are still enthusiastically celebrated.

2

DAVID YOUNG/S

VICTORIA EVELEIGH

VICTORIA EVELEIGH

1 Castle Hill view, Torrington. **2** Hunting the Earl of Rone in Combe Martin. **3** Packhorse Bridge in Allerford. **4** Cottages in Bossington. **5** Red Ruby cattle. **6** Hunting is popular on Exmoor. Here is the parade of hounds at the Dunster Country Fair.

BESIDE THE SEA

A speciality of the region is its hidden coves, only reachable on foot, but for families there are easily accessible sandy beaches, and the area is second only to Cornwall for surfing. What's more, everyone can enjoy a boat ride to observe seals and other marine life.

1 Woolacombe Sands. 2 Dramatic rocks around Hartland Point. 3 Ilfracombe's colourful harbour. 4 Donkeys at Clovelly. 5 Boat trips from Clovelly.

IAN WOOLCOCK'S

PHPIKVS

CLOVELLY ESTATE

6

6 Westward Ho! beach at low tide. 7 Outside the Museum of British Surfing in Braunton. 8 Catching the waves at Saunton Sands. 9 A short walk up the East Lyn brings you to Watersmeet tearoom. 10 The lighthouse at Hartland Point.

7

8

9

10

AUTHOR

Hilary Bradt's career as an occupational therapist ended when potential employers noticed that the time taken off for travel exceeded the periods of employment. With her then-husband George she self-published the first Bradt guide in 1974 during an extended journey through Latin America. Since then she has seen Bradt Travel Guides grow to be an internationally recognised and award-winning publisher. In 2008 she was awarded an MBE and in 2009 received the Lifetime Achievement Award from the British Guild of Travel Writers. Now semi-retired she writes regularly for the national press and travel magazines and currently has a monthly travel slot on BBC Radio Devon. She lives in Seaton, East Devon (✐ www.hilarybradt.com).

AUTHOR'S STORY

Exmoor was one of the first place names I knew – it was where Moorland Mousie, hero of one of my favourite pony books, came from, and I desperately wanted an Exmoor pony. A few years later I lived the dream and rode over the huge expanse of those moors, splashing through rivers and cantering along grassy tracks through the bracken. I was hooked. Even the mist and drizzle seemed romantic and my first cream tea extraordinary. It was over 40 years before I returned with a walking group, climbing Dunkery Beacon in a sea of purple heather and picnicking beside Tarr Steps. But only when researching the forerunner to this book, *Slow Devon & Exmoor*, did I really start to look at this extraordinary part of the West Country. In a small area it seemed to contain everything I liked best about rural England: dramatic coastal scenery, lovely little villages advertising cream teas, a tiny church half hidden in the woods – and Exmoor ponies.

Reprinted December 2016   First published March 2015
Bradt Travel Guides Ltd
IDC House, The Vale, Chalfont St Peter, Bucks SL9 9RZ, England
www.bradtguides.com
Print edition published in the USA by The Globe Pequot Press Inc,
PO Box 480, Guilford, Connecticut 06437-0480

ISBN: 978 1 84162 865 3 (print)
e-ISBN: 978 1 78477 119 5 (e-pub)
e-ISBN: 978 1 78477 219 5 (mobi)

British Library Cataloguing in Publication Data
A catalogue record for this book is available from the British Library

Photographs
© individual photographers credited beside images & also those from picture libraries
credited as follows: Alamy.com (A), Exmoor National Park Authority (ENPA), Gettyimages.
co.uk (G), Shutterstock.com (S), South West Coast Path (SWCP), SuperStock.com (S),
Visit Exmoor (VE), Visit Britain (VB)

Front cover Valley of Rocks (Jon Gibbs/G)
Back cover Red deer stags on Exmoor (ENPA)
Title page Appledore (Ted Forman/SWCP)

Maps David McCutcheon FBCart.S and Liezel Bohdanowicz
Typeset from the author's disc by Pepi Bluck
Production managed by Jellyfish Print Solutions; printed in India
Digital conversion by www.dataworks.co.in

CONTRIBUTING AUTHORS

Simon Dell, author of the Lundy chapter, first visited the island as a schoolboy almost 50 years ago, when he was introduced to 'The King of Lundy', Felix Gade, who had been Land Agent there since 1925. He has been visiting regularly ever since, and is the author of *Lundy Island Through Time* and *Walks on Lundy*. Simon is the mainland education volunteer for the Landmark Trust, visiting schools throughout the area and leading school trips to the island. He also gives lectures to adult groups and wildlife organisations, and is a member of the Lundy Field Society. He is currently working on a publication celebrating 50 years of the Landmark Trust on Lundy.

Janice Booth started her career 50-odd years ago as a professional stage manager, touring and working in reps around the UK. Later she worked for a Belgian charity, travelled haphazardly (Timbuktu, India, Greece, Madagascar, the Maghreb …) and sold haberdashery in Harrods. More recently she has edited two dozen or so Bradt guides to various far-flung countries, initiated and co-written *Rwanda: the Bradt Travel Guide*, and co-written Bradt's *Slow Travel: South Devon & Dartmoor*. She lives peacefully in East Devon, within sound of the sea.

CONTRIBUTORS

Victoria Eveleigh lives on an Exmoor hill farm with her husband, Chris. They keep Exmoor horn sheep, Devon cattle and Exmoor ponies, as well as horses for riding and driving. Besides farming, Victoria writes for the magazine *Exmoor* and is an author with Orion Children's Books. Chris illustrates her works. The Katy's Ponies series is set on Exmoor, Victoria's standalone novel *A Stallion Called Midnight* is set on Lundy and in North Devon, and she has also The Horseshoe Trilogy. Her website is ⬦ www.victoriaeveleigh.co.uk.

Alistair and Gill Campbell live in Porlock on Exmoor. They walk extensively and have written *Porlock Walks*, a guide to 12 lovely walks in the area. They also volunteer for the National Trust on Holnicote estate where their work includes restoring ancient stone walls.

ACKNOWLEDGEMENTS

Apart from my beloved contributors who slaved away in their free time for no recompense, and to whom I owe a debt that I can never repay (although I will try), I'd like to thank (in alphabetical order) Claire Barker for her Chambercombe ghost story, David Carter who steered my Hubbastone research in the right direction, Dave Edgcombe for explaining the Combe Martin area, Mike Harrison for his corrections stemming from his intimate knowledge of this coast, Seb Jay for showing me the stars, Ian Mabbutt, who conscientiously ate his way through the best restaurants of southern Exmoor, Tony Piper for filling me in on the Lynton/Lynmouth area, Florence Unwin who gave me a ten-year-old's view of North Devon, and finally all the volunteers at museums and tourist information centres (TICs) whose enthusiasm for their towns or regions is so infectious.

In the Bradt headquarters the dedicated work of Anna Moores and her team to get the text ready for the printer is beyond thanks; it is little short of miraculous.

FOUND SOME NEW SLOW PLACES?

North Devon and Exmoor are stuffed with people who have specialist knowledge of their part of the West Country and, although I've done my best to check facts, there are bound to be errors as well as the inevitable omissions of really special places. You'll find out before us when a fine new family-run hotel opens or a favourite restaurant changes hands and goes downhill. So why not write and tell us about your experiences? Contact us on ✆ 01753 893444 or ✉ info@bradtguides.com. I will put all updates onto my dedicated webpage (📷 www.bradtupdates.com/northdevon) as well as adding my own new finds. In addition you can add a review of the book to 📷 www.bradtguides.com or Amazon.

CONTENTS

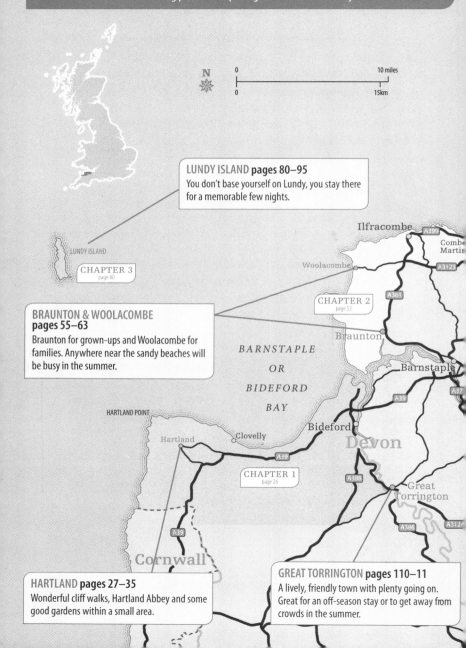

SUGGESTED PLACES TO BASE YOURSELF

These bases make ideal starting points for exploring localities the Slow way.

N

0   10 miles

0   15km

LUNDY ISLAND pages 80–95
You don't base yourself on Lundy, you stay there for a memorable few nights.

LUNDY ISLAND

CHAPTER 3
page 80

Ilfracombe | A399

Combe Martin

A3123

Woolacombe

CHAPTER 2
page 52

A361

**BRAUNTON & WOOLACOMBE
pages 55–63**
Braunton for grown-ups and Woolacombe for families. Anywhere near the sandy beaches will be busy in the summer.

Braunton

Barnstaple

A37

BARNSTAPLE

OR

BIDEFORD

BAY

A39

HARTLAND POINT

Hartland

Clovelly

Bideford

Devon

CHAPTER 1
page 26

A39

A388

Great Torrington

HARTLAND pages 27–35
Wonderful cliff walks, Hartland Abbey and some good gardens within a small area.

Cornwall

A39

A386

A312

GREAT TORRINGTON pages 110–11
A lively, friendly town with plenty going on. Great for an off-season stay or to get away from crowds in the summer.

LYNTON/LYNMOUTH pages 139–48
The most popular area in Exmoor – and it deserves the accolade. Superb walking and plenty of other happenings.

PORLOCK pages 158–66
Where Exmoor meets the sea: the best moorland scenery, lovely cliff and inland walks, and a great little town for relaxation.

DUNSTER pages 182–5
A perfect centre for a short break. There's lots to see in this medieval town, and the West Somerset (steam) Railway is nearby.

DULVERTON pages 185–8
A delightful small town, with good restaurants and a laid-back atmosphere. Ideal for exploring southern Exmoor.

Lynton Lynmouth

Porlock

Minehead

Dunster

Watchet

A39

A39

CHAPTER 5
page 120

BRENDON HILLS

CHAPTER 6
page 176

EXMOOR
NATIONAL
PARK

A396

Somerset

Wimbleball
Lake

A399

Dulverton

A361

CHAPTER 4
page 96

South
Molton

A361

A396

Devon

A377

Chulmleigh

A361

M5

TIVERTON

A396

Cullompton

A373

A3124

NORTH DEVON &
EXMOOR

This is a county of sudden surprises, spendthrift in its contrasts.
It is richly agricultural, richer in its virgin red soil than perhaps
any other county in England, and then, suddenly, it is maritime,
and the pastures give place to the blue sea, the second home of
Devon men since history became articulate.

L du Garde Peach, *Unknown Devon*, 1927

Recently I was asked by a travel magazine to list my five favourite places
in the world. After the expected exotics of Madagascar, Ethiopia and
Peru, I put North Devon. I'd just come back from a research trip for
this book, walking some of the coastal paths in glorious sunshine and
discovering new (to me) churches and unsung villages, and my heart
was full of how lucky I am to live in the South West and to be writing
this book. The region has so much to offer the Slow traveller: cliff paths
for walking, sea with rolling breakers for surfing and sandy beaches for
lounging, hidden coves, and wonderful Exmoor with its heathery hills
and deep valleys, combes, where rivers tumble over mossy stones on
their way to the Bristol Channel. Always there has been the sea, which
shaped the history of this county. It provided food – mainly herrings
– and adventure for the men of Devon and West Somerset. It allowed
invaders such as Hubba the Dane to threaten these shores, and it was
the means whereby the great explorers set forth to discover new lands;
it provided wealth to the smugglers and heartbreak to the victims of
wreckers. And for the present-day holiday-maker it is the reason they
come to North Devon.

In the course of my research I've been able to follow obscure leads and
find many places other guidebooks ignore. For one thing, I've been able
to indulge my passion for country churches, using a variety of specialist
books to ferret out the most interesting. I make no apology for my
enthusiasm for these 'storerooms of history' – they exemplify Slow travel,

being free (apart from what you put in the donations box), unpromoted and often mysterious to the uninformed. I hope my explanations on pages 12–16 will help gain some new enthusiasts.

This region, particularly Exmoor, is poorly served by guidebooks – a remarkable omission for one of the smallest, most diverse, and certainly one of the most beautiful of all our nation's national parks. Perhaps that is because the park is divided between two counties, with two different county councils involved in promotion and, to some extent, administration. I hope this book addresses the matter and helps visitors appreciate what so many ignore; the relative lack of visitors here is the Slow traveller's delight. But Exmoor deserves more.

THE SLOW MINDSET

We shall not cease from exploration
And the end of all our exploring
Will be to arrive where we started
And know the place for the first time.

T S Eliot, 'Little Gidding', *Four Quartets*

This series evolved, slowly, from a Bradt editorial meeting when we started to explore ideas for guides to our favourite country – Great Britain. We wanted to get away from the usual 'top sights' formula and encourage our authors to bring out the nuances and local differences that make up a sense of place – such things as food, building styles, nature, geology, or local people and what makes them tick. Our aim was to create a series that celebrates the present, focusing on sustainable tourism, rather than taking a nostalgic wallow in the past.

So without our realising it at the time, we had defined 'Slow Travel', or at least our concept of it. For the beauty of the Slow movement is that there is no fixed definition;

we adapt the philosophy to fit our individual needs and aspirations. Thus Carl Honoré, author of *In Praise of Slow*, writes: 'The Slow Movement is a cultural revolution against the notion that faster is always better. It's not about doing everything at a snail's pace, it's about seeking to do everything at the right speed. Savouring the hours and minutes rather than just counting them. Doing everything as well as possible, instead of as fast as possible. It's about quality over quantity in everything from work to food to parenting.' And travel.

So take time to explore. Don't rush it, get to know an area – and the people who live there – and you'll be as delighted as I am by what you find.

I want locals who thought they were familiar with the region to say 'I didn't know that!' And I want visitors from afar to learn that there's more to Devon and Exmoor than the beaches and commercial places that get into the tourist brochures (although they're also included here). That's what Slow is all about.

A TASTE OF
NORTH DEVON & EXMOOR

The taste of Devon is undoubtedly that of **clotted cream**. A Devon cream tea is as integral a part of a visit to this region as rain (indeed, the one often leads to the other). Clotted cream is quite unlike any other sort of cream, being as thick as butter and almost as yellow; it contains more fat (around 63%, while double cream is 48%), and traditionally was made by gradually heating fresh milk using steam or hot water, and allowing it to cool very slowly. The thick cream that rises to the top was then skimmed off. The original term was clouted cream, clout being the word for patch, referring to the thick crust that forms when the cream is heated.

Clotted cream is only made in Devon and Cornwall, and we Devonians are not only convinced that ours is better but that we got there first. After all, it was one of the wives of the Dartmoor giant, Blunderbus, who won her husband's affection by bringing the knowledge of clotted-cream-making to his kitchen. The story is slightly spoiled by the fact that Jennie was exiled to a cave in Cornwall at the time for being a lousy cook, and it was a Phoenician sea captain who taught her the process as a reward for saving his ship from wreckers.

Clotted cream is served with fresh scones, which should be warm from the oven not the microwave; purists prefer plain scones but others, myself included, love the fruit ones. In Devon we spread the cream on the scone first, instead of butter, and add strawberry or raspberry jam on top; in Cornwall it's the opposite: jam first, then clotted cream. Either way it's utterly delicious – and very filling. The Victorian prime minister William Gladstone was right when he called clotted cream 'the food of the gods'.

Talking of jam, an Exmoor speciality is **whortleberry jam**. Whortleberry is the Exmoor name for bilberry, a heather relative which grows on the moor. Brendan Hill Crafts, a preserves specialist, makes an award-winning whortleberry jam which is sold in a wide range of outlets across North Devon and Exmoor.

Back to clotted cream which is, surprisingly, the accompaniment to a traditional savoury recipe, **Devon squab pie**. Medieval dovecots are still found in the grounds of the great West Country estates, so it's not surprising that squab, or young pigeon, should feature in an ancient recipe. Except that it doesn't. Devon squab pie is made with mutton. The likely explanation for this misnomer is that until the 17th century squab, a luxury food,

"Devon squab pie is made not with squab, young pigeon, but with mutton."

could be consumed only by the lord of the manor and the parish priest. So perhaps the mixture of fruit and mutton tasted something like the sweet meat of a real squab. Be that as it may, this is a tasty dish composed of layers of mutton or lamb alternating with apples, prunes and spices. Some recipes add onion or leek. It's easy to make and, to add the authentic Devon touch, you need to serve it with clotted cream on the side.

RED RUBY CATTLE & EXMOOR HORN SHEEP

Two of England's rare breeds of meat animals are natives of North Devon and Exmoor, adapted over the centuries to the tough conditions of hill farming. The nickname for the North Devon breed of cattle, **Red Ruby**, is appropriate. These animals are a beautiful chestnut red, the colour of a ripe conker. Like so many rare breeds, the North Devon cattle nearly died out in the 19th century when meat prices shot up during the Napoleonic wars. It took the vision of Francis Quartly, of Great Champson, Molland, to reverse the decline. He outbid the butchers to build up a herd that represented the best of the breed. Red Rubies are prized for their docility, hardiness and ability to convert grass to succulent, marbled meat. Most of the herds you will see grazing in the North Devon and Exmoor fields are grown slowly, outdoors (though the climate is such that they need to be brought inside during the winter), with the calves staying with their mothers until they are weaned.

Exmoor horn sheep is another hardy breed which has adapted to the conditions on Exmoor over the centuries. And Exmoor has adapted to the sheep, so the landscape you enjoy today owes as much to these animals as it does to nature. They are all-white and, as the name suggests, both rams and ewes have horns. They are dual-purpose animals, raised for wool as well as meat. In the days when mutton was regularly eaten they were considered to have the finest meat of any breed, and the quality of their wool has been appreciated for centuries. Today, socks and knitting wool from Exmoor horn sheep can be bought from outlets in the Exmoor area or from the website ⬦ www. exmoorhornwool.co.uk.

cream is Devon, then **cider** is Somerset although western
⌐ ⌐s not in the heart of cider country. For this you need to go
east to flatter areas where the cider-apple orchards flourish. A popular
Somerset cider is Sheppy's (www.sheppyscider.com) near Taunton.
But for a total cider indulgence pop into Peeble's Tavern in Watchet
(page 191); they serve 20 varieties.

North Devon has five **breweries** listed by the Campaign for Real
Ale (CAMRA). They are Barum (Barnstaple), Clearwater (Bideford),
Country Life (Abbotsham), Forge (Hartland) and Wizard (Ilfracombe).
See www.northdevoncamra.org.uk for further details. Exmoor's
largest brewery is Exmoor Ales in Wiveliscombe (www.exmoorales.
co.uk). Their best-known cask ales are Exmoor Gold and Exmoor Beast
but they do a total of ten, some permanent, some seasonal. Another
popular brewery is Cotleigh (Ford Rd, Wiveliscombe TA4 2RE 01984
624086 www.cotleighbrewery.com). Their beers are named after
predatory birds: Tawny Owl, Golden Seahawk and Buzzard. They also
do seasonal brews such as Rednose Reinbeer. Groups of 18 or more can
take a brewery tour but the shop is open to everyone with a thirst.

North Devon and Exmoor are **game** regions: several hotels convert
to shooting lodges in the autumn and winter, so pheasant, partridge,
woodcock, rabbit and venison feature on many menus.

Foodies should try to visit Barnstaple in mid-October when the **North
Devon Foodfest** is held in the Pannier Market, and a few days later the
North Devon Food Fair pops up in Bideford. Further east, the **Lyn Food
Festival** is held in Lynton at the end of September.

THE APPEAL OF
COUNTRY CHURCHES

Some people go to church, others go to churches. I come into the latter
category. I love what rural churches can show us of village life through
the span of a thousand years. Simon Jenkins, in his wonderful book
England's Thousand Best Churches, sums up the appeal: 'Into these
churches English men and women have for centuries poured their
faith, joy, sorrow, labour and love.' In their artefacts and monuments
these little churches – for the best are usually little – tell the story of the
village, revealing the lives of the poor farm workers as well as their rich
employers up at the big house. They are recorded in the oldest Norman

font to the newest Women's Institute kneelers. Nowhere else will you find this unbroken thread of history.

No old church is devoid of interest. Start with the **lych-gate** where you enter the churchyard. Lych was the old English word for dead body, so a lych-gate was a corpse gate. A few retain the slab on which the coffin rested during the burial service. In medieval times only the rich were buried in coffins; the poor used the parish reusable one, the corpse being wrapped in woollen material for burial. And it had to be wool or they paid a fine – a canny way to protect the wool trade.

Look up at the eaves. Are there **gargoyles** with ferocious faces spewing water from the run-off from the roof? They may be there to protect the church from the demons and devils that are trying to get in.

Then visit the **tombstones**. The early ones from the 17th and 18th centuries often have beautiful, though worn and mossy, lettering, and carved cherub faces, angel wings or skulls as emblems of mortality. Sometimes the inscription can be unintentionally humorous: if the stonemason made a mistake there was no simple way of correcting it. More often they are poignant, with graves of babies and young children all bearing the same family name. The 19th-century Victorian enthusiasm for epitaphs and poems adds further interest. For real hyperbole about the worthiness of the dead person, however, you need to read the inscriptions on the **monuments** to the rich and influential inside the church. The unquestioning belief – at least of the family that paid for the tomb – that the ancestor was whisked up to heaven to an altogether more enjoyable immortality is clearly stated.

Old churches are full of words. You walk on ancient memorial slabs – **ledger stones** – from the 17th and 18th century, beautifully lettered with intriguing abbreviations and roman dates (so brush up on your Latin numerals). More recent memorials, on the walls in brass or marble, commemorate the rich, influential or brave. And painted on the wall of most churches is a **list of rectors** or vicars. They often start in the 1200s, with the French names of the Norman clergymen, and continue in an unbroken line to the women vicars of today.

Most intriguing of all are the carvings, because we can only guess at what they mean. These are what bring me such joy in Devon's churches. The tops of columns, **capitals**, are often carved with detailed and enigmatic faces of man or beast, but where the carver gave most expression to his imagination is in the wooden **bench ends** of the pews. Benches or pews in churches only came into being in the 14th century – before that the congregation stood – and were universal in the 15th, which is the date of the earliest of Devon's examples. The subjects of the carvings are quite extraordinary. Where you would expect religious motifs you find, instead, creatures of the wildest imagination. And even in the 14th century these weren't a new fad. The French abbot St Bernard of Clairveaux, who died in 1153, wrote: 'What mean those ridiculous monstrosities in the courts of cloisters; those filthy apes, those fierce lions, those monstrous centaurs, those half-men, those spotted tigers, those fighting soldiers and horn-blowing hunters; many bodies under one head, or many heads on one body; here a serpent's tail attached to a quadruped, there a quadruped's head on a fish; here a beast presenting the foreparts of a horse, and dragging after it the rear of a goat; there a horned animal with the hind parts of a horse?' He accurately describes the decorative church art that persisted for another five centuries until a more demure mindset took over. You will find many different explanations for the carvings in church booklets; personally I enjoy the mystery.

Dividing the nave, where the congregation sits, and the chancel leading to the altar, is generally a beautifully carved **wooden screen**, often called a rood screen since the rood, a beam on top, carried the figures of the crucifixion. These were all removed during the Reformation or by the Puritans in the Cromwell period. In the panels between the supports you can still find charming painted portraits of saints, rich with symbolism. These, too, were often damaged – literally defaced – by the reformers. North Devon and Exmoor churches, however, seem to have fewer painted panels than other parts of the county.

While on the subject of old wood, look out for the ancient **alms boxes** and **chests** used to store church documents. The oldest of these may be cut from a single log, and many are bound with iron bands and have more than one lock to secure them.

Carvings, both in wood and stone, are found on and over the **font**. This basin holds holy water for baptism, and is often the oldest thing in a church. Rough-hewn Norman stone fonts are quite common, as are more intricately carved ones from the same period, sometimes depicting strange creatures or faces. These may represent the demons being expelled through baptism. In the 13th century the Archbishop of Canterbury ordered that fonts should be covered to prevent the theft of holy water. The carved wooden covers became increasingly elaborate until they could only be raised by pulleys.

The aristocracy have their own lavish memorials. Some **marble tombs** occupy quite a large proportion of the church, with elaborate canopies, heroic inscriptions and depictions of the nobleman either in life or death. Dead knights in armour have their feet resting on lions, to symbolise courage, whilst their wives often have a dog for fidelity. Studying these effigies and the **memorial brasses** set into the floor is an excellent way to learn the history of costume and armour.

Finally the most eye-catching and least enigmatic features of a church: the **stained-glass windows**. Being vulnerable to storm and sabotage, many of the medieval ones have perished and most are now Victorian. But early ones do survive and charmingly represent the contemporary idea of the Bible stories.

Churches in Devon and Exmoor are rarely locked during the day. Give them the time and attention they deserve.

Here are my five favourites (in chapter order): Littleham (page 49), Tawstock (page 108), Horwood (page 110), Parracombe (page 133) and Culbone (page 167).

GLOSSARY

Finding your way around a church using the information leaflets is helped by understanding church terminology. To begin with you need to know that the altar is almost always positioned in the east end of the church; you can then easily work out which is the south aisle and so on.

boss Carved and painted knob at the intersection of roof beams.

choir stalls The seating in the chancel, between the altar and the screen, where the choir and clergy sit.

Green man A face, usually carved in stone in the capitals above columns, with foliage coming from its mouth and ears, and incorporated into its hair. Thought to be of pagan origin representing fertility.

Hunky Punk An imaginary malevolent creature sometimes depicted on bench ends.

misericord A hinged shelf in the choir stalls to support the standing occupant during long services.

nave The main body of the church where the congregation sits.

piscina A small basin, usually in the chancel, for washing holy vessels.

poppyhead A carved, three-dimensional figure on top of a bench back or end. The word derives from the Latin *puppis* or French *poupée* meaning doll or figurehead (as in a ship).

Reformation The separation of the official church from the Roman Catholic faith leading to the adoption of Protestantism. It was started by Henry VIII in 1534, led to the Dissolution of the Monasteries in 1539. In 1549 the order went out to destroy 'superstitious images'; this is when the most damage was done to country churches, completed a century later by Cromwell's Puritans.

reredos A painted or carved screen behind the altar.

wagon roof Also known as a barrel roof, a semi-circular beamed roof running the length of the nave.

FURTHER READING FOR CHURCH ENTHUSIASTS

A Cloud of Witnesses: Medieval Panel Paintings of Saints in Devon Churches Wilks, Diane, Azure Publications 2013. Many of Devon's churches contain historically important paintings of saints; some of the finest are illustrated here, with intriguing background details of the saints themselves, many of whom had unexpectedly colourful lives.

Devon's Ancient Bench Ends Gray, Todd, The Mint Press 2012. A detailed examination of the history and significance of these often enigmatic carvings illustrated in colour.

Devon's Fifty Best Churches Gray, Todd, The Mint Press 2011. A beautiful book, with some fine photos of the churches and their carvings, accompanied by location maps and informative text.

England's Thousand Best Churches Jenkins, Simon, Penguin 1999. The essential companion for any churchophile: knowledgeable and atmospheric descriptions of the churches (33 of which are in Devon) and their locations, in Jenkins' seductive prose.

The Pilgrim's Guide to Devon Churches Cloister Books 2008. A practical, helpful little handbook, small and sturdy enough to carry in a backpack, systematically listing all of Devon's Anglican churches, with a small photo and brief description of each. Location maps are included.

NGS GARDENS & OPEN STUDIOS

Each year householders from all over England and Wales open their gardens for the **NGS Gardens Open for Charity** scheme (www.ngs. org.co.uk). Since this guide aims to get under the skin of North Devon and West Somerset, a visit to one of these open gardens is the perfect way to understand the locals or – if you are a visitor from overseas – the English. We are the most passionate gardeners in the world and the West Country, with its rich soil and mild climate, makes enthusiasts out of even reluctant horticulturists. The gardens that are open in this scheme come in every size, from manor house grounds to the kitchen gardens of semi-detached cottages. And it's not just the gardens you'll enjoy. Almost every householder taking part in the scheme adds to the money raised by offering coffee and tea with a wonderful array of cakes.

The NGS publishes *The Yellow Book* annually which lists all the participating gardens in England and Wales, but there's one for just Devon and also a separate one for Somerset. These can usually be picked up free at tourist offices or accessed through the website. There are gardens to be visited throughout the year, from January to December, although more, of course, in the spring and summer months. Some only open for one weekend a year so you need to plan ahead.

A somewhat similar scheme, in that it brings you into contact with the locals, is the **Open Studios** fortnight which takes place annually in September in Devon and the following fortnight in Somerset. The Devon one is an initiative of the Devon Artist Network (www. devonartistnetwork.co.uk) and participating studios are listed on its website. Somerset's Open Studios are run by Somerset Art Works (www. somersetartworks.org.uk). Throughout the counties, artists open up their studios to show their work and to talk to art enthusiasts. Some exhibit in groups, in galleries, others set aside a room in their homes. For art lovers it adds a hugely enjoyable element to their visit to the West Country.

CAR-FREE TRAVEL

The mode of lionising the neighbourhood is on pony or donkeyback, or, far better, on foot. The roads are ill-equipped for carriages, being steep and circuitous.

A Handbook for Travellers in Devon and Cornwall, 1872

The Slow traveller prefers to get around under his or her own leg power or by bus, but that can be quite a challenge in this region of poor public transport. Detailed information on getting around without a car is given in each chapter, but do bear in mind that bus timetables change and buses are being withdrawn with an unnerving frequency. If you are relying on public transport for any part of your visit in Devon you should check the excellent website ◊ www.journeydevon.info. Its interactive bus map and timetables are kept up to date. For planning a journey, Traveline (◊ www. traveline.info) is invaluable and you can phone from a bus stop (✆ 0871 200 2233) and ask what's happened to your bus.

In Somerset the best website for bus information is ◊ www. exploremoor.co.uk.

HORSERIDING

Exmoor, the home of one of Britain's most distinctive native ponies, is perfect for riding, and information on its trekking stables is given on page 130. However, there are several accommodation providers who will also provide a field or stabling for your own horse, so a riding holiday using the information in this book plus a bit of additional research is entirely realistic.

CYCLING

Mike Harrison, compiler of Croydecycle maps (see page 21), writes: 'Cycling in North Devon is a pleasure, being far from cities so most of the rural lanes are quiet. The Tarka Trail (NCN3 and 27) on the old railway lines around the Taw and Torridge estuaries is ideal for families and there are other quiet and level lanes around Braunton. Coastal roads can be busy at peak times and often a bike is the quickest way round the narrow lanes but be wary of cars.'

The Tarka Trail (see *Chapter 4*) is one of the country's best-known cycle routes, running 180 miles from Braunton to Meeth, but there are plenty of other routes and circuits. The free booklet *Cycling Trails in Devon* (◊ www.visitdevon.co.uk; click on 'brochure request') is useful, but for more specific information buy Bryan Cath's *7 Cycle Rides around North Devon and Exmoor Challenge* and *7 Cycle Rides around North and Mid Devon*. They're available in the region and from ◊ www. westcountrywalks.co.uk. Croydecycle's map ❀ *Braunton & Ilfracombe* at 1:30,000 is perfect for cyclists who want to explore this area.

WALKING

The South West Coast Path is the long-distance national trail in this region. It begins in Minehead and follows the coast, with occasional forays inland, for 124 miles to the Cornish border before completing its 630-mile journey round the Cornwall peninsula to Poole Harbour in Dorset. This section is considered by many to be the most beautiful as well as the most challenging of the entire route. All keen walkers who visit Devon and Exmoor will do parts of the coast path, most utilising the inland footpaths to make a circular trip or doing one of the 'Bus-assisted walks' suggested in this book. However, there are several inland long-distance footpaths on Exmoor, including the **Two Moors Way**, which runs from Lynmouth to Ivybridge on the far edge of Dartmoor; the **Macmillan Way West** from southeast Exmoor to Barnstaple; the **Samaritans Way South West** from Bristol to Lynton; and the **Coleridge Way** from the Quantocks to Lynmouth. These are just the named trails; a network of minor footpaths and excellent maps (page 20) allow you to devise your own walk. Suggestions and detailed walk descriptions are given in each chapter, and chapter maps include the ♀ symbol to indicate that there is a described walk in that area.

GOOD TIDINGS

Janice Booth

North Devon and Exmoor has some beautiful stretches of coastline, particularly tempting for visitors fascinated by cliffs, beaches and the shore. However, lifeboats are all too often called out to rescue people who've wandered too far and are trapped by the incoming tide. These call-outs can be dangerous and costly, and can be avoided by always checking the **tide tables** (available in local shops and TICs) before a seashore wander; used sensibly, they open up a wealth of safe exploring.

Non-seawise visitors don't always realise how much the extent and timing of a tide's ebb and flow vary with the phases of the moon. The fact that you could walk past the tip of that promontory yesterday at midday and return safely doesn't mean you can do the same tomorrow, even if you calculate the time correctly: the tide may not ebb as far, or may rise higher, and you'll be trapped. (If this happens, don't try wading, particularly in rough weather; there can be dangerously deep pools close to rocks.) These timings and differences vary from place to place and from day to day, throughout the year, so – better safe than sorry!

For those who prefer to walk with a group, led by a local expert in history and/or nature, there's the **Exmoor Walking Festival** (⏣ www.exmoorwalkingfestival.co.uk). This takes place in late April to early May, over the bank holiday period, when the weather and scenery are at their best.

Walking maps & guides

Walkers and cyclists have a bonus in this region – Mike Harrison's marvellous pocket-sized Croydecycle maps (see box opposite). There are two 1:15,000 maps just for the South West Coast Path, but it's the 13 maps that cover all of the North Devon and Exmoor coast at a scale of 1:12,500 or five inches to a mile which are such a joy. It's not just the scale that makes them special, it's Mike's snippets of explanatory or helpful text. So footpaths may have the warning 'May be muddy after rain' or the reassuring 'sheep grazed' or 'firm grass'. Places of historical or geological interest will have a little block of explanatory text, and any other bit of empty space is filled with hard information on buses, phone numbers, and other bits of tourist information. And because Mike is stringent about accuracy, I can guarantee that these will be correct unless details have recently changed. The maps are regularly updated and an added bonus is the street plans of some of the larger towns. All this for £2.

In addition to the series of walking maps there are larger-scale cycling maps at 1:30,000, also *North Devon* and *Exmoor & Taunton* at 1:100,000 which are more useful to car drivers than any other maps I've found.

The maps are widely available in the region but you can also order them direct from ⏣ www.croydecycle.co.uk.

For inland areas not covered by Croydecycle you'll need the Ordnance Survey Explorer maps. The OL9 double-sided one covers all of Exmoor at a scale of 1:25,000, so is ideal for walking, though its size makes it unwieldy to use in wind or small spaces such as a car. At the same scale are two single-sided Explorer maps, 126 and 139, covering the North Devon chapters of this book.

❋ Ordnance Survey is also producing internet-based, pocket-sized MiniMaps, which are site-centred. You choose the place you want your map centred around, and the scale, and they will deliver them the next day; see ⏣ www.MyMiniMap.co.uk.

MIKE HARRISON, MASTER MAP-MAKER

Mike Harrison is certainly a popular person in Devon and Exmoor. Not that most users of his Croydecycle maps even know his name – they just know that these are by far the best walking maps of the area.

I visited Mike in his centuries-old stone-built cottage next to the church in Croyde. 'It belonged to my great grandmother' he told me. 'She bought it in 1900 for £150 and it's been in the family ever since.' When Mike was made redundant from his teaching job in Hereford, he had little idea that, at an age when most men have retired, he would be selling tens of thousands of maps, produced by himself in Rose Cottage. I asked him how it all started. 'Really from my love of orienteering. When I lived in Hereford I drew orienteering maps using specialist software and also produced a Herefordshire cycle map and guide. I printed 2,000 and they did well.' Then, in 2001, foot and mouth disease put a stop to orienteering and, without a job and his favourite sport, Mike decided to move to Croyde and work on the restoration of the cottage.

A trip to Greece in 2002 reignited his enthusiasm for maps. He met a Russian with a beautiful, large-scale map which actually turned out to be useless when it came to knowing where to find water. Mike's locally bought smaller-scale map had bits of text giving vital information for walkers – such as the location of water supplies. 'I thought, we don't have anything like this at home and, as a keen cyclist, I also found the size of the Ordnance Survey maps unwieldy.'

A venture into producing cycling maps of Devon and Cornwall had limited success, but 'I produced my first large-scale walking map – for Croyde – in 2006 and suddenly here was a product that was popular.' Popular is an understatement. Once you've used a Croydecycle map (the original name stuck, even though walking rather than cycling is now the emphasis) you feel unsatisfied with anything else. It's the way Mike squeezes all the information you could possibly want on to a pocket-sized map. Despite his output, with a total of 40 maps on Devon and Exmoor, this is still a one-man show. When researching a new map, Mike will walk up to 20 miles a day, checking out all the footpaths, in both directions, and taking notes on every feature of use or interest to the walker. The base map comes from six-inch-to-the-mile Ordnance Survey maps published in 1880 and 1905, which necessitates getting copies from the record office. 'Not that much has changed, but I add information from satellite pictures. Remember, a plan is accurate, a map is about giving the right impression.' An example is that if a map showed roads in their real width in relation to the scale, they would be the thickness of a hair. Junctions may need to be exaggerated for clarity.

Each map takes about two months to create. The profit from this venture is modest for one who works seven days a week. 'But it's fun, isn't it?'

Specific map information is given in each chapter – look out for the ❊ symbol within the text.

For those who prefer to follow written instructions, there's the 'no map reading' series of walking and cycling leaflets put out by Bryan Cath, Devon's walking expert, who runs West Country Walks (✆ 01271 883131 ✐ www.westcountrywalks.co.uk) also known as Combe Walks. In addition to organising the annual North Devon and Exmoor Walking Festival, Bryan will provide guided walks for groups of eight or more.

A number of **guidebooks** detail walks in the area. *Shortish Walks in North Devon* and *Shortish Walks in Exmoor* by Robert Hesketh (✐ www.bosinneybooks.com) are easy to follow with clear maps. Other regional self-published walking guides are listed in each chapter.

For walkers doing the South West Coast Path one guide stands out: *Exmoor & North Devon Coast Path* by Henry Stedman and Joel Newton, published by Trailblazer. This has the hallmark of all Trailblazer's walking guides: clear, hand-drawn maps, masses of background information, accommodation and eating suggestions. As an added bonus it's written with wit and observation.

HOW THIS BOOK IS ARRANGED

A book that spans two counties is always going to be a little awkward to organise. It was easy enough to know where to start – at the Cornish border, and then moving east, cutting each section into similar-sized chunks, the boundaries determined by rivers or main roads. Exmoor National Park, however, was a bit of a challenge, since it is the main focus of the book and a homogeneous whole under one authority, and I didn't want to divide it up. So it's a massive chapter. Then there are the gateway towns to the east of the national park which deserve a mention, though they're not technically in Exmoor, so the final chapter incorporates these, together with the attractions just outside the park as well as its extreme east.

MAPS

The map at the front of this book shows the area covered in each of the six chapters, along with suggestions on where to base yourself for a holiday in this region. Each chapter then begins with a sketch map of the area, highlighting the places mentioned in the text or in the accommodation section. The numbers on the map correspond to the numbers against the headings or emboldened names in the text. The ♀ symbol on these maps indicates that there is a walk in that area. There are also sketch maps for some of these featured walks.

LISTINGS

These are usually alphabetical, unless logic dictates that they should be geographical, such as grouping places in the same town together.

FOOD & DRINK

I've listed some of my, and local residents', favourite pubs, cafés and restaurants, favouring those places that serve local produce or are just exceptionally good or atmospheric. The list is by no means exhaustive, and some exploration and curiosity will yield many other splendid places.

ACCOMMODATION

There are some accommodation ideas for each area on pages 194–205 – a mixture of camping, glamping, self-catering, B&B and hotels. (*Glamping* derives from 'glamorous camping', with accommodation and facilities more luxurious than those associated with traditional camping.) The hotels, B&Bs and self-catering options are indicated by ♠ under the heading for the area in which they are located. Campsites are indicated by ▲. One self-catering provider that differs from the others is the Landmark Trust, which leases Lundy Island from the National Trust. This charitable organisation's role is to rescue historic buildings in danger of dereliction, restore them, and rent them out as holiday accommodation. Apart from those on Lundy, there are just two Landmark Trust places in North Devon and Exmoor. Both are included (pages 195 and 199).

Prices change regularly so are not mentioned, but I have tried to suggest whether a place is an upmarket option or more suited to the budget-conscious. Some accommodation providers keep their prices consistent all year but many, especially those by the coast, charge peak rates in July and August. For further reviews and additional listings, go to ⊘ www.bradtguides.com/ndevonsleeps.

ATTRACTIONS

When useful I have given contact details and it is always worth checking websites for any changes. I have not listed admission fees as they change regularly; always check them beforehand to avoid an unpleasant shock.

If a description does not say admission is free, you should expect to be charged. Opening hours are generally from 10.00 to 16.30 or 17.00. I have only given opening times if they differ from this norm.

Note that no charge has been made for the inclusion of any business in this guide.

USEFUL WEBSITES

Exmoor National Park Authority ⟨⟩ www.exmoor-nationalpark.gov.uk
North Devon Area of Outstanding Natural Beauty ⟨⟩ www.northdevon-aonb.org.uk
North Devon Biosphere ⟨⟩ www.northdevonbiosphere.org.uk
Visit Exmoor ⟨⟩ www.visit-exmoor.co.uk
Visit North Devon & Exmoor ⟨⟩ www.northdevon.com

FURTHER READING & MEDIA: NEWSPAPERS & LOCAL RADIO

One of Exmoor's most venerated characters, Hope Bourne, died in 2010 at the age of 91. Having spent her childhood and young adulthood in Hartland she moved to Exmoor on the death of her mother and lived a self-sufficient life spending around £5 a month. Her books, which she illustrated herself, include *Living on Exmoor* and *My Moorland Life*.

Children will love the Katy trilogy of pony books written by Victoria Eveleigh. Set in Exmoor they bring the landscape and farming to life, along with the management of Exmoor ponies. *A Stallion Called Midnight* does the same for Lundy Island.

If you buy a local newspaper while in Devon and Exmoor make it the *Western Morning News* (⟨⟩ www.westernmorningnews.co.uk). Published since 1860, it is an excellent paper with lots of information and reports on local events as well as politically unbiased international news. Taking the longer view is the monthly magazine *Devon Life* (⟨⟩ www.devonlife.co.uk), with in-depth articles on a range of town and country issues. Radio Devon (103.4MHz FM), broadcast from the BBC studios in Plymouth, is one of the most listened-to of the BBC's local radio stations. Tune in to hear traffic news as well as local-interest stories and interviews.

SOURCE MATERIAL (BOOKS)

I have drawn on the information in several out-of-print books by inspirational authors. These include:

A Handbook for Travellers in Devon and Cornwall (no author credited) John Murray, 1872. Extraordinarily detailed information on how and where to travel around using horse-drawn carriages and 'post buses'.

A Handbook for Travellers in Somerset John Murray, 1899. As above. Delightful.

Devon Hoskins, W G, Collins 1954; reprints 2003 & 2011, Phillimore & Co. Hoskins is *the* authority on Devon. No place is too small or insignificant to merit an entry in the gazetteer.

Devon: A Shell Guide Jellicoe, Ann & Mayne, Roger, Faber & Faber 1975. The erudite research and literary style that you would expect in a Shell Guide.

Early Tours in Devon and Cornwall Pearse Chope, R (ed) James G Commin, 1918; reprinted 1967, David & Charles. A fascinating look at how early travellers in Devon saw the county. The writers include John Leland (travelling 1534–43), Celia Fiennes (1695), Daniel Defoe (1724), W G Maton (1794–6) and Robert Southey (1802).

Glorious Devon Mais, S P B, Great Western Railway Company, 1932. A warm and human account, in Mais's masterly style, bringing the scenery and the people enjoyably to life.

The Coasts of Devon and Lundy Island: their towns, villages, scenery, antiquities and legends Page, John Lloyd Warden. Originally published in 1895 by Horace Cox, reprinted in facsimile by Ulan Press. Page travelled, observed, listened and wrote exhaustively about Devon. His fat book is stuffed with observations, legends and history.

The King's England: Devon Mee, Arthur, Hodder and Stoughton. Various editions since 1928. Arranged alphabetically as a gazetteer, Mee's descriptions of the places are affectionate and his style is very readable. He includes some unusual details and a sprinkling of old tales and legends. In the same series is Somerset.

Unknown Devon du Garde Peach, L, Bodley Head, 1927. An entertaining and interesting account of an exploration of Devon by motor car.

NORTH DEVON & EXMOOR DESTINATION PAGE

For additional online content, accommodation reviews, articles, photos and more on North Devon and Exmoor, visit ⊘ bradtguides.com/northdevon.

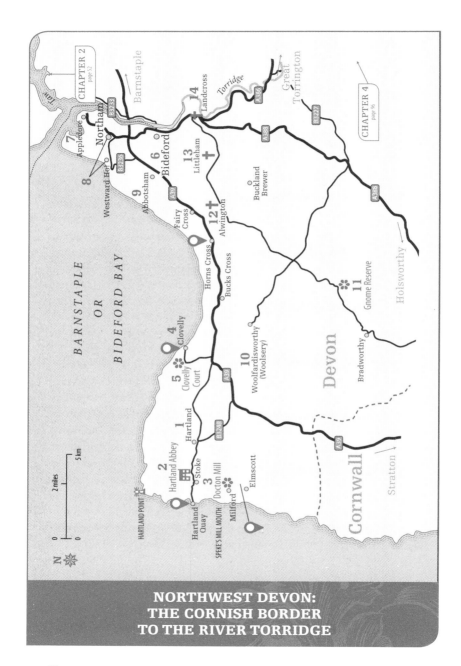

**NORTHWEST DEVON:
THE CORNISH BORDER
TO THE RIVER TORRIDGE**

1

NORTHWEST DEVON:
THE CORNISH BORDER
TO THE RIVER TORRIDGE

This remote north-western corner of Devon is a place to dream
in … The deserted coast is backed by a rich hinterland, full of
sleepy little villages which have never awakened for long enough
to find a place in the history books. They are still fast asleep, just
perhaps turning and muttering a little if they happen to lie by
the great highway along which the purposeful motorist does his
thirty or forty miles in the hour towards Cornwall.

L du Garde Peach, *Unknown Devon*, 1927

This 'wild west' of the county is perhaps my favourite part of North
Devon. Here there are no sandy beaches (unless you count Westward
Ho!'s low-tide sands) but the ever-changing wood and cliff scenery from
the coast path is sublime; the region's most charming fishing villages
are here (**Clovelly** and **Appledore**), as are the splendid **Hartland Abbey**,
some good gardens (**Clovelly Court**, **Docton Mill**) and a clutch of
villages whose churches are crammed with curiosities. And talking of
curiosities, there is even a **Gnome Reserve**.

Charles Kingsley and Sir Richard Grenville share the honours of
being the region's favourite son. Kingsley's name is everywhere, though
few 21st-century readers appreciate his flowery, moralistic prose (he
wrote *The Water Babies* and *Westward Ho!*), whilst Grenville, who met
his death when his ship, *The Revenge*, tackled a vastly superior Spanish
fleet, is mainly celebrated in his home town of Bideford.

GETTING THERE & AROUND

Few Slow travellers will grumble that the region is so poor in transport
infrastructure – for there lies the secret of its wildness. The nearest
railway station is Barnstaple, from where regular buses run to Bideford

TOURIST INFORMATION

Appledore Visitors' Association ⌀ www.appledore.org
Bideford Burton Art Gallery, Kingsley Rd, EX39 2QQ ✆ 01237 477676 ⌀ www.northdevon.com
Clovelly EX39 5TA ✆ 01237 431781 ⌀ www.clovelly.co.uk
Westward Ho! ⌀ www.westwardhodevon.com

and Westward Ho! The only main road is the A39 which runs close to the coast until a few miles from Clovelly where it loses its nerve and takes a short cut to Bude in Cornwall. However, the 319 bus does a pretty good job of servicing this road every two hours or so, with diversions to the impressively named Woolfardisworthy and Clovelly before finishing in Hartland.

CYCLING & WALKING

There are no dedicated cycle paths here and, although the network of lanes carries little traffic, they are narrow and visibility is poor so cyclists need to take particular care.

Walkers, on the other hand, can enjoy the splendidly rugged section of the South West Coast Path above the layered and crumpled rocks of **Hartland Quay** and **Hartland Point**, heaved up by geological forces millions of years ago and cut by streams and waterfalls. This is reckoned, by some, to be the finest walking in Devon. There are also numerous inland footpaths where you won't meet a soul.

Walking maps & guides

✾ Ordnance Survey's 1:25,000 Explorer series 126 covers the region, along with Croydecycle's 1:12,500-scale Walking Maps, *Hartland & Clovelly* and *Appledore & Westward Ho!*.

For the South West Coast Path, you're well set up with Trailblazer's *Exmoor & North Devon*.

 WET-WEATHER ACTIVITIES

Burton Art Gallery & Museum Bideford (page 42)
Hartland Abbey (house) Hartland (page 30)
North Devon Maritime Museum Appledore (page 45)
Exceptional churches (pages 48–51)
The Gnome Reserve (page 48)

THE HARTLAND HEARTLAND

It is not the height of Hartland Point that makes it so striking, it is the perpendicular wall of rock, dark and forbidding, with nothing but a few clumps of heather to soften its grimness; its wild and indeed mountainous appearance, which gives it a look of grandeur shared by no other headland in the Bristol Channel.

J L W Page, 1895

The area west of the A39 is the wildest corner of North Devon – literally a corner, since the coastline makes a right-angle turn at Hartland Point. There's no better place in Devon to see the effects of a mighty collision of tectonic plates around 300 million years ago, which folded the rock like an accordion or pushed it up on its side. Different types of rock erode at varying rates so they tip and slide forming cliffs and sea-stacks.

To experience these remarkable formations fully you need to walk a stretch of the coastal path, but there are two car access points at **Hartland Quay** and **Hartland Point** where the less mobile can admire the seascape. There are no bus-assisted walks here – the A39, and therefore the bus, runs too far from the coast.

Between the coast and the main road is a network of narrow, high-hedged and confusing lanes, but persevere for the wonderful manor house of **Hartland Abbey**, the alluring gardens at **Docton Mill**, and the lonely church of St Nectan at **Stoke**.

1 HARTLAND

🏠 **Blegberry Farm** Hartland (page 195) ⛺ **Koa Tree Camp** Welcombe (page 195), **Loveland Farm** Hartland (page 196)

The main settlement in the area has a long history. Hartland was a gift from King Alfred to his son Edward, and passed down a line of kings until Canute and eventually William the Conqueror. Seven hundred years later, however, it was described by W G Maton as having 'an air of poverty that depresses it to a level with a Cornish borough'. These days it has regained its confidence and enjoys a nice community feel, a village store that stays open late and has a microwave oven for heating your pasties, and a free car park. There are also pubs and tea shops. The 319 bus passes every two hours or so (but check the latest timetable), enabling you to do a fair amount of sightseeing even without a car.

The principle sights are some distance from Hartland, but both conveniently in the direction of Hartland Quay. The glorious Hartland

:y is about a mile away and **St Nectan's Church**, whose tower – at
feet the highest in Devon – provides a landmark for walkers, is a
mile further on at Stoke. You enter it via an unusual swivel lych-gate
with a counter-balance weight to keep it closed. Inside are numbered
pews from the days when parishioners had to pay 'pew rent' for their
seat in church, a huge, intricately carved screen with typical Devon fan
vaulting, and carved bench ends. The font is interesting, not only for its
carved sides but for the heads that glare at each other from the base and
below the bowl. The ones on the base are gloomy grotesques, whilst their
opposites – visible only if you lie on the floor – are wise old bearded
men. You can draw your own conclusions as to what they mean.

There are memorials, inside and out, to the Lane family who founded
Penguin Books.

FOOD & DRINK

The Hart Inn The Square, EX39 6BL ✎ 01237 441474 ⏱ www.thehartinn.com ⊙ closed
Mon. A traditional, 14th-century former coaching inn with an enviable reputation for good
dining. Locals come here for the real ale and conversation, but for foodies it's the restaurant.
All the produce is locally sourced – and they tell you where it comes from – and their menu
usually includes game such as rabbit, pheasant or woodcock.

2 HARTLAND ABBEY

EX39 6DT ✎ 01237 441496/441234 ⏱ www.hartlandabbey.com ⊙ Apr–Oct, Sun–Thu;
tea room & gardens ⊙ 11.30–17.00; house 14.00–17.00. Some variation so check website
or phone before visiting.

W G Maton may have had a poor view of Hartland, but he loved the
house which stands in the location of an old abbey, now disappeared.

> Every advantage has been taken of the spot to create a
> picturesque and agreeable scene, the slopes on each side being
> planted very judiciously, and the intermediate lawn opened to a
> little bridge that crosses a swift, bubbling brook . . . Though built
> in a monastic fashion, with Gothic windows, the Priory [sic] is
> wholly modern, no remains of the old structure being left. It is
> at present the residence of Colonel Orchard.

The house was indeed wholly modern when Maton saw it in the
1790s; Paul Orchard had completely rebuilt it only 20 years earlier.
Nothing remains of the original abbey, which survived longer than
any other monastery in England. When Henry VIII finally got round

to dissolving it in 1539 he gave it to the appropriately named William Abbott, who was Sergeant of his Wine Cellar at Hampton Court (nice job; nice perks!). In 1583 Prudence Abbott married into the Luttrell family of Dunster Castle who retained ownership until the house passed, again through marriage, to Paul Orchard. The Orchards held it for a hundred years before it passed to the Stucleys in the mid-1800s; it has been with their family ever since. The Orchards and the Stucleys demolished, rebuilt and altered parts of the house over the centuries, so the current building is a hodgepodge of different designs – but it works, perhaps thanks to architects like Sir George Gilbert Scott who was commissioned by Sir George Stucley to design the entrance and front hall which give the arriving visitor such a positive impression.

"Hartland Abbey is gorgeous: far superior to most other great Devon houses, which sometimes struggle to justify their entrance fee. This is undisputedly grand."

Hartland Abbey is gorgeous: far superior to most other great Devon houses, which sometimes struggle to justify their entrance fee. This is undisputedly grand, with magnificent fireplaces, splendid furniture and paintings, many of them from Poltimore House near Exeter (the heiress of Poltimore married a Stucley), and stunning views from the huge windows. The quality of the contents is one of the advantages of a house that has never been sold, but passed down through the centuries by inheritance.

A peep into the guest rooms makes one envious of the wartime evacuees from London's Highgate Junior School, who hit the jackpot when they were sent here. Until recently the surviving ones came back each year to relive those extraordinary times, but these days most are too old to make the journey, although some individuals do still manage it including 'one amazing gentleman who made his way here using public transport and enjoyed tea and cake with Lady Stucley'. Scattered around the house are laminated newspaper cuttings which add snippets of intrigue: Princess Margaret in a bath wearing a tiara, for instance.

The library was built within the walls of the original abbey, and is hung with portraits including one by Sir Joshua Reynolds and two by Gainsborough. And there are quite a few books. Before the war it used to have a lot more – 8,000 more, in fact. In 1939 these books were found to be surplus to requirements and taken to the local tip. A canny farmer intercepted the cart and decided they would be just the thing for building a boundary wall: cheaper than bricks. This literary wall contained such rarities as a copy of a Hebrew grammar from 1597. There will have been some erudite cows in North Devon.

The gardens are as rewarding as the house, and the lived-in, or rather worked-in, feeling is even stronger since almost all of the work has been

Elmscott to Speke's Mill Mouth or Hartland Quay

❋ OS Explorer map 126 or Croydecycle *Hartland & Clovelly*; start: Elmscott ♥ SS23122 21831; 3½ or 5½ miles; easy (no steep climbs or descents)

In contrast to the rugged walk around Hartland Point, this is a gentle, mostly level stroll which still gives you the chance to admire the tortured rocks that characterise this bit of coast.

A clearly signed path runs from opposite Little Elmscott Farm through a field to join the coast path, where you turn right and keep going. Ahead is the high tower of St Nectan's Church and the dome of the radar station marking Hartland Point; below is a series of inaccessible beaches and jagged rocks. I walked it in sunshine after days of rain which had encouraged edible giant parasol mushrooms to appear among the gorse and heather. Talking of gorse, this was

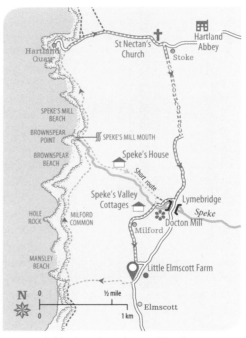

the first time I'd noticed the parasitic common dodder, draped over the gorse like a fragrant mauve bedspread. It kills the gorse, but in this case I prefer the parasite to the host.

After about half a mile you'll come to a seat made from the wreckage of the tanker *Green Ranger* which broke up on the rocks during a gale in November 1962. Heroic Appledore lifeboatmen rescued the crew. Part of the wreck is still visible. The unfolding panorama of rocks at the sea's edge is extraordinary: jagged, furrowed or tilted. At **Speke's Mill Mouth**

done by the Stucley family themselves. They only employ 1½ gardeners, so to have achieved this amount of order in such a vast garden is an inspiration to us inept amateurs. The information leaflet describes this challenge in detail; it is clearly written by gardeners for gardeners. Make sure you pick up a copy before setting out to explore. I recommend a

(or Spekesmouth) a spectacular waterfall pours, unhindered, over a vertical rock face, popular with climbers. J L W Page in *The Coasts of Devon and Lundy Island* (published in 1895) describes this with his usual enthusiasm: 'This, perhaps the finest cascade on the coast, is at least fifty feet high, and against the black glistening wall of rock, the spray shows white as snow.' Such a beauty spot could not stay hidden and now, over a hundred years later, car drivers can find their way down to the foot of the falls, with consequent litter and general peopleness, so prepare to be a bit disappointed.

This is where you leave the coast if you are doing the shorter walk. Apart from the easier distance, this gives you the option of visiting **Docton Mill** with its lovely gardens and excellent cream teas (page 35). Retrace your steps for a short distance, but continuing straight on rather than taking the right fork to the coastal route. Then just stay on the main path, keeping the River Speke on your right and ignoring the first fork left to Speke's House. You'll reach Lymebridge and Docton Mill in less than a mile. Replete with tea and cakes, you've a stroll of under a mile back to your car.

By the longer route, **Hartland Quay** is only 20 minutes away from the waterfall, and the views are magnificent. The rocks now look like purple ploughed fields, broken by high, smooth chunks topped with green. The closer you get to the quay, the more dramatic the seascape, until you reach Hartland Quay Hotel with a view to die for, and snacks or full meals available from the bar. If you want to linger, there's a small shipwreck museum, a good reminder of the days when this was a busy port. In the late 18th century W G Maton commented that 'Hartland-quay consists of about a dozen decent cottages, and has a commodious little pier, at which commodities of various kinds, for the supply of this part of the country, are landed from Bideford and Barnstaple; and here the fishermen and coasters find good shelter against the south-westerly winds, by mooring under the eminences.' The quay was still in use 50 years later when Hartland Abbey's Sir George Stucley landed a load of Maltese stone from his yacht, destined for the fireplace in the billiard room.

Head inland to look at **St Nectan's Church** in Stoke and/or **Hartland Abbey**, then return to your car via the narrow lanes.

visit to the Bog Garden where narrow paths wind around huge stands of giant rhubarb, *Gunnera manicata*, and more delicate ferns and other water-loving plants. Some way from the house is the walled kitchen garden, where when I visited runner beans dangled temptingly and a gardener or a Stucley was tying up the raspberry vines. This garden helps to feed the present-day hungry family. Beyond the car park is a path 'to the beach'. It joins the South West Coast Path at Blackpool Mill, and, since it misses out the first up and down of the Hartland Point walk, makes a sensible alternative to starting the walk at Hartland Quay. On a high point, just before meeting the coast path, is the recently restored gazebo with a super view over the sea to Lundy Island.

Around Hartland Point

❋ OS Explorer map 126 or Croydecycle *Hartland & Clovelly*; start: Hartland Quay
♥ SS23122 21831; 5 miles; strenuous

Local walks expert Bryan Cath warned me: 'It may look short but there are five up and downs and no escape route; it's more than some people can cope with.' Indeed, it looks easy to follow the coastal path round Hartland Point to the lighthouse and beyond, but it is certainly strenuous. However, I've known worse elsewhere on the South West Coast Path and the scenery is superlative, so the above is a warning not a deterrent. And it's easy to make it a circular walk, with a chance to see St Nectan's Church and Hartland Abbey too. If you plan to visit Hartland Abbey (do double-check the opening times), you can park there and take the private path to Blackpool Mill, thus cutting out one of the hills. Or achieve the same objective by parking at Stoke and taking the path that follows the south bank of Abbey River.

If you park at **Hartford Quay**, take the path round **Warren Beach**. After meeting and leaving the road, start your first climb, admiring the pleated and puckered cliff rocks as you go, to **Dyer's Lookout**. Dropping down to River Abbey and its bridge, you'll see Blackpool Mill Cottage ahead.

Another up, another down – and again, and again, and again – and you'll be at **Hartland Point** with its lighthouse sitting coyly at the base of the cliff (closed to visitors) and the big radar 'football' on the hill, used during World War II to track enemy vessels and aircraft. The hills are hard work but from every summit there's a splendid view. The steeply sloping rock faces here are used for **climbing and abseiling activites** run by Skern Lodge (✆ 01237 475992 ⏚ www.skernlodge.co.uk).

At the end of the track there's a car park and refreshment kiosk. After a reviving cuppa turn your sights to the church tower and follow the often muddy tracks to **Stoke** and thence to your vehicle.

3 DOCTON MILL

Lymebridge, Hartland EX39 6EA ✐ 01237 441369 ✐ www.doctonmill.co.uk ☉ Mar–Oct daily (check website for exact dates)

This delightful place combines an excellent tea room with a beguiling garden full of winding mossy paths through mature woodland, a bog garden and lawns bordered by the little River Speke which later cascades over a slab of rock at Speke's Mill Mouth. When there is sufficient water in the river it runs the mill which is still operating. Both the tea room and the gardens have won awards, and plenty of people come here for lunch (fish and salads are specialities) or cream tea without visiting the garden – which is a pity. There is so much variety here in a relatively small

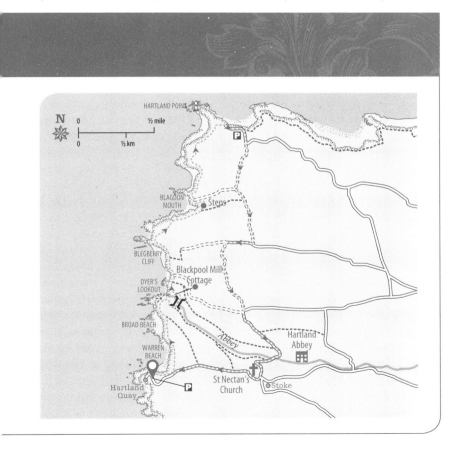

area, and always something to see whatever the time of year. Lana and John Borrett, the owners, have been here for 15 years and are responsible for creating the Magnolia Garden and many of the herbaceous borders.

"A beguiling garden full of winding mossy paths through mature woodland, a bog garden and lawns bordered by the little River Speke."

I asked Lana which was the very best month to visit. 'Probably early June, when it's full of bluebells, although the snowdrops are often wonderful when we first open. But there's always something colourful to see.'

In your wanderings you'll come across a mystery slate tombstone carved with just initials and a single date. No-one knows anything about it. My rather unromantic guess is that it was a trial stone for an apprentice learning his craft. The letters and date contain a variety of straight lines and curves which are the tricky part of good letter carving.

The car park is small, so the owners ask you not to leave your car there while you go walking; it is for tea room and garden visitors only.

If using a sat nav to reach Docton Mill, be careful not to follow it blindly up the narrow lane to Milford, as I did, but keep an eye on the signs which direct you to the entrance on your right just after the bridge.

THE CLOVELLY AREA

At Clovelly is a little pier for vessels, and the harbour is noted for the herring-fishery. The land, as it juts out into the promontory of Hartland, is by no means remarkable for fertility, nor is it either novel, or varied enough to be pleasing to the eye.

W G Maton, travelling during 1794–96

4 CLOVELLY

🏠 **New Inn Hotel** Clovelly (page 194), **Bridge Cottage** Peppercombe (page 195)
🖉 www.clovelly.co.uk

The village has certainly changed since Maton's visit, but it took another century for its charms to become widely known. The man credited with this is Charles Kingsley who, in 1885, described Clovelly in typically overblown fashion in his novel *Westward Ho!* Visitors began arriving by boat and as the herrings, which had provided the village with income for centuries, declined in number, so the tourists increased. After Kingsley came Christine Hamlyn, who ensured that this tiny fishing village

A CHILD'S VIEW OF NORTH DEVON

Florence Unwin, aged 10

I love Devon. I think it must be the greenest place in England – not because it's eco-friendly but just from all the plant life growing in every hedgerow. This is easy to appreciate when it is warm and sunny, with a gentle breeze drifting in off the sparkling blue sea. But on our last holiday the weather wasn't as good and I wasn't always in the mood to gaze at the greenery – particularly during one seemingly endless walk in the hail, when my parents were going on about the 'idyllic scenery' and pointing at a random, not particularly interesting, lighthouse. What I had been looking forward to most about this holiday was going to the beach – like we had at Woolacombe the year before, when we went body boarding and sandcastle building. That wasn't looking very likely.

My gloomy mood quickly cleared up when we reached a tiny café tucked just out of sight of the dreaded path. Soon we were all gripping steaming mugs of hot chocolate or, in my case, munching my way through the marshmallows that floated around the surface and pinching a scone from my mum's Devon cream tea.

When we reached the village of Clovelly it started raining again, so we all huddled inside an old bookshop. When the sun came out, we wandered through the quaint cobbled streets and stopped to coo over the retired donkeys that the villagers once used to drag their luggage up and down the hill. And then we had another long tramp, of course, all the way back to our warm, dry holiday cottage.

remained in the time-warp that you see today. It has no cars, two hotels, and 2,000 visitors a day in summer.

Clovelly has been owned by one family since Zachary Hamlyn, a wealthy lawyer, bought the estate from the last of seven generations of the Cary family in 1738. Christine married Frederick Gosling in 1889, persuading him first to change his name, and secondly to earmark a portion of his large fortune for improving the estate. Many of the cottages were run down, so they and the entire village were restored and prettified according to Christine's taste. Her initials and the date of restoration can sometimes be spotted above a doorway. It was she who ensured that the village remained car-free, the only transport up and down its stepped, cobbled main street being donkeys and sleds. Tourist sentiment has put paid to the pannier-laden donkeys that used to carry supplies and mail; we love seeing working horses, but apparently not working donkeys. The animals now live in a sanctuary and pose for photos or give rides to children. But the sleds are still used, and you'll see them tied up outside the cottages. Souvenir shops are restricted, and all cottages must be leased as the primary home of their owner. Thus, although Clovelly is extraordinarily picturesque, it is a lived-in, working village, but with about 70% of its inhabitants commuting to the real world. In the 1920s the author S P B Mais wrote: 'Clovelly has been overphotographed. It cannot be overpraised. It bears no resemblance to any other place in the world. With its one street full of tourists, you might as well not try to see it, because it is no longer there to see. Its whole virtue goes when full.' That sentiment still holds true so plan to spend as much Slow time in the area as possible; walk into Clovelly if you can, or stay the night (page 184) so that you can see the village when it is there to see. And, away from the crowds, you cannot help but be enchanted by the little whitewashed cottages with grey slate roofs and flower-crammed gardens, stacked almost on top of each other. The cobbled road is called Up-a-Long and Down-a-Long, and is so steep, and so slippery after rain, that for centuries visitors – and locals – have grumbled about it. A local remarked to the author J L W Page: 'The folks do only dare get tight at one inn – the one at t'bottom o' the hill. Them as lives three doors away must keep always sober'.

"Away from the crowds you cannot help but be enchanted by the whitewashed cottages with grey slate roofs and flower-crammed gardens."

If you arrive the conventional way, by car, you will be processed through the visitor centre, paying an entrance fee before watching a film about the village's history. Then you're funnelled down the narrow cobbled street to peer into the windows of private houses, choose a few souvenirs, and buy a beer and Cornish pasty from the **Red Lion** pub, before returning to your car. If the steep climb back up is too daunting a Land Rover service will help you out. But stay longer and get your money's worth. There is plenty to see: a **Kingsley Museum**, a **Fisherman's Cottage** showing life as it was in the 1930s, and craft workshops. And if you still resent paying the entrance fee bear in mind that it is this income that keeps the village as it is, free from fast-food outlets and amusement arcades.

Each year, in mid November, the **Clovelly Herring Festival** is held; it focuses on everything herring, including traditional sea shanties and plenty of local beer and cider.

BOAT TRIPS

As befits an erstwhile fishing village, there are plenty of boat trips available, including one to **Lundy Island**.

Clovelly Charters ✆ 01237 431042 (daytime) or 01237 431405 (evenings Apr–Oct) or 07774 190359. Diving or fishing trips, swimming with seals, and visits to Lundy on the *Jessica Hettie*.

Independent Charters ✆ 01237 431374 ⊘ http://independentcharters.co.uk. A family-run business specialising in fishing trips, but other options available.

Lundy Charters ✆ 01237 424228 ⊘ www.lundy-charters.co.uk. Departures to Lundy from Clovelly or Appledore (page 45) on the *Lundy Murrelet*, plus a range of other trips including fishing and wildlife.

5 CLOVELLY COURT GARDEN & CHURCH

Clovelly EX39 5SY ✆ 01237 431781 ⊘ www.clovelly.co.uk/village/clovelly-court-gardens
⊖ Apr–end Sep; admission charge to village includes visit to the garden

Clovelly Court is the original seat of the Carys (their manor burned down in 1796) and now the Hamlyn descendants live here. The house is private but the kitchen garden is well worth a visit. Unlike the other gardens in North Devon which lure visitors by their beauty, this is mostly given over to growing food. And what food! The combination of a sheltered walled garden in a warm climate, and splendid glasshouses, allows the harvesting of peaches, apricots, grapes, oranges and lemons, peppers, tomatoes . . . and so on. There are plenty of flowers and shrubs to provide colour, but organically grown fruit and vegetables are the main thing here and there is generally a good selection offered for sale.

All Saints' Church is old, as can be guessed by the Norman arch above its door. The tower is also Norman. The graveyard is full of Carys, the original owners of Clovelly and residents of Clovelly Court, and there are several memorials to them inside. Charles Kingsley is also commemorated – his father was a popular rector here.

WALKS TO OR FROM CLOVELLY

If you contrive to arrive in Clovelly on foot you will avoid the feeling of entering a theme park (with the accompanying entrance fee) and see it for what it is: an extraordinarily picturesque working village. There's a short circular walk from the car park at Brownsham or two possibilities for bus-assisted walks.

Bus-assisted walks to Clovelly from Hartland or Horns Cross

The 319 bus running along the A39 makes two sorties inland, to Clovelly Visitor Centre and to Hartland, enabling you to do a linear walk along the **South West Coast Path** between these two points or from Horns Cross, east of Clovelly, partly along the level track known as **Hobby Drive**. Either way, this allows you to walk into Clovelly, bypassing the visitor centre, and then take the bus back to your starting point (make a note of the times before heading out). Hobby Drive was a carriage way constructed, as a hobby, by James Hamlyn during the Napoleonic Wars, perhaps using the labour of French prisoners of war. During those times of high unemployment, land owners thought up schemes to provide work for their labourers, and carriage ways were popular projects.

From Hartland, use the Croydecycle map (or Ordnance Survey) to access the coast via **Beckland Farm** and **Brownsham**, a distance of

Circular walk to Clovelly from Brownsham

✵ OS Explorer map 126 or Croydecycle *Hartland & Clovelly*; start: NT car park at Brownsham
📍 SS2852325973; 5½ miles; easy

Leave your car in the National Trust car park at **Brownsham** and take the path through **Beckland Woods**, following the signs to **Mouth Mill**; it has some ruined buildings from the old lime kiln in which you can shelter if it's raining, and a pebble beach with the sea-sculpted **Blackchurch Rock** in view. The rock formations are splendid, like multi-tiered sandwiches laid on their sides. You are now only about 45 minutes from Clovelly, walking through Brownsham Wood, which is owned by the National Trust and knee-deep in imbecile young pheasants in the late summer. About a third of the way along you'll pass the beautifully carved 'Angel Wings' seat, put there by Sir James Hamlyn Williams in 1826. Soon you'll get glimpses of Clovelly tucked into the cliffs and have a choice of routes into the village: either the road, and a steep walk downhill to emerge near the Red Lion pub by the quay, or the footpath that leads you to the centre of the village.

Returning takes about an hour, and is straightforward except for one confusing bit. Walk out along the road to the main gate of the estate, and pass through the side gate, past the church, then follow the bridleway. Once you see the cottage marked Snackland on the Croydecycle map (or Snaxland on the OS map), leave the track and bear right across the field. The bridleway is signposted where it enters Brownsham Wood; after that simply follow it to the car park.

From Horns Cross (or Bucks Cross) to Clovelly

❋ OS Explorer map 126 or Croydecycle *Appledore & Westward Ho!* plus *Hartland & Clovelly*; start: Horns Cross bus stop ♀ SS3847523145; 6.3 miles; moderate

This walk can be shortened by two miles by starting at Bucks Cross rather than Horns Cross. From the latter the **Coach and Horses** pub might delay your start, but once refreshed head seawards for less than a mile down the shady, ferny valley until you reach the remains of an Iron Age fort, Peppercombe Castle, and the coast path. From here you are mainly in woodland, continuing through first Sloo and then Worthygate woods (bluebells in the spring) until you come to the scatter of cottages that is Bucks Mill. The 1939 Ward Lock guide to the area states that: 'At one time all the inhabitants of Bucks were Braunds and many of that name live there still. They seem to be a distinct race, swarthy to a degree, and are held to be descended from a party of Spaniards who some say were wrecked near, and others contend were taken prisoners, at the time of the Armada.' That theory entertained some guidebook writers in the first half of the 20th century, but has now been dismissed.

From Bucks Mill the path passes by some magnificent beech trees and carpets of bluebells in the spring, before joining Hobby Drive which provides an easy three-mile stroll into Clovelly.

about 2½ miles, to join the walk described opposite. Then it's around 3½ miles to Clovelly, making a total distance of under six miles. The full, dramatic, wonderful walk from Hartland Quay is just over ten miles.

The six-mile walk from the bus stop at Horns Cross is very different, being mainly inland through woods and including Hobby Drive.

BIDEFORD & AREA

🏠 **Beara Farmhouse** Buckland Brewer (page 195), **South Yeo** Yeo Vale (page 195)

The Bridge at Bedeforde is a very notable Worke… A poore Preste began thys Bridge; and, as it is saide, he was animated so to do by a Vision. Then al the Cuntery about sette their Handes onto the performing of it, and sins Landes hath bene gyven to the maintenaunce of it. Ther standith a fair Chapelle of our Lady at the very ende of it, and there is a Fraternite in the Town for perservation of this Bridge; and one waititth continually to kepe the Bridge clene from al Ordure.

John Leland, travelling during 1534–43

Bideford's **Long Bridge** over the River Torridge is still its most notable feature, although an even longer modern one carries most of the traffic from Barnstaple. The old bridge has linked the town with its neighbour across the Torridge, East-the-Water, since about 1280. Two hundred years later the wooden structure was reinforced with stone; the original wooden arches varied in width, and this irregularity has been preserved with each rebuilding. Leland's 'fraternite in the Town', the Bideford Bridge Trust, continued to maintain the bridge until 1968 when the western arch collapsed; the Department of Transport then decided that enough was enough and took over responsibility.

The Grenville family owned Bideford from Norman times until 1744, but until the late 16th century it was mainly a centre for shipbuilding, and largely overshadowed by Barnstaple. After Sir Richard Grenville's 1585 voyage to establish colonies in Virginia and Carolina, trans-Atlantic trade took off, along with Bideford's fortunes. The quay was built in 1663 and quantities of tobacco and Newfoundland cod were landed there. The town's surge of prosperity began towards the end of the 17th century when it was the main port for the transport of goods to and from the American colonies. Tobacco was the main import.

Down river is the still-charming town of **Appledore**, and, turning west, the resort of **Westward Ho!** and its older neighbour **Northam** (page 46).

6 BIDEFORD

Generally accepted as being the most attractive town in northwest Devon, Bideford has its Long Bridge (see above), a rich maritime history, good shops and restaurants, and the excellent **Burton Art Gallery and Museum**. This is beyond the statue of Charles Kingsley at the north end of the quay, set in the Victoria Park. The town's **tourist information centre** is also here (✆ 01237 477676). In this peaceful, flowery place are eight guns captured from the Spanish by Grenville or his contemporaries.

Of the narrow streets rising steeply from the quay, the most interesting architecturally is Bridgeland Street. Above Bridge Street, which leads up from the old bridge, is the elegant 1884 building which houses the **Pannier Market** on Tuesdays and Saturdays.

St Mary's Church (🕙 10.00–12.00 only), nearby, is crammed with maritime memorials. The Norman font is one of the few old things in the church, and it is here that the first native American to be brought to England was baptised in 1588. His name was Raleigh, in deference to Grenville's contemporary, and he was from the Algonquin tribe. He only survived a year, dying, presumably, of an infection against which he would have had no immunity.

If you're in Bideford at dusk watch out for flocks (murmurations) of **starlings** making patterns in the sky before roosting under the bridge.

FOOD & DRINK

Green Goose 25/26 Mill St, EX39 2JW ✆ 01237 459599 ⬦ www.thegreengoosecafe.co.uk. An informal and very friendly place with good, wholesome food and excellent service.
L'Eau de Vie 16 High St, EX39 2AA ✆ 01237 476813. A very friendly French restaurant serving a variety of authentic French dishes, beautifully cooked, along with French conversation once a month. A favourite with locals.

7 APPLEDORE

🏠 **Poacher's Cottage** (page 195)

Reminiscent of Clovelly, with its car-free streets sloping steeply down to the long, curved quay, this still feels like a working maritime village – as indeed it is. Once the centre of North Devon's ship-building industry, it still has the Appledore Shipbuilder's Yard, an impressively large dry dock.

ROPE-MAKING

In Appledore's maritime museum is a working model of how rope was made when every seaside village had its Ropewalk. A straight stretch of at least 300 yards was needed to make the rope that was an essential part of the shipping industry. The process was similar to the way a sheep's fleece is turned into yarn, but on a much larger scale.

The hemp, usually grown locally, was dried and then 'heckled' or 'hatchelled' with iron spikes to separate the fibres, called 'streaks'. To twist the fibres, the spinner walked backwards, feeding streaks from the bundle round his waist into the 'yarn', while another worker turned the handle of a simple device which twisted the yarn into 'strands', their length depending on the length of the Ropewalk – anything up to 800 yards. Spinners worked 12-hour shifts and in the course of a working day could walk 18 miles – backwards.

The name Ropewalk is retained in many British towns and cities, as is Ropery. They are both throwbacks to the traditional skill of rope-making.

Back in the first millennium, this region was once thought to be the site of a fierce battle between the local Saxon population and Hubba the Dane (see box, below). A plaque marking the spot where the battle supposedly took place can be seen at the bend in the road still known as Bloody Corner, between Appledore and Northam. In fact, this is much more likely to be the site of a battle that took place between the native Saxons and the Norman invaders in 1069. But never mind, the defeat of Hubba the Dane is a good story, and one that Appledore clings on to. On Western Green stands a hunk of Lundy granite, the Hubbastone, erected in 2009 and carved with Nordic designs to commemorate

HUBBA THE DANE

Janice Booth

Hubba the Dane and Bloody Corner (between Northam and Appledore) are so tangled up in legend and conflicting historical reports that 'facts' about them need to be treated with a degree of caution. In the 17th century Tristram Risdon (1580–1640, author of *A Chorographical Description or Survey of the County of Devon*) and Thomas Westcote concluded that the 9th-century battle of Cynuit had taken place at Henniborough near Northam, and that Hubba (who died in it) was buried at Wibblestone – which was renamed Hubbastone in his honour. The story was embraced locally and expanded over the years, as happens with such things. A plaque erected at Bloody Corner by one Thomas Chappell in 1890 instructs: 'Stop stranger stop/Near this spot lies buried/ King Hubba the Dane/Who was slayed in a bloody retreat/By King Alfred the Great'.

However, current research suggests that the battle in which Hubba died took place elsewhere (probably near Beaford) and that he wasn't slain by Alfred. He was indeed a 9th-century Viking leader, possibly named Ubba Ragnarsson; tradition claims that in ad878 he landed his ships at Boathyde with conquest and pillaging in mind, and marched on Kenwith, where he was defeated and killed. A version of this story appears in Thomas Cox's *Devonshire* (1738):

In this place [Appledore] it was that Hubba the Dane, having wasted South Wales with fire and sword, landed in the days of King Alfred with 33 sail of ships, and laid siege to the castle of Kenwith, now called Hennaborough. The Devonshire men bravely opposed their ravagers, and having slain Hubba, their general who lies buried at Hublestone, and many of his followers, obliged them to fly to their ships and make their escape.

this battle. The cherry on this slice of historical cake is that the local stonemason who worked on the modern memorial was named – appropriately – Gabriel Hummerstone.

The booklet *Appledore Heritage Trail* describes, and illustrates, buildings and places of interest which include an exceptionally rewarding museum. **The North Devon Maritime Museum** is all about Appledore's relationship with the sea, but the exhibits are so varied that it is never dull. One room is given over to the town's history, including the exploits of Hubba the Dane and seafarers Stephen and William Borough. Other rooms contain intricate models of historically important ships, together with stories about the lifeboat service and the fleets of boats that went all the way to Newfoundland for cod, as well as the rather surprising fact that a collar and cuff factory in the town once employed a hundred women.

"Other rooms contain models of ships, together with stories about the fleets of boats that went all the way to Newfoundland for cod."

Good **shops** abound and there are six pubs and an award-winning café/delicatessen, **John's** (✆ 01237 425870 ⇱ www.johnsofappledore. co.uk), which has a range of delicious take-away picnics, pastries and fresh produce for sale as well as a café. It is also the village post office and has some tourist information leaflets.

The village turns literary in late September for the **Appledore Book Festival** (⇱ www.appledorebookfestival.co.uk), a week-long event with big-name authors.

The ferry service to Instow (⇱ www.appledoreinstowferry.com) is run by volunteers, operating a few hours each side of the high tide. Look for the signs on the quay. Bicycles can be taken if there's room.

BOAT TRIPS

Appledore Leisure Cruise or Fishing Trips ✆ 07866 314260. Trips on an 18-foot open boat, the *Fender*, up the River Torridge for sightseeing or fishing.

Appledore Pleasure/Fishing Cruises ✆ 01237 476191. Trips on *The Cheeky Monkey*, a 20-foot traditional wooden boat. Up the River Torridge for seven to eight miles.

Appledore Sails ✆ 01237 423163 or 0780 2713435 ⇱ www.appledoresails.co.uk. Charter a skippered yacht for a short or long trip on an Appledore-made lug sail boat.

Lundy Charters ✆ 01237 424228 ⇱ www.lundy-charters.co.uk. Departures to Lundy from Appledore or Clovelly on the *Lundy Murrelet* (page 39).

8 WESTWARD HO! & NORTHAM

🏠 **Yeoldon House** Northam (page 194)

Writing at the end of the 19th century, J L W Page quoted a contemporary journalist as saying that **Westward Ho!** was 'a tedious place, that no one would visit had they anywhere better to go to.' Over a hundred years later it is hard not to agree with him, although the resort is beloved by families and certainly everyone I met there was having a very good time.

This is the only town to be named after a book rather than the other way round, and also the only one to have an exclamation mark. It is entirely the creation of a 19th-century development company which saw the benefits of cashing in on Kingsley mania. They got it right. In addition to the beach scene there is a splendid golf course and an area of wild coastal vegetation, **Kipling Tors**, named after the town's more erudite literary connection who was at school here.

Stretching for two miles behind the sandy beach to **Northam Burrows Country Park** (The Burrows Centre, Sandymere Rd, EX39 1XS ✐ 01237 479708 ☉ May–Sep, park open to walkers year-round) is the Pebble Ridge. In former times maintaining this natural defence against the sea was the responsibility of 'Potwallopers', local people who could claim a vote because they had boiled their own pot in the parish for six months. They held the grazing rights to the Northam Burrows, so it was in their interest to keep the sea out.

"In former times maintaining this natural defence against the sea was the responsibility of 'Potwallopers', local people who had boiled their own pot in the parish for six months."

The Northam Burrows are now part of the UN Biosphere Reserve, and a Site of Special Scientific Interest with saltmarsh and sand dunes, very similar to Braunton Burrows. Natural History information is available at the Burrow Centre.

The village of **Northam** is altogether more tranquil than its brash neighbour, Westward Ho!, with a touching memorial near the square to the local men who were lost at sea. Each man is represented by a boulder carried there from the beach. The village has a rich history which it shares with Appledore (see box, page 44). The tall tower of its church was traditionally a landmark for sailors, and until the mid 19th century was regularly painted white to make it stand out more clearly.

9 ABBOTSHAM

Driving between Northam and Clovelly on the A39 you will pass prominent signs to **The Big Sheep** (✆ 01237 472366 ⌂ www.thebigsheep. co.uk). This large-scale family attraction began by being centred entirely on sheep; it still has some demonstrations of sheep management and, entertainingly, sheep racing but you need to be with small children to enjoy the rides and other entertainments. Adults will find more quiet pleasures in the lovely **St Helen's Church** at Abbotsham described on page 50.

♍ FOOD & DRINK

Bell Inn Rectory Lane, Parkham EX39 5PL ✆ 01237 451201 ⌂ www.thebellinnparkham. co.uk. Even if it hadn't won the North Devon Pub of the Year Award in 2013, this 13th-century thatched pub in the little village of Parkham just south of Horns Cross would be worth the detour. It's everything a Devon pub should be: oak beams, open fires and real ales. It also has an impressive menu featuring some traditional Devon recipes, and regular community events.

Coach and Horses Buckland Brewer EX39 5LU ✆ 01237 451395. Buckland Brewer is a village to the south of Littleham, and this charming 13th-century thatched pub is the place to go if you are looking for a tranquil piece of rural Devon. Good food.

Memories 8 Fore St, Northam EX39 1AW ✆ 01237 473419. A small, personable restaurant which makes a point of serving ethically produced local meat (free-range, outdoor reared) and a wide range of imaginative dishes in unfussy surroundings and at affordable prices. Try the sticky date and ginger sponge pudding! Popular, so book ahead.

Soyer's Restaurant Yeoldon House, Durrant Lane, Northam EX39 2RL ✆ 01237 474400. A quality restaurant in this upmarket hotel serving seriously good food, beautifully presented. You can enjoy the whole hotel experience here, even as a non-resident, with coffee in the comfortable lounge.

SOUTH OF THE A39

You can feel delightfully cut off pottering down the narrow lanes that meander through this very rural region. Apart from the **Gnome Reserve**, there are few established tourist attractions which is, perhaps, an attraction in itself for walkers or cyclists.

10 WOOLFARDISWORTHY

More of a curiosity because of its name – surely one of the longest unhyphenated village names in England – than because it has anything of spectacular interest, but this is a pleasant, large village with a handy shop and an interesting church. For convenience, and fitting on signposts, the name is often shortened to (and pronounced) Woolsery.

The church has a Norman doorway, with carved heads that make a convenient shelf for the swallows that nest there. The interior is airy and spacious, with some carved bench ends and an effigy of Richard Cole (1614), in full armour, propped uncomfortably on one elbow. Parts of the church, most notably the tower, are 14th century. It is unusual in that the staircase is on the outside of the tower.

If you drive to the Gnome Reserve from Woolfardisworthy you'll pass through a beautiful arbour of beech trees leaning over the road forming a tunnel: an excellent example of a beech-topped earth bank, as described below.

11 THE GNOME RESERVE

West Putford, Nr Bradworthy EX22 7XE ✆ 01409 241435 ✎ www.gnomereserve.co.uk
☉ 21 Mar–31 Oct daily 10.00–17.00

The little fellows deserve their reserve; after all there are over 2,000 of them, dotted around the dark mossy woods and involved in every activity you can imagine. You'll find them cycling, skateboarding, wielding a tennis racket, a javelin or a violin and riding anything that moves: a bicycle, aeroplane, duck, pig, and a snail (at least I think it's a snail). There are two gnomes on their potties, mooning at delighted children, and one luxuriating in his bath. All in all they are having a wonderful time, and visitors are expected to play their part. You are greeted by the indefatigable owner, Ann Atkin, who asks you to select an 'almost compulsory hat' to wear as you tour the garden. Trained as an artist, she has been collecting gnomes since 1979 and it remains a family concern, with her daughter-in-law Marg baking the scones for the cream tea that any visitor should indulge in before going gnome.

"There are two gnomes on their potties, mooning at delighted children, and one luxuriating in his bath."

SOME EXCEPTIONAL CHURCHES

Dotted around the area are some wonderful little churches with that hallmark of Devon, carved bench ends. So if you love these storehouses of history and folk art, it's worth making a diversion.

12 ALWINGTON

The lovely little **church of St Andrew** (EX39 5DA), which has some fearsome gargoyles glowering down from the tower, is famous for its complete depiction of the Bible, Old and New testaments, carved into the bench ends. Not all these are old – many were carved by a local man, Reuben Arnold, in the early 20th century, but some date from the 16th century and the carving, and subject, is exceptional. The name associated with Alwington from these times is Coffin. There is a wall memorial to Richard and Elizabeth Coffin and their 15 children. The Coffins married into the Pine family and became – almost unbelievably – the Pine-Coffins.

The church is kept locked but the address and phone number of the nearby key-holder are on the porch noticeboard.

13 LITTLEHAM

The **church of St Swithun** (or Swithin; EX39 5HR) sits on its own, nearly a mile from the village but well signposted. I was lucky to find the warden, Andrew Tregoning, mowing the graveyard. He gave me a guided tour: 'I'll show you the walrus.' Not an animal you expect to find carved into a church screen, but it was a pun on the name of the rector who, in 1892, took on the tremendous task of restoring the dilapidated church. His name was the Reverend George Morse, and morse (or something similar) is the Nordic name for walrus. The striking bench ends are in light-coloured oak so are the first thing you notice on entering the church. Some of the subjects of these carvings defy description. There are men whose faces are starting to morph into foliage, some with long tongues (I guess) disappearing into some sort of vessel. And is that an eagle wearing a horned headdress? One can only agree with Andrew when he says 'Of course a lot of the carvers were high on LSD' (it is known that mould – ergot alkaloids – growing on rye bread could produce hallucinations).

At the back of the church is a chest hollowed out from a solid oak trunk. Dominating the south side is the huge tomb of General Crealock, who lived and died in Victorian times. The tomb is topped by a beautifully carved effigy of the general who evidently did not die in poverty. Or modesty. His descendants spared no expense on the memorial; he is surrounded by 12 angels, with female figures representing the virtues of Truth, Hope, Faith, Justice, Fortitude and Wisdom. The latter has a man's face carved at the back of her head; make of this what you will.

POLACCA

Unique to North Devon were the little boats which plied the Bristol Channel in the 18th and 19th centuries bringing coal and limestone for the many lime kilns which are a feature of this part of the county, where 'burnt lime' or quicklime was needed to improve the fertility of the acid soil. Polacca were small vessels which could be sailed backwards to navigate the tricky Bideford Bar. The name was also spelled poleacre, referring to the single pole mast which allowed the sail to be hoisted or lowered quickly in an emergency.

The memorial arrived, in pieces, in 1894 when Morse was in the middle of his restoration which must have been somewhat inconvenient. Originally the tomb was surrounded by a railing which has since been removed to try to make a little more space.

Andrew Tregoning has painstakingly copied out Morse's even more painstaking diary of the restoration. It makes fascinating reading before or after visiting this church: ⚓ www.littleham-landcross.org.uk.

There is an old (but restored) painting of St Swithun on the wall which probably dates from the 14th century. He was an Anglo-Saxon bishop of Winchester (and later patron saint of the cathedral) who went out of his way to help the poor. His humility decreed that he be buried outside the church so under the feet of passers-by and subject to the rain falling from the cathedral roof. The story goes that when his remains were dug up and reburied in a shrine within the cathedral, he showed his anger through a downpour which persisted for 40 days. Hence the belief that if it's raining on St Swithun's Day (15 July) it will continue for 40 days.

14 LANDCROSS

In the same parish as Littleham, the sweet little **Holy Trinity Church** (EX39 5JA), which lost its tower to lightning over a hundred years ago, sits high above the River Torridge. There is plenty here to engage the visitor, with medieval tiles on the floor and some carved bench ends, including two contortionists. The pulpit is also made up of old carvings.

ABBOTSHAM

The church, **St Helen's** (EX39 5AP), is joined to the old school, which suggests it played an important part in education. It has a quaint, stubby little tower, a high, white wagon roof with painted bosses, and some wonderful bench ends, although – even with the lights on – a torch is useful to see the detail. These are a mixture of religious pictures, workmen's tools, and 'village art' which is open to interpretation although the chained ape is supposed to represent drunkenness. Here, also, is a contortionist similar to the ones in Landcross. A very useful walk-around information board identifies each bench carving. It does not mention, nor could I find, the carving of a man riding backwards on a horse or donkey which is described and photographed in a couple of written accounts of this church. Perhaps it has been removed.

Near the altar is a fine chair carved with scenes from the crucifixion and, on a secular note, there is local honey for sale.

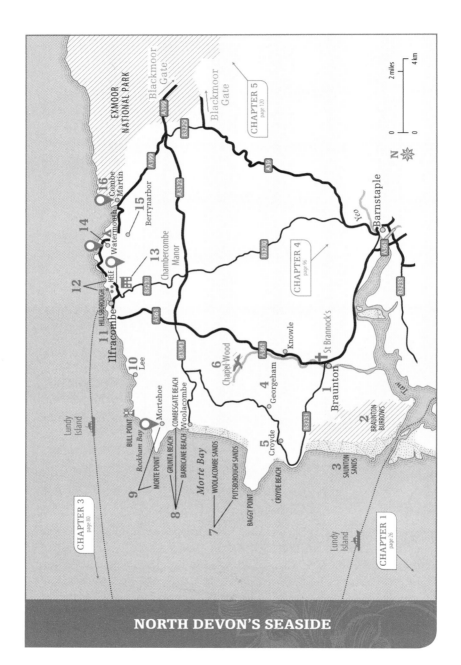

NORTH DEVON'S SEASIDE

2

NORTH DEVON'S SEASIDE

The finest scenery in Devonshire is to be found in the north, between Lynton and Ilfracombe, where the offshoots of Exmoor abut upon the sea, or are based in woods and subalpine ravines.

A Handbook for Travellers in Devon and Cornwall, 1872

North of the River Taw's broad estuary are Devon's most popular seaside resorts: the huge expanses of sand at **Saunton** and **Woolacombe**, with the smaller **Croyde Bay** tucked in between them, and the more intimate coves such as **Barricane**, **Grunta** and **Lee**, which take more effort to get to so are usually crowd-free even in the summer holidays.

The UNESCO Biosphere of **Braunton Burrows** lures nature lovers, with **Braunton** making an appealing base, and there's good birdwatching and marine wildlife viewing around the National Trust's **Baggy Point** and **Morte Point**.

Ilfracombe has its historic Tunnels Beach, great restaurants and the aquarium, while **Combe Martin** is a good centre for walking. In fact the latter is mostly in Exmoor National Park so should be in the next chapter, but is near enough to Ilfracombe to fit better here.

GETTING THERE & AROUND

Access from Exeter is via the A377 to Barnstaple, a reasonably fast road, or from Tiverton on the A361 North Devon Link Road. Thereafter progress will be slow in the holiday season when the smaller lanes in this pocket of North Devon get very crowded. Public transport is mainly limited to the 21A bus which runs frequently from Barnstaple to Braunton, Saunton, Croyde and Georgeham, whilst the 31 and 303 go from Ilfracombe to Woolacombe and Mortehoe. Check an up-to-date bus timetable for changes in the schedule.

CYCLING & WALKING

Often a bike is the quickest way round the narrow lanes and their bottlenecks of cars, but cyclists need to be wary of fast-driving locals.

Most of the famous **Tarka Trail** is described in *Chapter 4*, but it continues north through Braunton. Further east the region is served by the Ilfracombe–Woolacombe cycle circuit, part of NCN27, which gives you a 15-mile circular route largely along roads but with a traffic-free section from outside Ilfracombe to Willingcott Cross along a disused railway, and the coast at Woolacombe Sands. This route is described in detail in the free booklet *Cycling Trails in Devon*. Cycles can be hired in Braunton (Otter Cycle Hire, Station Rd ✐ 01271 813339).

The area is terrific for walking, with the South West Coast Path and its offshoots providing the best routes.

WET-WEATHER ACTIVITIES

Museum of British Surfing, **town museum** and **Countryside Centre**, Braunton (page 55)
Chambercombe Manor (page 70)
Combe Martin Museum (page 76)
Ilfracombe Museum (page 66)
Ilfracombe Aquarium (page 66)

WOOLACOMBE WAVES CERAMIC STUDIO

In Golden Coast Holiday Village ✐ 01271 871360

On wet days – or fine ones – if you've never tried painting your own pottery, you'll find this utterly absorbing even if you always thought yourself bereft of artistic talent. Children, of course, love it. Studios such as this one provide the ceramics, ranging from mugs to tiles to ornaments, inspiration and guidance. And if you can't stay to pick up your fired pots, they will post them to you.

BRAUNTON, THE BURROWS & SAUNTON SANDS

1 BRAUNTON

🏠 **Mill Cottage** (page 196)

This is one of North Devon's main surfing towns (actually it's officially a village), as you would guess from the surf shops displaying boards and their trappings, and the nation's only surf museum. It is a compact, visitor-friendly place with all the main attractions clustered around the Caen Street car park. Without having to open your umbrella you can find an exceptional small museum, the comprehensive Braunton Countryside Centre, and the Museum of British Surfing. Truly something for everyone.

When I visited the **Museum and Information Centre** they were having a derailment problem. The little model locomotive was soon back on its track and trundling around the perfect replica of the town in pre-Beeching days. It's so beautifully made I could hardly believe it was all the work of volunteers. 'I made the trees', Jane Fewings told me, 'but it was a combined effort, led by Barry Hodgson and Peter Constance.' That the museum and information centre is run by enthusiasts is obvious as soon as you step through the door, and the shifting exhibits show all aspects of rural and coastal life in times past, such as the Bulb Farm which was one of the region's biggest employers. 'You might wonder why the big houses belonging to captains were built on West Hill, far away from the sea,' Jane commented. 'It's said it was so the children could see their father's boat coming in and intercept dad and his money before he reached the Mariner's Arms.'

Across the car park, the **Countryside Centre** (✆ 01271 817171 ☉ Apr–Oct, Mon–Sat) gives detailed information on the Burrows as well as the agriculture of the area. The Great Field is a relic of Saxon cultivation where this very fertile land was worked in strips. It is still used for arable farming. Next door is the spacious **Museum of British Surfing** (⌘ www.museumofbritishsurfing.org.uk). I was surprised to learn how old this sport is, although Hawaii, not Devon, is its natural home. Duke Kahanmoku of Hawaii took a primitive surfboard to Australia in 1920 and started the craze which took off in the 1960s. Britain was not far behind in popularising this new sport, though the oldest surfboard dates back to the early 1900s. Agatha Christie used to go to Hawaii for the 'surf riding'.

If you feel hungry after all that virtual surfing, go round the corner to **Warrens Bakery** (15b Caen St) which calls itself the 'Guardian of the Cornish Pasty since 1860'.

On the outskirts of town, well signposted, is the **Elliott Gallery**, where a permanent exhibition showcases the work of the artist Walter Elliott, and there are temporary exhibits from other artists.

Some way out of Braunton, on the road to Ilfracombe and set in a graveyard full of orderly rows of tombstones and equally orderly and splendid elm trees, is **St Brannock's Church**, topped by a spire. There is some speculation that the missionary, St Brannock, arrived from Ireland as part of an invading force. Nevertheless, he must have been accepted pretty quickly by the populace if only for his ability to perform miracles. He usefully persuaded two deer – harts – to accept the yoke and to 'draw timbers thence to build a church'. A cow, which was slaughtered and partially butchered, reassembled itself at his request and carried on grazing. His first church was built on a hill overlooking Braunton, but the Devil kept rolling the stones down to the bottom at night (in a reverse

COASTGUARDS, SMUGGLERS & WRECKERS

The clifftop cottages that formerly belonged to coastguards are now highly sought after for their views and their often quite isolated position. Few pause to wonder why they were built so far from the centre of the seaside villages that they were protecting. Equally, few speculate on the origin of the South West Coast Path. The answers lie in Devon and West Somerset's long history of smuggling and, more shamefully, wrecking. Originally the coastguards' duty was to prevent the smugglers and wreckers from going about their business, and these were local people – smuggling was an integral part of Devon's economy – so the coastguards were not welcome neighbours. Their cottages were in the best position for patrolling the cliffs, watching out for the activities of the miscreants and, coincidentally, beating out the path that, in 1978, became the final addition to the South West Coast Path.

Favourite haunts for smugglers were sheltered coves, preferably with caves, and with a lime kiln nearby so accessible by boat. What one might call benign smuggling was done to escape the high duty on luxury goods. Wreckers were another matter. By tying lanterns to the tails of donkeys, they imitated the bob of a ship's light at anchor and lured their victim to the rocks. As the sailors swam ashore they were killed; the law stated that if no-one was left alive after a wreck, the cargo could be claimed by local people.

of the situation at Brentor on Dartmoor, where he moved the stones to the top of the hill; the Devil was particularly busy in Devon). Finally St Brannock had a dream that he should build the church where he came across a sow feeding a litter of piglets. The sow duly appeared and the church, built in the 13th century, is well worth visiting. The sow and her piglets are depicted on one of the roof bosses just above the font, but it is the carved bench ends that are special. The two stags or harts surely must be the ones that succumbed to the yoke, and on the third pew on the right from the altar is a hand grasping a severed head by the hair; presumably John the Baptist. Many of the bench ends are carved with the initials of the gentry who sat in those pews. Some are upside down; it is speculated that the carver, being illiterate, was unaware that it mattered.

"St Brannock had a dream that he should build the church where he came across a sow feeding a litter of piglets. The sow duly appeared."

Finally, if there's marmalade on sale (as there often is in Devon churches), don't miss this delicious homemade treat.

2 BRAUNTON BURROWS

⌂ www.northdevonbiosphere.org.uk

To a nature lover, the very word biosphere is alluring, conjuring up the image of rare species you wouldn't find elsewhere. And it's true of this UNESCO Biosphere Reserve, which recognises the uniqueness of this sand dune ecosystem. 'Sand' is misleading, since the dunes are clothed in vegetation, giving them a pleasing, green, blobby appearance. If you know your stuff, you could happily spend a few hours here. The casual visitor, however, will be hard put to recognise the rare plants or to spot a lizard or unusual insect. Enjoyment is further complicated by the confusing network of paths that criss-cross the dunes; you need a good sense of direction and perhaps a compass if you're to avoid getting lost. The botanical secrets of the Burrows are revealed in *Wild Flowers of Braunton Burrows* by Mary Breeds, who works at the Braunton Countryside Centre.

Perhaps the most rewarding way to see the area is by bike. The flat lanes are a godsend if coming from the hills of Exmoor, and cycling along the canal you'll see a good range of waterfowl. Braunton is also the start of the cycling section of the **Tarka Trail**.

3 SAUNTON SANDS

Saunton Sands was one of the beaches used to rehearse the D-Day landings, its 3½ miles of sandy beach being similar to those of Normandy. Now it is one of the region's best surfing beaches, and ideal for families, particularly those with dogs which are permitted on parts of the beach year-round. Those who don't like crowds have only to walk away from the car park and facilities to find their own private place.

GEORGEHAM & CROYDE

Most visitors drive straight through these villages on their way to the popular beach resort of Croyde. They're worth a stop, however.

4 GEORGEHAM

The town was just Ham in the Domesday Book, and gained its longer name through the church of St George, so the correct pronunciation is George-ham. Henry Williamson, author of *Tarka the Otter*, lived here and the little hut where he did his writing is now a listed building. He financed the building of the hut from the proceeds of *Tarka*. He is buried near the church tower, and it's worth pottering round the graveyard which is as enjoyable to browse as a second hand bookshop.

A MEETING WITH HENRY WILLIAMSON

Bob Dawe

In a way it feels as though Henry Williamson and I shared a childhood. We both flew kites and tobogganed on Hilly Fields in southeast London even though there was nearly half a lifetime's difference in our ages. This close identification, accompanied by my early fascination with World War I, prompted me to immerse myself in his 13-volume sequence *A Chronicle of Ancient Sunlight* rather than the more popular *Tarka the Otter*. I was keen to meet him and so wrote to him in 1973, shortly afterwards finding myself driving down to visit the lonely hut he wrote in,

high above Georgeham. He lived not far away in a terraced house in Ilfracombe. His mop of white hair and droopy World War I moustache were unmistakeable, but I was taken aback by the enormous weariness in his rheumy old eyes, due to the days and nights that he spent writing, writing, often by no more than the light of a candle. His small basement room was swimming in manuscripts which were piled up everywhere, on tables, the carpet, the floor. *Tarka the Otter* was in the process of being filmed and, much to his annoyance and confusion,

Almost every stone from the 1830s to the 1890s has a four-line (or longer) commemorative poem, usually assuring the reader that the deceased is better off under God's care. For example, a sad little grave of an infant proclaims: 'Grieve not for me my parents dear/Nor be forever sad/The shorter time I lived here/The lesser sin I had'.

To balance the many children's graves, there's one to a woman who died aged 100.

It seems that no-one dared to die in Georgeham at that time without commissioning the local poet to write a verse. One stone has just a poem without any name or inscription – possibly a marketing ploy?

5 CROYDE

Croyde is one of the places in which I am going to spend my declining years. It is an entirely delightful village, unspoiled and, one would almost say, unspoilable, but the modern builder is a fierce fellow. Croyde Bay is perfect; a real bay, this, not like Woolacombe or Saunton Sands, a mere ridge of sand. A real bay, to delight the eye, must curve out to a headland at either end … and between the headlands the great green rollers should run across hundreds of yards of hard, yellow sand before they break.

L du Garde Peach, *Unknown Devon*, 1927

Williamson had been repeatedly badgered to shorten the filmscript, hence the sea of paper as he struggled to complete the work.

Throughout his long life, Williamson had enjoyed the company of women. When I found him fretting in this nest of paper, he was bemoaning the fact that his latest young lady acolyte, who had been doing her best to help him sort it all out, had just left him in the lurch. We retreated to his 'local' where he was not too weary to do his best to impress my girlfriend by squeezing a bread-crust into the shape of an aeroplane and zooming it around her head. Later, we parted company on the sunny edge of Exmoor. As we left the pub, Williamson extravagantly and unnecessarily draped his greatcoat in an overtly protective gesture around my girlfriend's shoulders. As we drove away, I could see him in my rear-view mirror staring after us, a sagging, lonely, world- and work-weary figure. I felt a strange mixture of pity and respect. Not long after this the film *Tarka the Otter* was completed and not long after that, Henry Williamson died.

SURFING SCHOOLS

This region is the surfing capital of Devon so here's your chance to learn how to ride the waves. The following are listed geographically:

Lyndon Wake Croyde ✆ 01271 890078 ✐ www.lyndonwake.com

Surfing Croyde Bay Croyde ✆ 01271 891200 ✐ www.surfingcroydebay.co.uk

Surf South West Croyde & Saunton ✆ 01271 890400 ✐ www.surfsouthwest.com

Walking on Waves Saunton ✆ 01271 815438 ✐ www.walkingonwaves.co.uk

Barefoot Surf School Putsborough Sands ✆ 01271 891231 ✐ www.barefootsurf.com

Nick Thorne Surf School Woolacombe ✆ 01271 871337 ✐ http://nickthorne.com

The village has 26 listed buildings, mostly old farmhouses and associated barns, and some good pubs. The **beach**, still lovely, is renowned for surfing. When I visited, on a blustery day, the sea was speckled with swimmers and surfers having a great time in the breakers. Parking is expensive here, but if you continue north, towards the headland Baggy Point, you'll find the National Trust (NT) car park which is free to members and cheaper than the beach one for non-members. From here you have a choice: walk round **Baggy Point** to Putsborough Sands with a selection of footpaths to take you back to your car or, if it's low tide, investigate the tide pools at this end of the beach. There's a frequent bus service (21A) to Croyde Bay from Barnstaple and Braunton.

¶¶ FOOD & DRINK

The Blue Grove 2 Hobbs Hill, EX33 1LZ ✆ 01271 890111 ✐ www.blue-grove.co.uk. A lively place in Croyde village, serving local food (fish, Exmoor game, as well as international dishes such as Tuscan pork stew and spiced Thai mussels). Popular with locals for its themed evenings (curry, quiz nights) as well as visitors.

6 CHAPEL WOOD RSPB RESERVE

Tucked away only a couple of miles east of Woolacombe Sands (see opposite) is this haven of peace and birdsong. The reserve (♀ SS48175 41060) is small but rewarding, with streams and the remains of a 13th-century chapel. The RSPB has fixed nest boxes on several of the trees, so in the spring and early summer you can sit quietly and watch the feathery comings and goings, take a stroll along the various paths and admire the display of bluebells. The bird list includes nuthatches, tawny owls and woodpeckers.

BEACHES & HEADLANDS: MORTE BAY

Between the two horns of Baggy Point and Morte Point is Morte Bay and the 2½-mile stretch of sandy beach that makes up Putsborough Sands and Woolacombe Sands (the two morph into each other). **Woolacombe Sands** has been voted one of Britain's best beaches, so it's not surprising that it is so popular with families. There's room for everyone along this expanse of golden sand and white surf, and in the several holiday parks for camping and caravans. But tucked into recesses on the southern face of Morte Point are smaller, less crowded beaches, as well as a gorgeous headland walk.

7 PUTSBOROUGH & WOOLACOMBE SANDS

Putsborough is the southern, more isolated, end of the beach, sheltered by Baggy Point, with rock pools and fewer amenities than Woolacombe (and there is no lifeguard) so perhaps more appealing to adult Slow visitors. There's a dog-free area but otherwise it's dog-friendly, and the café serves good food. The car park is expensive (as they all are in this region) but if you park at the NT place in Croyde and walk over Baggy Point you can get the best of all worlds.

Woolacombe came into its own during the Victorian period when sea-bathing became all the rage and the large houses and hotels that we see today were built. The beach is privately owned and deserves its accolades. It has ample car parking close by, clean loos, plentiful refreshments including fish and chips, and is cleaned daily. Beach huts can be hired for the day. Lifeguards are on duty and there is a doggy stretch as well as a dog-free area in the summer. And there are tide pools. For families it really is ideal.

8 BARRICANE, COMBESGATE & GRUNTA BEACHES

If, like me, you prefer coves to huge expanses of sand, you may prefer the smaller, less accessible Barricane, Combesgate and Grunta beaches (a steepish climb down rough steps and grass to Grunta, a shorter flight of steps to Barricane and Combesgate) with their rippled sand and satiny grey rocks. Murray's 1872 guide says that Barricane Beach 'almost entirely consists of shells.' You have to search hard to find any these days.

Grunta is my favourite though; it has rocky alleys for children to explore, tide pools, plenty of sand at low tide – and good pickings for painstaking (or lucky) shell hunters, who may even spot a cowrie or blue-rayed limpet.

9 MORTEHOE & MORTE POINT

⋏ North Morte Farm (page 197)

Mortehoe, up a dauntingly steep hill above the beaches, is a bustling little place with several gift shops, three pubs, tea shops, an all-purpose village store, an interesting church notable for its carved bench ends, mosaic and stained-glass windows, and a **museum** (✆ 01271 870028

Mortehoe to Bull Point

❋ OS Explorer 139 or Croydecycle *Mortehoe & Woolacombe*; start: Mortehoe car park
♥ SS4576545214; 2.4 miles; moderate (some steepish hills)

Head up North Morte Road (signposted North Morte Farm) to a well-signed footpath to Rockham Bay. This soon leaves the houses and takes you on a good path towards the intersection with the coast path. **Rockham Beach** is perhaps the most rewarding of all the hidden beaches in this area, with grey sand and shingle. However, at the time of writing the beach is officially closed because the steps were destroyed in a cliff fall. These will be repaired. Continue on the path, through bracken, gently up and down along the coast path to **Bull Point** and the lighthouse, where you will meet the **Lighthouse Road** which leads you back to Mortehoe.

Alternatively, you can continue walking east along the coast path to **Sandy Cove** (shingle and some sand) from where, at low tide, you can walk to Lee and thence a further three (hilly) miles to Ilfracombe from where there are buses back to Mortehoe. Mortehoe to Ilfracombe along the coast path is just over seven miles.

☺ Apr–Oct 11.00–15.00, closed Mon & Fri off season, Fri Jul & Aug). This is in a lovely converted stone barn adjacent to a convenient car park. It is well worth a visit, with good displays of rural and maritime history, particularly shipwrecks; these are something of a speciality in this area, thanks to Morte Stone, the 'Rock of Death', a lethal projection beyond **Morte Point**. In one year alone, 1872, five vessels were lost. A local legend has it that 'No power on earth can remove [the rock] but that of a number of wives who have dominion over their husbands'; exactly how they are to achieve it remains a mystery.

A network of paths straggles from Mortehoe across the headland to Morte Point. From here you might spot seals or even dolphins. The coastal path is particularly glorious here, bright with gorse, heather and bracken; you feel miles from anywhere, rather than a pebble-throw from one of the most popular beaches in the South West. There is a stunning walk (see opposite) from Mortehoe via Rockham Beach to Bull Point and back along a quiet lane, or you can walk south to Woolacombe Sands, buy an ice cream, and toil up the hill back to Mortehoe. To reach Woolacombe Sands by an inland route, take the grassy footpath that leads from the far end of the museum car park. It climbs and then descends steeply through gorse and rocks, rejoining the road above Combesgate Beach.

10 LEE

The writer L du Garde Peach described Lee in 1927 as 'making some pretence at being a fishing village but the renown of Ilfracombe has made it rather the summer refuge of the more fastidious; the crowds which throng the Ilfracombe promenade, and bring fortune to its places of amusement, find little to their taste in Lee.' That sentiment holds true today: Lee is Devon as it used to be.

It was low tide when I arrived for the first time, and the sand, seaweed and rock pools stretched invitingly back to the surf, guarded by giant slices of rock. The remains of a concrete slipway provide access over the seaweedy rocks to the sand. You could spend hours here investigating the pools, collecting pink quartz, or walking up the fuchsia-lined footpath to the village and its delightful pub, **The Grampus Inn** (✆ 01271 862906). 'Bill was a fiddle player', Mike Harrison told me. 'He wanted to play in a pub so he bought one.' So the Grampus has live music from time to time and open mic on Friday nights. It also has real ales, cream teas and simple pub food. And there's a village shop.

Driving out of the village I passed a sign for 'Happy eggs'. I thought it summed up Lee rather nicely. It's only three miles via the coastal path to Ilfracombe, and the 35 bus connects the two places.

11 ILFRACOMBE & AREA

The situation of Ilfracombe is truly romantic. The port is a beautiful natural basin, sheltered by craggy heights that are overspread with foliage … The town consists chiefly of one street, full a mile long. It has a neat, healthy appearance, and is said to contain about two thousand inhabitants. The church stands on the upper part of the town and there is a chapel on a sort of knoll which may be called St Michael's Mount in miniature, being joined to the main land only by a narrow neck.

W G Maton, travelling during 1794–96

As Dr Maton noted, Ilfracombe's position is superb. The town fits where it can between giant crags and grassy mounds, with some imposing houses set high on the surrounding hillsides. It was a major seaside resort in Victorian times, when the arrival of the railway brought up to 10,000 visitors a day and encouraged the building of some grand hotels. One guest at the Ilfracombe Hotel in 1878 was the 19-year-old German grandson of Queen Victoria. Legend has it that the young prince was throwing stones at the ladies' changing huts on Rapparee Beach, and was asked to desist by 16-year-old Alfred Price, whose family had looked after the beach for generations. A fight ensued and, when his assailant became world famous some three decades later, Alfie was proud to boast that he had 'given the Kaiser a bloody nose'.

"Some three decades later, Alfie was proud to boast that he had 'given the Kaiser a bloody nose'."

When the railway closed in 1970 the visitor numbers slumped, and the town has had to strive to reclaim them. If you arrive by car and park on the seafront, you may find the pervading smell of fast food, the jangle of amusement arcades and the blast of live music venues discouraging. Approach on foot, however, via the coastal path from Hele (see opposite), and your first view of the town and its harbour spread out below you is thrilling, even if the two conical towers known by some locals as Madonna's Bra (though the tourist office prefers Sand Castles) come as a bit of a surprise. They house the tourist information centre,

LUNDY

Lundy is truly special. Although you can easily visit for only a day, for some people this is just the beginning of a lifelong love affair. Lundy means Puffin Island and this is the most southerly place in Britain where you can see these delightful birds.

1 View south towards the jetty. 2 A puffin with a beakful of sand eels. 3 The Old Light. 4 Lundy cabbage. 5 Atlantic grey seal.

EXMOOR NATIONAL PARK

One of the smallest – and least visited – national parks in England, Exmoor is superb. Within its boundaries are true moorland, purple with heather in the summer, and rivers bordered by ancient woodland. Add to this a rugged but accessible coastline, and you have something for everyone.

TRICIA GIBSON

1 Typical August view on Exmoor. 2 The East Lyn River. 3 Feral goat in the Valley of Rocks.
4 Snowdrop Valley near Wheddon Cross. 5 Red deer stags in the rutting season. 6 Exmoor
ponies have evolved to deal with the harsh conditions on the moor. 7 The 13th century
clapper bridge at Tarr Steps, one of Exmoor's most popular visitor attractions.

DEVON ODDITIES

Fancy a Gnome Reserve or a Bakelite Museum? You'll find it here, along with the flowerpot men that disport themselves around Berrynarbor and the eccentricities of some ancient churches. There's plenty to smile about in the region.

1 The Bakelite Museum, Williton. **2** In Old Cleeve church the effigy's feet rest, not on a lion but on a cat which has just caught a rat. **3** One of Berrynarbor's many flowerpot men. **4** A reflective gnome at the Gnome Reserve.

museum and Landmark Theatre. As your eyes adjust to the scene, you will see Damien Hirst's extraordinary sculpture, *Verity*, standing, sword upraised, at the entrance to the harbour. Approached from the quay it is the sheer size that impresses (she is over 66 feet high) but otherwise the statue appears to be of a beautiful, and pregnant, woman. But go round to the other side and you get the zombie shock; her skin has been peeled back to show the underlying muscles – and globules of fat – and her womb sliced open to show the developing foetus. A child I know had nightmares after seeing it. Hirst says that *Verity* stands for Truth and Justice, although the symbols of justice – the legal books and scales – are underfoot and held

A bus-assisted walk from
Hele Cornmill to Ilfracombe

❊ OS Explorer 139 or Croydecycle *Ilfracombe & Berrynarbor*; start: Hele Cornmill
♀ SS5345347521; 1.6 miles; moderate (some steep bits)

By parking at Hele Cornmill (and indulging in the best cakes in the area) you can approach Ilfracombe from its most flattering side as well as taking in Hillsborough Fort on the way. It's a treat of a walk, short but with steep ups and downs, and some wonderful views.

Walk to Hele Beach and take the coastal path up to Beacon Point. This is a tough climb (made easier with steps) but the view of Ilfracombe from the top makes it all worthwhile. On a sunny day it's just gorgeous: the little squared-off harbour full of boats is backed by pink-, blue- and cream-coloured houses, behind which tower the incongruous cones of Madonna's Bra. The craggy green Lantern Hill provides a contrast on the right.

After your descent to Ilfracombe, walk up Fore Street to Portland Street from where regular buses run to Hele Bay.

behind her back. Truth is clearly the dominant one. Perhaps justice is the last resort when the full disclosure of truth has failed. It's a controversial sculpture for such a traditional town, which is no bad thing.

From *Verity* you need to run the gamut of ice cream licking, vinegar-dripping crowds on the quay before escaping up Fore Street, where there are some good restaurants, leading into High Street which is the main shopping centre. Keep closer to the shore and you will come to Madonna's Bra – I mean the Sand Castles – and the excellent **Ilfracombe Museum**. This merits an hour or so, being full of all sorts of unusual treasures. Here you can read the story of the original Tom Thumb, who married an equally tiny person and was exhibited at Barnum's circus. There's a Lundy room which will set you up information-wise before you visit the island, and the Mervyn Palmer room dedicated to one of those polymath naturalists in which the Victorian era specialised. This man collected everything: butterflies, an assortment of animals including an enormous python, and some pre-Columbian and Zulu art. Anything, really, that took his fancy. The museum also has a beautiful model of the *Bounty*, as in 'Mutiny on the'. The label explains that it was originally built to transport breadfruit trees to the West Indies to feed the African slaves. But they preferred plantains, so the whole endeavour was doomed.

> *"This man collected everything: butterflies, an assortment of animals including an enormous python, and Zulu art."*

The **Landmark Theatre** has a wide variety of live performances, and a very nice uncrowded **café** with a sea view.

Ilfracombe has an exceptional **aquarium** (✆ 01271 864533 ✆ www.ilfracombeaquarium.co.uk). Instead of gawping at tanks of tropical fish, here you can learn exactly what's in the waters of a typical local river, from its source high up in Exmoor, to its fast-flowing central stretch and down to the estuary and harbour. A typical rock pool is on show and finally the diverse and often surprising inhabitants of the Marine Conservation Zone around Lundy (the first such site in England). Handily near the parking area at the end of the quay, this is perhaps Ilfracombe's main attraction.

Ilfracombe celebrates **Victorian Week** in June with much dressing up and festivities, and in early August the **Birdman Festival** sees the spectacle of young men (mostly) attempting to take to the air by throwing themselves off the pier.

ILFRACOMBE'S BEACHES

The town's **public beaches** are small and grey-sand, but provide enough entertainment for children when the adults have finished looking at the town. Further east is the more secluded **Raparree Cove** where the future Kaiser received his bloody nose. The number-one spot, however, goes to **Tunnels Beach**, which is more of a museum than a beach. You pay a small fee to pass through a tunnel built by miners, to emerge, magically, on a beach surrounded by an amphitheatre of vertical black rocks topped with green. There are tide pools galore, and an artificial 'safe' bathing pool fed by the tides. Along the tunnels are some delightful cuttings from the local newspaper of the time, *The North Devon Journal*, reporting various outrages. One (dated 1859) described the intrusion of two gentlemen on the ladies' bathing area. They swam round the point and 'not only mounted the rocks but plunged into the basin while the female bathers were engaged in their ablutions.' (Remember the female bathers would have been covered from neck to knees in their swimwear.) There are also stern rules governing the use of boats by gentlemen: 'Gentlemen unaccustomed to the management of a boat should never venture out with Ladies. To do so is foolhardy, if not criminal … Great care must be taken not to splash the Ladies … neither should anything be done to cause them fright.' Inevitably this lovely beach gets crowded in the holiday season.

FOOD & DRINK

All good restaurants in Ilfracombe are heavily booked up during the holiday season. Don't risk turning up without a reservation in July and August, particularly on weekend evenings.

The Quay 11 The Quay ✆ 01271 868090 ⏲ www.11thequay.co.uk. Owned by Damien Hirst, this is the smartest restaurant in Ilfracombe. Herbs and salads come from their own nearby farm.

Relish Bar & Bistro 10–11 Fore St ✆ 01271 863837 ⏲ www.relishbarandbistro.co.uk. A classy, popular place with a truly yummy menu focusing on locally sourced food such as Lundy crab and game casserole, with an emphasis on seafood, all beautifully presented.

Seventy One 71 Fore St ✆ 01271 863632 ⏲ www.seventyone.biz. An unpretentious and very popular place offering a limited, affordable menu focusing on locally sourced meat and fish. Try the slow-roasted pork belly or crusted rack of Exmoor lamb.

The Ship and Pilot 10 Broad St ✆ 01271 863562. A thoroughly traditional English pub, serving a huge range of drinks and no food. The multi-year winner of the CAMRA (Campaign for Real Ale) Cider Pub of the Year, it also has a great range of local ales. Interesting décor, and popular with locals and visitors alike.

BOAT TRIPS

For Lundy Island on the MS *Oldenburg*, see page 84.

Bristol Channel Charters ✆ 07827 679189 ⌂ www.bristolchannelcharters.co.uk. Specialise in fishing and diving.

Chopper's Crazy Boat Trips ✆ 0781 6304383 ⌂ www.chopperscrazyboattrips.com. Fishing, wildlife (including snorkelling with seals around Lundy) or charters.

Ilfracombe Sea Safaris ✆ 07827 679189 ⌂ www.ilfracombeseasafaris.co.uk. Trips along the coast or to Lundy Island in small (35-foot) inflatable Rib boats; length varies from one to four hours.

Wildlife cruises Pier kiosk, Ilfracombe Harbour ✆ 01271 879727 ⌂ www. ilfracombeprincess.co.uk. Wildlife and coastal cruises on the 100-passenger *Ilfracombe Princess*. Seals, porpoises and dolphins may be sighted. Trips last from 45 minutes to 1½ hours.

12 HILLSBOROUGH, HELE BEACH & CORNMILL

To the east of Ilfracombe is the **Hillsborough earthwork**. This was probably once a fortress – it commands an impressive view of the harbour, and two ramparts are just visible – but it could equally well have been a ceremonial centre. In 1896 it was purchased by the Ilfracombe Urban District Council for 'public enjoyment'; it is now a nature reserve and affords the best views of Ilfracombe.

Hele Beach is a (grey) sand and shingle beach, particularly rewarding at low tide for its rock pools. Nearby is the exceptional **Hele Cornmill and Tearoom** (✆ 01271 863185). This has been a working mill since 1525. In 1830 it was owned by John Hele, who managed to be a blacksmith, dentist, policeman and miller all at once, but over time the mill became derelict. It was bought in 1972 by Chris Lovell who restored it to working order. The current owners, Kathy and David Jones, bought it in 2011 although they had no previous experience of milling. 'We've learned on the job, so to speak,' David told me and then went on to describe the technicalities of using water power to grind wheat, and the catastrophe of being flooded in 2013. 'It took us three months to get the mill working commercially again.' A tour of the mill is well worth it; there's local history and legends, as well as the story of the mill itself. The baked goodies in the tea room are yummy (as you would expect with home-milled flour) and I learned that cheese scones

"In 1830 the mill was owned by John Hele, who managed to be a blacksmith, dentist, policeman and miller all at once."

THE GHOSTS OF CHAMBERCOMBE MANOR

Claire Barker

Claire Barker is the author of *Magical Mail* and the Knitbone Pepper trilogy. She lives on a small North Devon farm with her family and an assortment of slightly wonky animals.

To my eyes, Chambercombe Manor – a charming white manor house, set in pretty gardens and bathed in early autumn sunshine – didn't look very scary. In fact it looked more like a location for a magazine photo shoot. As a children's author researching locations for ghost stories, I reluctantly decided that it didn't look quite spooky enough for my purposes. But as I had already paid at the gate, I had little choice. I put away my notebook, deciding not to mention my reason for visiting and to enjoy the afternoon anyway.

Soon the tour guide appeared at the front door. As I trailed from room to room she was very knowledgeable and enthusiastic about the history of the house. She informed me that the place was positively heaving with ghosts and television's *Britain's Most Haunted* had even filmed there.

Rather thrillingly, every so often she would stop mid-sentence and say 'Can you hear that?' as if to suggest the presence of a wayward spirit, but all my skeptical ears could hear was the resolute cheerfulness of the blackbirds outside. However, I enjoyed looking at the suits of armour and the unusual furniture. After a while even the stubborn lack of ghostly activity became entertaining.

Then as the end of the tour approached, I climbed the stairs to a narrow landing and took a small step down into an adjacent bedroom. To my great surprise, my whole body instantly began to tingle, from the top of my head to the tip of my toes. 'How peculiar,' I thought, and stepped back out again. The tingling promptly stopped, so I put my foot back into the room and it began again. I repeated this experiment several times with the same results. Throwing caution to the wind I stood in the middle of the room, tingling fiercely, only to become suddenly and inexplicably overwhelmed with tears. The tour guide nodded sagely as if she had seen all this before. 'Ah yes,' she said, 'this is the children's room. They like you. Do you work with children?'

I was shown several things after this but truthfully it's all a bit of a blur. All I wanted to do was get back in my car and drive home very, very quickly. My visit to Chambercombe Manor was the best piece of research I did all year, but I don't think I'm brave enough to return in a hurry!

with cream cheese and jam compete admirably with the traditional cream tea. If you are here sheltering from the rain, so have some time in hand, ask to try the nail puzzle.

The cornmill is the start of a short bus-assisted walk; see page 65.

13 CHAMBERCOMBE MANOR

Chambercombe Lane, EX34 9RJ ✐ 01271 862202 ✎ www.chambercombemanor.org.uk
⊙ Easter–30 Oct Tue, Wed, Thu 11.00–15.00, Sun 12.00–15.00

Inland from Hele Beach, down a lane described by S P B Mais as one 'we shall be unwise to resist', is this manor house. It was built in the 12th century, and was once the family seat of a branch of the Champernowne family – and is reputed to be one of the most haunted houses in Britain. How it gained its ghosts is the stuff of legend. There are many versions of the story but the one recounted by J L W Page is the most appealing:

One summer evening the farmer, smoking his pipe in the garden, fell to studying the roof of his house, which needed repairs. While considering which of the windows would most readily give access to the roof, he was puzzled at noticing, for the first time, a window for which he could not account. Calling to his men to bring tools, he hurried upstairs and at once attacked the wall of the passage opposite the mysterious casement. In a few minutes the plaster gave way, and the farmer, creeping through the breach, found himself in a long, low room furnished with tables and chairs of ancient date, and hung with moth-eaten tapestry. But the object to which his attention was first attracted was a bed with close-drawn faded curtains. With trembling hand the farmer tore them aside and started back in horror, for before him lay a skeleton.

Page goes on to pour cold water on the story since, he claims, there is no room that fits this description and no window. This is backed up by Claire Barker (see box, page 69), who was shown a windowless, dark, forbidding room, almost like an attic, concealed between two other bedrooms. But the story of the skeleton persists; it is thought to be Kate Wallace, who was mortally wounded by wreckers in the 17th century – one of whom turned out to be her own father.

The house and gardens are open to the public, and you can participate in a guided or self-guided tour. You can even arrange to stay the night for a bit of intensive ghost-spotting.

COMBE MARTIN & AREA

You are now approaching the western edge of Exmoor National Park, and the region's most strenuous walking country. Before that, however, there's a more gentle landscape.

A bus-assisted coastal walk from Watermouth Castle to Combe Martin

OS Explorer 139 or Croydecycle *Ilfracombe & Berrynarbor*; start: Combe Martin car park, SS5775247248; 2 miles; moderate (some steep bits)

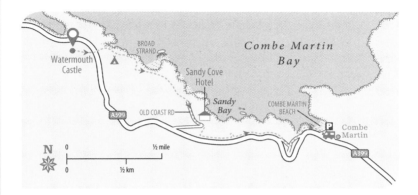

The coastal path between Ilfracombe and Combe Martin has two sections following the A399 (although a huge amount of money has been spent creating a safe walkway beside the busy road). However, if you park in Combe Martin and take the number 301 bus, which runs hourly, to Watermouth Castle you can stroll back the two miles to enjoy some of the best cliff views of this section.

From the castle the coastal path meanders along the cliff edge to bring you to one of the most heart-stoppingly lovely beach views in Devon. A curve of grey slate sand culminates in a tree-topped rock nodule, and is backed by high wooded cliffs. In true Slow form you must walk to Broad Strand Beach, and the final descent involves 227 steps so it's worth checking a tide table since it is certainly more rewarding at low tide. The steps were washed away in the storms of 1990; they were mended by paratroopers, but whether this service would be repeated is debatable. Further sea and beach views bring you to Sandy Cove Hotel and the road, which you must follow, with periods of respite, to Berry Lane and Combe Martin.

14 WATERMOUTH

Little Meadow (page 197)

Heading east by car or bus, you can hardly fail to be surprised at the neo-Gothic **Watermouth Castle**, a grey hulk which is not as old as it first appears. It is now a popular family attraction, part theme park and part museum, but its history is interesting. The castle was built during the early 1800s when grandeur was all the rage amongst the privileged classes, of whom the wealthy Bassett family was one. There is some mystery as to why it took 20 years to build when there was plenty of money available, but eventually it was inherited in 1880 by Walter Bassett who became obsessed with Ferris wheels, and built one in the grounds as well as in other parts of the world including the famous one in Vienna which featured in the film *The Third Man*. However, this was his eventual downfall. The patent was owned by George Washington Ferris, an engineer who created the world's first giant wheel for the World's Columbian Exposition in Chicago in 1893. This was a magnificent achievement, powered by a steam engine and 265 feet high (still dwarfed by the London Eye which is 443 feet), and probably the first major engineering project to be built entirely for pleasure. It was an instant success but Ferris gained little profit from his invention, and litigation to try to protect the patent not only reduced him to poverty but virtually bankrupted the Bassett family and they had to sell up.

"Eventually it was inherited in 1880 by Walter Bassett who became obsessed with Ferris wheels."

Watermouth has another claim to fame. In 1942 a 27-mile prototype oil pipeline was laid, stretching between Swansea oil refinery and Watermouth Bay via the Bristol Channel. During its three-week trial it delivered 38,000 gallons of oil daily. This was to test the theory that fuel could be pumped under the English Channel to France to supply the army. PLUTO, an acronym for Pipe Lines Under The Ocean, was a success and in 1944, after the Normandy Landings, a similar pipeline provided vital fuel to the allied forces fighting in France.

15 BERRYNARBOR

⌂ **Langleigh Guest House** (page 196)

Sitting above and to the west of Combe Martin, this lofty village has much to commend it. There's a free car park so it's a useful starting point for the region's walks, and the church is one of the most beautifully located in Devon, high on a hill with the billowing landscape behind it. The village of whitewashed houses, tucked into the hillside, is equally attractive. Beatrix Potter used to holiday here; no doubt she would have enjoyed the more modern addition of 'flowerpot men' who may be spotted in gardens, up drainpipes, or dangling from the roofs of some of the houses.

No-one remembers the name of their original creator, but they were taken over by Greg and Sue Elstob when their relatives bought Langleigh Gift Shop, where you can now order your own flowerpot men.

The village has a pub, a post office and village store, and a tea room.

16 COMBE MARTIN

Pack o' Cards (page 196), **West Challacombe Manor** (page 196) **Longlands Farm** Coulsworthy (page 197), **Under the Milky Way** (page 197)

> We found Combe-Martin placed in a dale, along which it extends at least a mile from the sea-shore. The scenery of the latter is really magnificent: its more prominent parts are singularly striking, and have the happiest accompaniments imaginable. The sea enters a little cove at Combe-Martin, commodious for the mooring of small vessels; and here the produce of the mines is shipped for Wales and Bristol.
>
> W G Maton, 1794–96

Squeezed into the crease between two hillsides, this straggly town once claimed to have the longest High Street in England. This has now been modified to the longest street party in England, and perhaps the largest number of name changes in one street: five. Once over 70 shops lined this road; now there are only a handful and few noteworthy houses, so that a walk from one end to the other is unrewarding, although it hardly merits Charles Kingsley's comment that it was a 'mile-long manstye'. It's useful for visitors to know that there's a general store at the service station near the top end of town (if coming from Blackmoor Gate), a post office not far from the church and its car park, and a small supermarket at the main car park, with the TIC and museum, near the beach.

There's more to a town than its High Street, and Combe Martin has plenty to interest the visitor including its history. The Martin part of the name comes from Sieur Martin de Turon, who was granted the lands by William the Conqueror. Legend has it that the last Martin failed to come back from a hunting trip so his father, assuming the lad was staying the night elsewhere, ordered that the drawbridge over the moat be raised. The unfortunate hunter returned in the dark, fell into the moat and was drowned, thus ending the Martin line. His father was so consumed with grief and guilt that he left Combe Martin for ever.

The family seat passed to the Leys, a descendant of whom built the town's most extraordinary building, the Pack o' Cards.

Once silver ore was discovered in the region, Combe Martin's fortunes blossomed. The first recorded extraction of the metal was in 1292, in the reign of Edward I.

Miners had no choice of occupation: they were impressed from the Peak District and Wales to serve various kings and finance their wars in France. Both Edward III and Henry V paid for their claims on French territory through the wealth of Combe Martin. The harbour allowed the metal to be easily transported along with agricultural products, most notably hemp. One of the village industries was the spinning of this hemp into shoe-makers' thread and rope for the shipping industry (see page 43 for more on the rope-making business). More recently, but before refrigeration and polytunnels, the town became renowned for its strawberries, which ripened earlier in this sheltered valley than elsewhere in the country. The mines finally closed for good in 1880. For further information on mining in the area see ⌀ www. combemartinminers.co.uk, a website run by a group of enthusiasts who are researching the history.

These days there are really only two buildings of interest in the town: the **Pack o' Cards** pub and the church. The former is a piece of 18th-

HUNTING THE EARL OF RONE

⌀ www.earl-of-rone.org.uk

One of the most bizarre, colourful, historical and highly charged events to take place in the British calendar is Hunting the Earl of Rone in Combe Martin each Spring Bank Holiday. No-one knows how old this event is, but we do know that it was banned in 1837 because of the drunken and licentious behaviour which accompanied it. J L W Page, writing in 1895, describes a conversation with an old lady who remembered the festival with great affection. 'She told me with what an awful joy she would give her halfpenny to escape the jaws of the … hobby horse which laid hold of any non-paying delinquent'. She is quoted as saying 'My

dear soul, I should like to have 'un again!' It was revived, only a little more soberly, in 1973.

The hunt begins on Friday evening, when men dressed as Grenadiers, in scarlet jackets and beribboned conical hats, parade the length of the village, to the beat of drums and the firing of their muskets. Their quarry is a shipwrecked fugitive thought to be hiding out in the woods and subsisting on ship's biscuits. Perhaps he is Hugh O'Neill, the Earl of Tyrone, an Irish traitor who was indeed wanted by the government some 400 years ago. The Grenadiers are accompanied by a Fool carrying a besom, and a Hobby Horse, a

century eccentricity created by George Ley, a gambler, in homage to his success. All its numbers echo those in a pack of cards, hence its four floors (suits), 13 doors and 13 fireplaces (cards in a suit), and originally 52 windows (cards in a pack); also the whole thing looks like a house of cards. Ley, who died in 1709, has a memorial in the **church of St Peter ad Vincula** (St Peter in Chains). Its 100-foot-high tower has been dated at 1490, and was probably built by the same stonemason as neighbouring Berrynarbor and Hartland. A local jingle describes these towers: 'Hartland for length, Berrynarbor for strength, and Combe Martin for beauty'. It is indeed a decorative tower, with statues set in niches. Inside are all sorts of treasures. The rood screen, which dates from the 16th century, has recently been expertly cleaned, bringing out the colours and details of the painted saints in the panels. There are some carved bench ends and more recent poppyheads (three-dimensional wood carvings) in the choir including a Combe Martin fisherman and a whale. Carved on the capitals above the pillars are the usual vine leaves and grapes, but look out for the rare green woman. On the wall, but too high up to see the detail, is a highly regarded marble sculpture of Judith Ivatt, wearing an exquisitely carved lace collar.

grotesque twirling figure in a huge, hooped beribboned skirt and a teeth-clattering horse's head. This procession ends at the 'stable' at the Top George Inn. A miniature (in that it's enacted by children) procession takes place on the Saturday. The highlight of this day is the enormous strawberry cake, celebrating Combe Martin's fruit speciality. Sunday sees another procession, but on Monday things really hot up. After three days of noisy searching, they catch the man in Lady's Wood at the top of the village and, dressed in sackcloth, he is put backwards on a donkey, decorated with ship's biscuits and flowers, and marched along with drums and music. Now and then he is shot and falls to the ground, only to be revived by the Fool or the Hobby Horse. He's then replaced, again backwards, on the donkey and continues his sad journey. Women and maidens carry beautiful flower garlands. Eventually the procession reaches the church where people are dancing and the bells ringing and the Earl of Rone is shot once more.

Then it is all the way down to the sea, where the dead Rone (now replaced by a sackcloth effigy), is thrown into the waves from the quay, and the women throw their garlands after him.

Combe Martin loop: cliffs, beach & silver mines

🌸 OS Explorer 139 or Croydecycle *Combe Martin & Hunter's Inn*; start: Combe Martin (beach) car park, 📍 SS5775247248; 2.6 or 3 miles; moderate (some steep climbs)

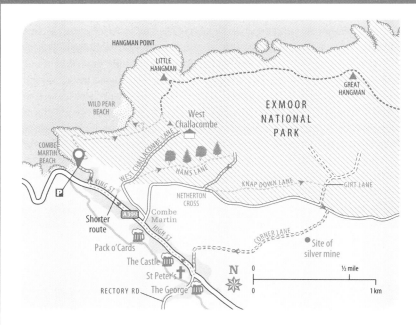

This walk is mainly along quiet lanes, though with very few level stretches. It gives you the option of descending to Combe Martin's loveliest cove, Wild Pear Beach, for a swim and also takes you by Challacombe Manor and near some reminders of the town's silver-mining past.

At the opposite end of the long street from the Pack o'Cards is the town's pretty beach, shingle at high tide and sand at low; cliffs climb steeply up from it on each side. Combe Martin lies within an Area of Outstanding Natural Beauty, and you really need to approach it on foot from the coastal path to appreciate this setting.

The town also has an excellent **museum**, staffed by volunteers, with a varied collection showing village life and the mining trade. Here children can bring in their finds from the beach to study under a microscope

Park in the west-end car park near the beach; from the upper end of the car park follow the track signposted South West Coast Path. It climbs steeply uphill to the cliff's edge before turning sharply right, and follows the cliff until you reach the narrow path which leads down to **Wild Pear Beach**, once busy with the traffic of limestone-carrying boats but now blissfully secluded.

At the point where the path starts to climb steeply towards **Little Hangman**, look for a turning to the right where you'll join West Challacombe Lane, passing **West Challacombe Manor** which is now owned by the National Trust and let as self-catering holiday accommodation (page 196). This is a beautiful 15th-century manor with a splendid Great Hall which retains its medieval roof. No-one is certain what it was used for, but it could have housed the impressed miners brought from Wales and the Peak District.

The lane leads to Combe Martin's main street (King Street at this point) so if you want to cut your walk short here you are less than half a mile from your car. To continue, turn sharp left along Hams Lane for a half mile or so, until it curves round and descends steeply to Netherton Cross. You'll catch some lovely views of Combe Martin strung out along its valley. Turn left at the junction then left again, climbing steeply up Knap Down Lane. At the junction with Girt Lane you've reached the highest point and it really is downhill all the way now, as you turn right, then left, then right again to join Corner Lane which descends steeply into the town. As you start down the lane, look for the tall remains of a **double-cylindered engine house** used in silver mining, a landmark for miles around.

Then it's a just a matter of walking down the High Street/King Street back to your car. However, you emerge close to two pubs, the George and the Castle, so if it's that time of day … Or for more spiritual refreshment you're also near the church.

or join an organised beach safari. There are ropes and pulleys to play around with as well, to understand how heavy cargo such as limestone could be loaded on to a boat. The **tourist information centre** is also here, along with information on Exmoor National Park.

A lively **carnival** is held during the second week of August, when a giant 'grey mare', ridden by Old Uncle Tom Cobley and All, parades around the town on Wednesday evening, presumably looking for Widecombe Fair. There's also a **Strawberry Fayre** in June, celebrating the town's history as a major fruit-growing region, and the bizarre but hugely enjoyable **Hunting the Earl of Rone** (see box, page 74), which takes place on the Spring Bank Holiday. 'They like dressing up in Combe Martin,' the lady in the tourist office told me. Indeed!

BEACHES

The town's little beach is easily accessible with a car park nearby, but by far the prettiest beach in the area is **Wild Pear Beach** to the east which is sandy, secluded, sheltered – and involves a walk of around a mile along the coastal path and a descent (and ascent) of 400 feet (page 77). However, the rewards are many, particularly at low tide when the rock pools are exposed. And talking of exposed, this is a popular beach with naturists.

FOOD & DRINK

Black & White Fish & Chips Borough Rd, EX34 0DG ☎ 01271 883548. A long-established, very popular chippie which sells seriously good take-away fish and chips. Located at the beach end of town.

The Pack o' Cards High St, EX34 0ET ☎ 01271 882300 ⬦ www.packocards.co.uk. Straightforward food nicely prepared by James Batchelor who, after his award as Student of the Year, went on to work at the Hilton in the Arctic Circle with Gordon Ramsay. Consequently he is as expert a snow-boarder as he is a chef.

BEYOND COMBE MARTIN

Next to Combe Martin are some of the highest cliffs in the country: **Hangman Cliffs**. Above them are Great Hangman and Little Hangman, and climbing them from sea level is quite a challenge, though the views

"On the top of Great Hangman, you are at the highest point of the South West Coast Path."

are said to make it worthwhile. When you stand on the top of **Great Hangman**, you are at the highest point of the South West Coast Path (1,046 feet). The name comes not from a desperate walker nor from the rather appealing alternative, sometimes suggested, that a sheep-thief managed to strangle himself on the animal's rope as he made his getaway. Rather it's a corruption of 'An Maen', Celtic for The Stone or Stony Head. There are some good circular walks that include the peak, but the one described on page 80 cunningly avoids it and gives you some doses of history instead of exhaustion.

It is a rewarding circuit that takes you above Wild Pear Beach and near **West Challacombe Manor**.

If you decided to do the hard slog to the top of Great Hangman you may be tempted to continue east along the **South West Coast Path**. This is, after all, one of the most spectacular and varied stretches of the entire route. However, there is no bus link until you reach Lynmouth, 13 miles away; given the hilly terrain, this is a lot to do in one day. A good solution is to split the walk into two days, staying overnight at Hunter's Inn (page 137) on the River Heddon.

UPDATES WEBSITE

You can post your comments and recommendations, and read the latest feedback and updates from other readers online at ⊘ www.bradtupdates.com/northdevon.

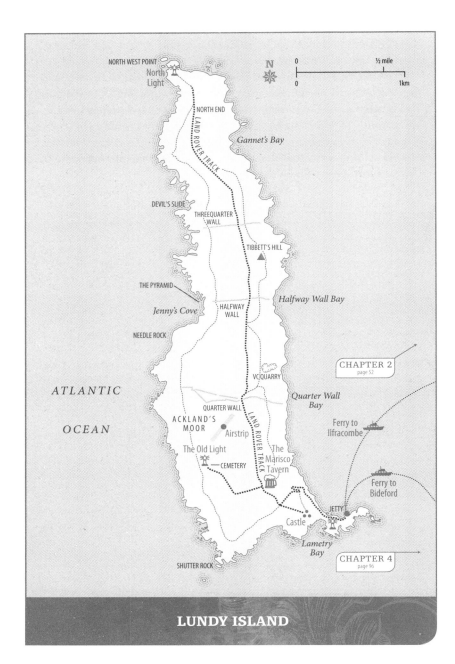

LUNDY ISLAND

3

LUNDY ISLAND

Simon Dell

I saw the Isle of Lundy which formerly belonged to my grandfather, William, Lord Viscount Say and Seale, which does abound with fish and rabbits and all sorts of fowls – one bird that lives partly in the water and partly out, and so may be called an amphibious creature; it is true that one foot is like a turkey, and the other a goose's foot; it lays its eggs in a place the sun shines on and sets it so exactly upright on the small end that there it remains until taken up, and all the art and skill of persons cannot set it up so again to abide.

Celia Fiennes, *Through England on a side saddle*, 1695

Although this description will not immediately strike a bell with modern ornithologists, one semi-amphibious bird that is indeed associated with Lundy is the puffin: the island was called after them. 'Lunde øy' is Norse for Puffin Island. The island was well known to the Scandinavian pirates who harried the shores of Wales and Devon, and is first mentioned by name in the *Orkney Ingasaga* (1139–48).

Lundy lies about ten miles north of Hartland Point in the entrance of the Bristol Channel where it meets the Atlantic. It is a granite island measuring three miles long and about half a mile wide. Just over two dozen people live there – all employees of the Landmark Trust which leases the island from its owner the National Trust.

Until 1969 Lundy was in the private ownership of the Harman family and upon Albion Harman's passing the future of the island looked bleak indeed. Previous owners had included the Heaven and Christie families, as well as the Sovereign, and it had also been in the lease of famous Devon names such as the Grenvilles. Lundy's history is steeped in tales of enforced slaves living there, of plots against the king and of being a stronghold for pirates. In 1969 the National Trust acquired it after Sir Jack Hayward donated the asking price at auction; the island's future was secure. The Landmark Trust took on a 60-year lease and the responsibility to repair buildings, manage the land and employ the staff.

"The only place in the UK where you can find all five British species of shallow-water cup coral."

Lundy inspires much interest, both nationally as well as further afield, enjoying, as it does, an unspoiled habitat (both terrestrial and marine) and a wealth of archaeology. It is now a Site of Special Scientific Interest (north of the Quarter Wall) and the first National Statutory Marine Reserve, with a No Take Zone. It is the only place in the UK where you can find all five British species of shallow-water cup coral.

While the sea and its shore abound with life, there are almost no indigenous terrestrial mammals. The pygmy shrew and pipistrelle bat seem to be the only creatures that have always been here. There are no

SEABIRDS

Hilary Bradt

Lundy is famed for its growing population of puffins, formerly known as 'the Lundy parrot', but when J L W Page visited the island in the 1890s he wrote about an abundance of seabirds of all sorts: 'In the breeding season they literally swarm – as one islander put it "You can scarcely see the sky, sir". The sea is covered with them, the land is covered with them; they sit in regiments and battalions on ledges of rock.' They were hunted for their feathers, with 379lb of feathers being recorded as plucked by the women in 1816. Eggs were also collected and sold to visitors, causing more than one islander to fall to his death from the cliffs.

These days, while the birdlife can hardly be described as blotting out the sky, Lundy is a favoured place for birdwatchers. Seabirds include shag, herring and black-backed gulls and, in the breeding season, the famous puffins, razorbills and guillemots, fulmars and Manx shearwaters which, like the puffins, are benefiting from the eradication of rats.

Puffins are best seen in the breeding season, from May to July. If you miss them on the cliffs around Jenny's Cove you can sometimes spot their characteristic flight, with rapid wing beats, skimming close to the ocean's surface. Puffins only sport their brightly coloured bills in the breeding season. The outer part is later shed, leaving a duller-coloured beak. Although puffins feed on a variety of small fish, sand eels are much favoured, and the classic photo of a puffin holding a quantity of these fish in its specially adapted beak is the photograph all puffin enthusiasts long to capture.

reptiles (perhaps St Patrick stopped off here on his way to Ireland) but there are plenty of rabbits, with a disproportionate number of black ones. They were introduced here by the Normans, and Lundy became one of the first Royal Warrens in the country. More recent introductions, by the Harman family, are Sika deer and Soay sheep. There are also some feral goats. The tough Lundy ponies are of mixed ancestry: mainly New Forest, Welsh Mountain and Connemara.

Since 1929 Lundy has had its own stamps ('puffinage') introduced by the owner at that time, Martin Coles Harman, and for a while it also had its own coinage.

Archaeological interest ranges from Bronze Age huts and enclosures at the north end to Romano-British inscribed stones in the burial ground near to the Old Light. There are also the remains of the Victorian granite quarries on the east side. On and around Lundy there are no fewer than 14 Grade II listed buildings and 41 scheduled sites and monuments, plus two scheduled wreck sites.

Lundy is divided by three main walls: Quarter Wall, Halfway Wall and Threequarter Wall. Land in between these walls differs considerably; farmed fields round the village at the south end, rough grazing in the middle, and bare granite encrusted with heather and lichens at the north end.

There are many letting cottages available for holidays, as well as facilities for campers, and the availability of winter transport by helicopter from Hartland means that the year-round occupation rate is high. All accommodation is self-catering and handled by the Landmark Trust (page 197). The island shop is fully stocked to meet all visitors' requirements, while the Tavern caters for all meals and provides a social centre. Dogs are not allowed on Lundy.

"Why do people come to Lundy? For the character of the island itself, and the tranquillity that is found there. For bird-watching... or the history."

Why do people come to Lundy? For the character of the island itself, and the tranquillity that is found there. For birdwatching, rock climbing or diving; for interest in the plants, the fungi, the lichens, or the archaeology and history; for walking; or simply for a rest with a few good books. One thing is for sure – after one visit most people are caught by the Lundy spirit and return time and again to this special corner of North Devon.

GETTING THERE

Lundy is accessible year-round, by sea in summer and by helicopter during the winter months.

BY SEA

Between the end of March and the end of October the **MS** *Oldenburg* carries both day visitors and staying passengers from the ports of either Bideford or Ilfracombe. Sailing timetables can be found on the Landmark Trust Lundy website (⌂ www.lundyisland.co.uk). Departure ports depend on the tides because Bideford is tidal-dependent (high tide) whereas departures from Ilfracombe can take place at any level of tide. The sea trip takes about two hours from either port.

Parking in Bideford is available at the end of Bideford Quayside in the long-term car park and in Ilfracombe on the opposite side of the harbour in Longstone car park.

If you have a choice of departure ports for a day trip, Bideford will give you twice as much time on Lundy as Ilfracombe because you'll leave and return on the morning and evening high tides. Quite often at the end of a Bideford sailing day the *Oldenburg* will also do a 'round the island' trip for a small fee. It will be announced when you dock, lasts about an hour, and provides an excellent opportunity to see seals and, in the breeding season, puffins.

THE MS *OLDENBURG*

The *Oldenburg* takes 267 passengers and is a really comfortable vessel. She has upper and lower decks with a forward saloon, and a rear buffet and shop.

Built in 1958 in Germany, she operated ferry services between the German mainland and the Friesian Island of Wangerooge and to Heligoland until coming to Lundy in 1986, where she has given faithful service ever since. The crew are friendly and helpful and are a mine of information.

A local tip is that if you have a choice of dates for the sailing, try to go on the third day of three consecutive calm days – the Bristol Channel is much calmer having had a few days to settle down.

Another insider's tip is to make sure you use the toilets on board before you get off. There are no facilities on the island until you reach the village itself. It is best to use the toilets once the ship is moored up and people have started to disembark.

SHORE OFFICES

The Lundy Booking Office The Pier, Ilfracombe EX34 9EQ ✆ 01271 863838 ✉ info@
lundyisland.co.uk
The Lundy Shore Office The Quay, Bideford EX39 2EY ✆ 01271 863636

Private charters are also available, one of the most popular running from Clovelly on the *Jessica Hettie* (✆ 01237 431042 day or 01237 431405 evening). See also pages 39 and 45.

BY HELICOPTER

The *Oldenburg* sea trips do not run between the end of October and the end of March, but Lundy is still open for staying visitors: seven-minute helicopter flights operate on Mondays and Fridays from Hartland Point, where parking is available (✆ 01271 863636 ◌ www.lundyisland.co.uk).

STAYING ON LUNDY

There are 23 **self-catering properties** available for short breaks and weekly holiday lets; a **campsite** near the village with room for 40 people; and a **hostel** (The Barn), with beds for 14 – see pages 197–8.

As is normal for Landmark Trust accommodation, only essential electrical equipment is provided; this doesn't include radios, TVs, washing machines or dishwashers.

Some of the properties have open fires, but many rely on electric storage heaters, so take as much warm clothing as your luggage allowance will permit. Even in summer it can be surprisingly cold, so make sure you have a warm sweater. The island has its own electricity supply which is turned off between about midnight and six in the morning, so bring a torch, also a simple first-aid kit.

There is no need to bring any **food supplies** with you: the village shop stocks everything you might need, and there is even a *Lundy Cook Book* written by a frequent visitor using everything that is available in the shop. See page 94 for *Food & drink*.

GETTING AROUND ON LUNDY

Cars, apart from the Land Rovers used by staff, are not permitted on the island; visitors can bring bicycles but should check with the shore office (see page 85) for current requirements. Canoes can also be carried on the hold deck by prior arrangement, as can mobility scooters providing they are robust enough to go up the steep road and rough lane. They will need to be lifted by crane on to the front hold deck. The rule of thumb is that you need to be able to walk up and down the gangplank, which has handrails either side, with a little help from the crew if needed.

Once you arrive on Lundy the ship moors up against the **jetty** in the sheltered easterly harbour.

It is a 350 foot climb to the village, but you can ask (in advance) for a lift in the Land Rover.

Basically Lundy is for walkers. The more energetic can head for the north end; this way it's quite possible to get a seven-mile walk, or even longer if you use the footpaths around the perimeter.

MAKING THE MOST OF A DAY VISIT

If you are only visiting for a day, you need to make best use of the time available. Plan ahead.

WHAT TO BRING

Make sure you dress for inclement weather with stout boots or shoes for walking across open ground. Umbrellas are not really a good idea because Lundy can be windy. Seasickness pills are useful for the sea journey.

You will need binoculars; there are some available for hire on the ship if you forget to bring them. Also take a packed lunch so you are not tied to having lunch in the village – the Tavern can get quite busy on sailing days (a good tip is to leave the Tavern until the end of your visit, but always make sure you give yourself 30 minutes to get to the jetty for boarding time).

A guidebook of Lundy walks, available in the shore offices and on board the *Oldenburg*, helps focus your attention on interesting aspects of the island. A good free map is also available at the shore office and on board.

WHERE TO GO & WHAT TO SEE

Some of Lundy's most important and interesting sights are on the lower southern half, so are easy to visit on a day trip – especially from Bideford, when you have a longer day on the island.

THE LUNDY CABBAGE

The Lundy cabbage (*Coincya wrightii*) is a species of primitive brassica growing only on Lundy, with its nearest relative found in southern Spain and North Africa. It is likely that Lundy is sufficiently far from the mainland to have allowed the plant to evolve into a separate species. It is one of only about a dozen endemic plants in the British Isles but, even in this select company, it stands out, uniquely having its own endemic insect(s). There is a bronze Lundy cabbage flea beetle (and, possibly, another flea beetle and a weevil) which live only on the plant. The Lundy cabbage flowers from mid-May until early July.

Highlights would include the **Old Light**, a disused lighthouse constructed in 1819 at the highest point on the island, and the **cemetery**, site of some Roman burials; you can climb to the very top to enjoy wide panoramic views over the whole island and further still, with the coast of North Devon and Cornwall visible as well as the Welsh coast. The **castle** is also one of the most significant buildings here. It overlooks the landing bay, with its hidden **Benson's Cave** underneath.

If you are visiting between May and July you will want to try to see some puffins at their nest site above **Jenny's Cove**. Other highlights are **VC Quarry**, just beyond Quarter Wall and **North Light**, which you'll have time to walk to if you're staying overnight on the island.

EXPLORING LUNDY & ITS HISTORY

I devised this circular walk on the southern half of the island to keep within the limited time available and take in the most interesting historical sights. If you are staying on Lundy overnight, you may like to explore further afield and follow the longer route (page 92). For both walks, use the map on page 89.

A WALK THROUGH LUNDY'S HISTORY FOR DAY VISITORS

Start: jetty; 3 miles; easy, with some optional steep descents/climbs

MS *Oldenburg* moors up to the jetty which was constructed between 1998 and 1999. At the top of the jetty is the former Christie's Quay which was built in the early 1920s as a small sheltered harbour tucked beneath the South Lighthouse. Carry on past the steep flight of steps on the left which lead up to the **South Light**.

The landing place is marked by the 'TH Landing Place' stone which commemorates the construction of the original lighthouse on Lundy in 1819. This area of the landing beach has been renovated over the past few years with a new slipway constructed over the top of the old one.

The road winds its way along the cliff edge with views to the north along the east side of Lundy, up past the quarries where the eagle-eyed will spot the ruins of quarry dwellings on the top of the cliffs.

At 'Windy Corner' the road turns left and inland under the oak trees where you have a fine view of **Millcombe House**, built by the owner of Lundy, William Heaven, after he purchased the island in 1836.

Instead of heading towards Millcombe House and the tavern at the top of the hill, turn sharp left past the gates; carry on up the hill and back towards the east coast and the landing bay to find the **battlements**, a low wall built where the lane doubles back to the right.

While you are at the battlements you will notice the Goat Track leading up from the landing beach. Look up above the track and southwards towards a black wooden bungalow, Hanmers, and you will notice that the Goat Track doubles back on itself and carries on up the steep grass bank in the direction of the castle. Take this track up some stone steps and to **Hanmers** which was built by fishermen in the 19th century. Carry on uphill along the grass path, through the defensive ditch which surrounded the **castle**, until you reach the castle itself. Through the iron gate you can see the three Landmark Trust cottages which huddle within the castle walls.

The castle was built in 1244 by Henry III after the downfall of the piratical Mariscos who leased the island. You can go left around the castle on to the parade ground, with fine views over the landing bay and Hartland Point on the North Devon coast.

From the parade ground walk back up to the left of the castle and find the footpath which leads down to Benson's Cave below. Walk down towards the **South Light** with the cliff on your right. If you don't like heights don't go down – you will be returning the same way. Carry on towards the South Light and down some steps on the right. Follow them down and along a clifftop path to the end of the headland. You will find the cave entrance back on your left, going under the parade ground and castle.

Benson's Cave is named after the notorious Thomas Benson (see box, page 90) who brought convicts to Lundy to work for him on the island; some left their initials carved in the cave walls.

After leaving the cave, go back up to the castle while looking out along the coastline to the west and left. You will see what looks like a wooden telegraph pole high on the cliff in the distance. Head for this along the pathway which leads over the grass from the castle. Your route takes you beside the cliffs to a stile, which you cross; in a few yards look to your left and over the cliff to find **Benjamin's Chair**, a ledge where the Heaven family used to enjoy picnics in the 19th century.

Carry on with a stone wall on your right until the wall turns north towards the old lighthouse. At this point walk towards the wooden pole ahead and after ten yards turn right into the long grass to find the deep pit of an ancient **Bronze Age burial chamber**.

Carry on to the **Rocket Pole** which was used as a ship's mast for attaching breeches-buoy equipment when practising rescue techniques in the 19th century.

Leave the pole and head uphill and slightly right to the large **Rocket Pole Pond** which is a flooded quarry.

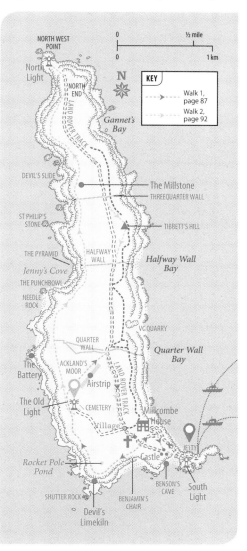

NORTH WEST POINT

0   ½ mile
0   1 km

North Light

NORTH END

N

KEY

Walk 1, page 87
Walk 2, page 92

Gannet's Bay

LAND ROVER TRACK

DEVIL'S SLIDE

The Millstone
THREEQUARTER WALL

ST PHILIP'S STONE

TIBBETT'S HILL

THE PYRAMID

HALFWAY WALL

Halfway Wall Bay

Jenny's Cove

THE PUNCHBOWL

NEEDLE ROCK

VC QUARRY

QUARTER WALL

Quarter Wall Bay

The Battery

ACKLAND'S MOOR

LAND ROVER TRACK

Airstrip

The Old Light

CEMETERY

Millcombe House

Village

JETTY

Castle

Rocket Pole Pond

BENSON'S CAVE

South Light

SHUTTER ROCK

BENJAMIN'S CHAIR

Devil's Limekiln

THOMAS BENSON

Hilary Bradt

This Bideford-born merchant trader's story is one of power and corruption. He inherited the family fortune at the age of 37 in 1743, and built up a fleet of ships which traded with the American colonies of Virginia and Maryland, as well as sending fishing vessels to the Newfoundland cod banks. Deciding that a place in parliament would be beneficial, he presented the Corporation of Barnstaple with a magnificent silver punch bowl, and was duly elected as their MP in 1947.

In 1748 Benson became a tenant of Lundy, under lease from the then owner, Lord Gower. One of his contracts was for the transportation of convicts but, instead of shipping them to America, he brought them to Lundy where they worked as his unpaid servants. At night they were shut up in the cave that now bears his name.

His next enterprise was smuggling, but he was caught and fined heavily. Page takes up the story: 'Benson went rapidly from bad to worse. Among other little villainies he insured a vessel's cargo and then caused her to be put back to Lundy where he stored the cargo – probably in the very cave that bears his name – and then had the ship scuttled and claimed the insurance money.' When his accomplices were caught he fled to Portugal and his connections with Lundy ended.

The stone here was removed to build the new South Lighthouse in 1896. You can usually find ducks on the pond.

Continue to the southwest corner of the island to a rocky promontory with fine views over the coast and **Shutter Rock**, looking like a pyramid below, where seals are often spotted along with a multitude of seabirds.

Just below you to the south is the **Devil's Limekiln** – a natural feature of a huge hole in the clifftop where the end of a sea cave collapsed. Some intrepid walkers do stroll down and around the limekiln but that excursion might be best left to the more sure-footed and adventurous.

The **Old Light** can be seen ahead as you follow the coastal footpath with the sea on your left. After a small valley with an animal-drinking reservoir on the cliff edge, its sloped ramps allowing livestock access to the water, you'll continue to the lighthouse but just before going in to the enclosure turn right briefly and pay a visit through the five-bar gate to the **cemetery**. Here you will find graves from the 19th and 20th centuries as well as four standing stones erected beside the wall. These are Roman gravestones dating back to the first century AD and are engraved with the names of their Roman burials.

From the cemetery continue to the lighthouse and enjoy the shelter of the building for a picnic lunch. You can go into the building, turn left and ascend the stairs to the very top for magnificent views across the whole island and, on a clear day, as far as Wales to the north.

The lighthouse was in use until 1896 when the new North and South Lights were built; the Old Light was over 500 feet above sea level so often obscured by low cloud.

"Ascend the stairs to the very top for magnificent views across the whole island as far as Wales."

Once you have explored the lighthouse go around to the far side of the building and over a stile in the back wall. This leads you out on to **Ackland's Moor**, and to the east side of the island by cutting diagonally across over the **airstrip**. The runway is marked by white painted boulders. Head to the far end of the airstrip and to the main vehicle track at **Quarter Wall gate**.

If you have had enough and want to return to the village early, turn right and south along the track back to reach the village in 15 minutes. To continue with the walk pass through the gate where Lundy ponies often congregate. You will see the big boulders marking the way of the track for lighthouse keepers in the fog. Over to the right and eastwards towards the coast are the ruins of some cottages. Carry on along the track a short way and turn right along a grass path downhill towards the ruined cottages, once homes of the quarry manager and doctor. After visiting the ruins head north along the pathway to the quarries, the first of which is flooded and contains golden orfe fish introduced in 1929 by Mr Harman.

Continue uphill and north to the Time Keeper's Hut which has a small round memorial to Felix Gade who lived on Lundy for over 50 years as agent.

Pass the hut and go downhill along the tramway past the willow trees to the quarry on the left. This first quarry is known as **VC Quarry**; here you'll find a memorial to John Harman, who was killed in Asia during World War II and was awarded the posthumous Victoria Cross at the Battle of Kohima. He was the son of the island's owner at that time (see box, page 95).

A visit to the next quarry will then lead you up around a left-hand bend in the track and on to the main road which runs the length of the island. Turn left, south, back to the village, its shop and the **The Marisco Tavern** about 25 minutes away. When you arrive in the village the building on the right is the shop and on the left is a small detached hut which houses the island interpretation centre and museum.

Once in the village there is plenty to see including the **church**, built in 1896 and dedicated to St Helena. This is on the track south out of the village complex, five minutes' walk away.

It takes about 25 minutes to stroll down to the jetty from The Marisco Tavern; the quickest and most direct route is to come out of the tavern and turn right down to the kissing gate by the toilets. Carry on downhill over the grass through another gate and follow the path downhill past Millcombe House and out down the driveway to re-join the track which you came up on arrival.

EXPLORING FURTHER AFIELD: PUFFINS, SEALS & LIGHTHOUSES

Start: Old Light; 6 miles; fairly easy, though some steep climbs & descents. This walk is for visitors staying on the island.

Head north from the Old Light, keeping to the coastal path. As you start to drop into a small valley, look out for a pile of stones beside the path in the bottom of the dip. This marks the point where you turn towards the sea and walk a few yards to find a path beside a wall which takes you steeply down to **the Battery** by the sea. This diversion, which will take about an hour, allows you to visit the **Trinity House** fog signal station, constructed in 1862 to supplement the old lighthouse. From here two cannons were fired every ten minutes to warn ships in thick fog. The cannons were cast in 1810 and bear the cipher of King George IV. They were replaced by signal rockets in 1878, and the Battery was abandoned in 1897 when the new North and South lighthouses were built. The two cottages were homes to the Battery keepers and their families.

"Find some conveniently placed natural boulders to sit on when watching the puffins on the cliffs."

Once you have visited the Battery return back up to the main west-side path and continue northwards over a stile in a fence to **Halfway Wall**, with the big granite formations known as the Cheeses on your left. Before you cross the wall look back at the coast and south to the cliffs where **Needle Rock** sticks out of the sea. If you are here between May and July, leave the path and go to the cliff edge; you will find some conveniently placed natural boulders to sit on when watching the puffins on the cliffs to the south above **Jenny's Cove**, which is named after an African trading ship which went aground in the 18th century with a cargo of ivory and gold dust.

Keep an eye on the grassy banks with binoculars; the puffins stand out once you see their orange feet amongst the similar razorbills and guillemots. When you have finished puffin watching, cross Halfway Wall and continue to **Threequarter Wall** and over the stile. After crossing the wall go towards the sea on the cliff outcrops; find somewhere to sit and look south towards the cliffs by **St Philip's Stone**, the triangular rock that you can see in the distance. It's cut off by the sea at high tide. There are more puffin nests in this area in the season.

Continue north for about 200 yards and you'll pass the **millstone** in the grassy path. A number of granite millstones were produced on the island's west side; this one is actually incomplete and was abandoned during construction. You get a better view of it once you have passed it and are looking back over your shoulder southwards.

Look out for the **Devil's Slide** ahead of you. It is the longest single slab of granite in the country and popular with climbers.

From here it is not far to the north end of the island: you can see the Land Rover track winding its way there. You can either stay on the west coast path or simply head towards the main track, depending upon how tired you feel.

Carry on to the far end of the Land Rover track to where there is a turnabout in the lane for vehicles. This is where the footpath continues

THE LUNDY ATLANTIC GREY SEALS

Lundy is home to a breeding colony of around 60 grey seals (with up to double this number in the summer). They can be seen all around the island, particularly at their 'hauling-out' spots – favoured rocks and ledges for basking in the sun. Seals can often be seen in the Devil's Kitchen, bathing and hauling themselves on to rocks just offshore. The same seals also come into the Landing Bay from time to time for an inquisitive look at visitors. Brazen Ward is also a good spot for seal watching.

In the 1890s, J L W Page reported that 'the natives, by the way, have the most exalted idea of the ferocity of these creatures. One youth actually told me that they had been seen to take up large stones in their flippers and hurl them at the head of an intruder'.

north to the metal bridge and steps which lead down to the **North Light**. This was built in 1896 to replace the Old Light.

When you get down to the lighthouse you will find a tramway. This was constructed in 1896 along with the North Light and was used by the keepers to transport heavy equipment and goods from the loading crane to the lighthouse. Turn right along this tramway and, just before you reach a concrete platform at the end, look to your left: you will find the steps which lead down to the water's edge where the lighthouse keepers used to be landed by boat. There are usually seals around this landing place but be warned: it is quite a steep climb down and up again.

When you rejoin the Land Rover track you'll follow it south, all the way back to the **village**, a walk of about 1½ hours.

FOOD & DRINK

The Marisco Tavern ✆ 01237 431831. Not just a pub, the Tavern provides a restaurant and social centre for island staff and staying guests, as well as catering to the large numbers of day-trippers arriving on the *Oldenburg* or visiting ships such as the paddle steamer *Waverley*. It also doubles as the island library; this is where evening talks take place in the Wheel House room, and there are plenty of games available. Day-trippers' lunches are modestly priced – you do not

GIANTS' GRAVES

Hilary Bradt

In 1851, some farm workers discovered two huge granite coffins, one of them ten feet long and the other eight. When these were opened they were found to contain two skeletons. The larger one had its head resting on a 'pillow' of granite, and both graves were covered with limpet shells. In or beside the coffins were some blue stone beads and fragments of pottery.

J L W Page takes up the story: 'Mr Heaven was sent for, and the skeletons carefully measured. The larger had a stature of 8ft 2in. Mr Heaven was present the whole time, and not only saw the measurement taken, but, as he himself told me, saw one of the men place the shin bone of the skeleton against his own, when it reached from his foot half way up his thigh, while the giant's jawbone covered not only his chin but beard as well ... Mr Heaven exclaimed, when he saw the larger skeleton, "The bones of Hubba the Dane!"'

The bones were reburied and have never been found again, so the age of the skeletons – and indeed their size (the second, probably female, was of normal height) – has never been ascertained. Medieval seems to be the favoured period.

JOHN PENNINGTON HARMAN VC

Hilary Bradt

At the site called VC Quarry on Lundy is a memorial to John Pennington Harman who was posthumously awarded the Victoria Cross for outstanding bravery in Burma in 1944. During the siege of Kohima, about 500 men stopped the advance of 15,000 Japanese into India for 15 days until the British Second Division could fight their way through to relieve them.

There have been fewer than 1,400 recipients of the Victoria Cross since its inception in 1856 so John Harman has a special place in history.

The quarry was chosen for the memorial as it was John's favourite place to play as a boy.

Diana Keast, John's sister, recalls that he was a keen beekeeper, and kept bees on Lundy. There is a rural superstition that if the owner of a hive of bees dies and the bees are not told, they will pine away or desert the hive. The news of John's death was delayed by two weeks, but his father immediately sent word to the resident agent and asked him to tell the bees. Felix Gade went to the hive and found that all the bees had vanished.

get the impression that the Tavern takes advantage of being the sole food outlet on the island. It offers a comprehensive range of quality food, at prices which even on the mainland would be considered competitive. The chef uses mostly the island's own produce: their own selectively bred lamb and rare-breed pigs, plus the wild Sika deer, Soay sheep, goats and rabbits. However, if you are a day-tripper who has forgotten to bring a packed lunch, don't think you can walk in and just buy a packet of mass-produced sandwiches from a chiller cabinet!

For stayers, breakfast (which includes their own pork sausages), lunch and dinner are served every day. Lundy lamb is always on the menu, as are homemade burgers and pasties. Evening meals include a selection of desserts as well as a separate blackboard of vegetarian specialities.

Tables may not be booked in advance; they operate on a first come, first served basis.

SEND US YOUR PHOTOS!

We'd love to follow your Slow explorations — why not send us your photos and stories via Twitter (@BradtGuides) and Instagram (@bradtguides) using the hashtag #northdevon. Alternatively, you can upload your photos directly to the gallery on the North Devon & Exmoor destination page via our website (www.bradtguides.com).

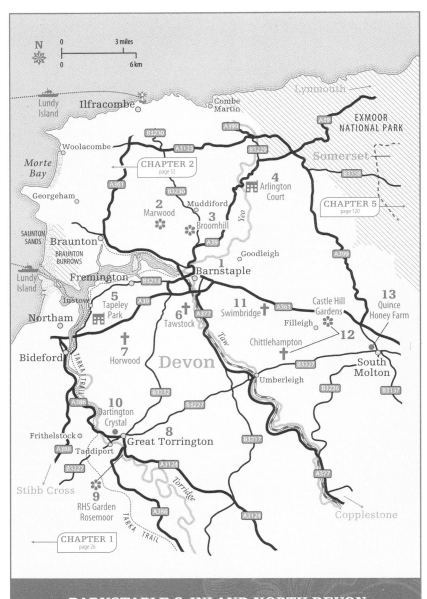

BARNSTAPLE & INLAND NORTH DEVON

4

BARNSTAPLE & INLAND NORTH DEVON

> I crossed the river Tau and found another sort of face of the country, the red soil with the red sandstone, and all of the country full of rising ground, and small hills beautifully improved.
>
> Richard Pococke, *Travels through England*, 1750

This region shows the marketing power of a popular book. **Henry Williamson** was one of the finest nature writers ever. His love for North Devon stemmed from a childhood holiday, and shines through his subsequent writing. Utterly out of his environment as a soldier in World War I he wrote vividly of life in the trenches (*A Chronicle of Ancient Sunlight*, considered, by some, to be one of the greatest series of novels of its time). In the latter part of his life he became embittered and succumbed to extreme right-wing views, but that doesn't diminish the importance of his most famous work, the 1927 *Tarka the Otter*, written in Georgeham (page 58) where he lived for eight years and is buried. His otter ranged widely over the rivers of North Devon, hence the Tarka label attached to the oblong of countryside stretching from the north coast's sandy shores to the edge of Dartmoor.

The selected attractions here are scattered over a wide region: some of the loveliest **gardens** in North Devon and a handful of **exceptional churches**. More peaceful than the busy seaside resorts, it's a good area to base yourself in the crowded holiday season.

GETTING THERE & AROUND

Barnstaple, as the main town in North Devon, has excellent **road** links with Tiverton, Exeter and Plymouth, as well as Cornwall. However, the **rail** link between Exeter and Barnstaple, the Tarka Line, is so scenic, and the bicycle hire shop in the station so conveniently placed,

i TOURIST INFORMATION

Barnstaple North Devon Museum, The Square, EX32 8LN ✆ 01271 375000
♿ www.staynorthdevon.co.uk
Great Torrington South St, EX38 8AA ✆ 01805 626140 ♿ www.great-torrington.com

that a combination of train and bike is an obvious alternative to the car for exploring the region. The local **bus** service isn't bad either, with routes fanning out from Barnstaple and covering almost all the areas in the North Devon chapters. The *North Devon* timetable (♿ www.journeydevon.info) covers this region. For current bus times (or help) phone Traveline (✆ 0871 200 2233). If you get stuck, taxi companies in Barnstaple include A1 Taxis (✆ 01271 322922), Value Taxis (✆ 01271 327777) and Barnstaple Taxi Service (✆ 01271 379455).

THE TARKA LINE

This branch railway from Exeter to Barnstaple is one of the most scenic in the county. It runs for 39 miles from the River Exe to the Taw estuary, following much of the river and countryside that featured in *Tarka the Otter*. The leisurely journey takes an hour. Bicycles are carried free, but are normally limited to two.

The Tarka Rail Association (♿ www.tarkarail.org) is a group of enthusiasts who are working with First Great Western and other bodies to improve the service. One of their initiatives is *Tarka Line Walks* and *More Tarka Line Walks*, detailed guides to a variety of linear and circular walks from the railway using the 11 stations along the line as start/finish points. This excellent scheme opens up an area of Devon which is walked much less than the South West Coast Path or the Two Moors Way.

CYCLING & WALKING

The area hosts the West Country's most famous cycle path, the Tarka Trail, but there are also quiet, fairly level country lanes to explore so the bicycle remains an effective way of getting around. Biketrail at Fremington Quay (page 100) offers a mobile repair service if you are stuck somewhere in North Devon.

Walkers can use the Tarka Trail, but its popularity as a cycle route means they may feel crowded out. The best option for some gentle inland walking is the selection of Tarka Line walks between train stations (see page 98). Walkers arriving at Barnstaple station booted and poled and ready for a hike will find a board with descriptions of suggested walks from the station varying from 2½ miles to 8½ miles.

The Tarka Trail

This 180-mile, traffic-free recreational route runs along a disused railway line from Braunton to Meeth. Families who pedal happily in the sunshine have reason to bless Dr Beeching who closed this unprofitable branch line in 1965. Freight trains continued to use it until 1982 and the line was purchased in 1985 by Devon County Council. It must carry far more cycles on its level and scenic route than ever it did rail passengers, and deserves its popularity. From the ease of hiring cycles in Braunton, Bideford, Barnstaple and Torrington (page 100) to the informative signs and lovely waterside scenery, this is a great way of spending a summer day.

Probably the most popular section for cyclists is Barnstaple to Instow and back (see box, page 105) or, for the more energetic, to Great Torrington (14 miles), but some bike hire companies may collect you

DEVON & THE ENGLISH CIVIL WAR

The English Civil War was in fact three armed conflicts that ravaged the land and divided families between 1642 and 1651, but it is the first war, 1642–46, that features in Devon's history. Wars can never be simplified in a few words, but this book contains enough references to the conflict to make a little background information useful. Broadly speaking the dispute was between the Royalists, also known as Cavaliers, who supported King Charles I despite his despotism and enthusiasm for ruling England without the help of parliament, and the Parliamentarians or Roundheads (a reference to the shaven heads of the rabble-rousing London apprentice boys) who backed the Republican, Puritan ideals of Oliver Cromwell and Sir Thomas Fairfax, his superior (Cromwell was a better politician than a soldier).

A prominent name in Devon's Civil War was Sir Ralph Hopton, who led a small force of Royalist cavalry from Minehead into Cornwall, joining forces with Sir Bevil Grenville. Devon's most significant battle was in Great Torrington (page 111) in 1646 between General Thomas Fairfax's Parliamentarians and Lord Hopton's Royalist forces. This marked the end of Royalist resistance in Devon, Hopton surrendered to Fairfax in Truro, the Parliamentarians triumphed and King Charles I was executed in 1649.

and your bike from your end point, thus allowing you to ride a longer distance. The booklet *Tarka Trail Circular Routes*, available from TICs and from www.devon.gov.uk, gives many detailed suggestions along the whole length of the trail.

CYCLE HIRE

The following companies are organised geographically, north to south.

Otter Cycle Hire Station Rd, Braunton EX33 2AQ ℘ 01271 813339

Bideford Bicycle & Kayak Hire Torrington St, East-the-Water EX39 4DR ℘ 01237 424123 www.bidefordbicyclehire.co.uk. May offer a pick up/drop off service so you can do a linear route.

Tarka Trail Cycle Hire The railway station, Barnstaple EX34 8DL ℘ 01271 324202 www.tarkabikes.co.uk ☉ Mar–Nov daily

The Bike Shed Nr the Albert Clock, Barnstaple EX32 8LS ℘ 01271 328628

Biketrail The Stone Barn, Fremington Quay, nr Barnstaple EX31 2NH ℘ 01271 372586 www.biketrail.co.uk ☉ daily (but check beforehand out of season). Will pick up bikes by arrangement if you want to do a linear route and offer a mobile repair service. Fremington Quay is a pleasant two-mile walk along the Tarka Trail from Barnstaple.

Torrington Cycle Hire Old Town Station, Station Hill (behind the Puffing Billy pub) EX38 8JD ℘ 01805 622633 ☉ Feb–Nov, daily

WET-WEATHER ACTIVITIES

Arlington Court Carriage Museum (page 105)
Barnstaple Museum (page 101)
Dartington Crystal Great Torrington (page 113)
Horwood church (page 110)
Plough Arts Centre Great Torrington (page 111)
Queen's Theatre Barnstaple (page 102)
Quince Honey Farm (page 117)
Tawstock church (page 108)
Torrington Museum (page 111)

1 BARNSTAPLE

🏠 **Anderton House** Goodleigh (page 199)

Historically, Barnstaple has always been compared with Bideford, the fortunes of one rising as the other waned. It, too, has a bridge over the Taw which has an even more exciting history than its rival since it was begun,

HEDGES, TREES & WALLS

There is a saying that for every species of tree in a hedge you can add another hundred years to its age. Hedges served a dual purpose: they contained cattle and sheep in pasture, and they provided edible berries for rural households. Thus hawthorn, blackthorn (for sloes) and blackberry were popular, their spines making an effective barrier. Beech was introduced in the 18th century, having the advantage of keeping its dead leaves in the winter, so maintaining the visual effect of an impenetrable barrier. Earth banks were also constructed to provide shelter for flocks in Devon's stormy weather and faced with stone for stability. They were planted with beech trees to give additional height. Traditionally these were pollarded or cut and laid but, once mechanical flayers made this labour-

intensive task uneconomical, the trees grew unchecked and are now a common sight in Devon, their roots straddling the bank. Sycamore was introduced in the 1600s, as a fast-growing, salt-tolerant species but, compared with the native oak, it is a poor host. Where an oak can support up to 200 species of insect, the sycamore is home to only 12.

Dry stone walls are also a feature of the North Devon countryside, and the skill with which they were built is testified in their age: 200 years or more. The Dry Stone Walling Association of Great Britain is involved in encouraging the continuation of this traditional craft and you will see some beautiful examples of new walls as well as ancient ones.

so they say, by two spinster sisters who spun the first two piers with the help of local children. John Leland called it a 'right great and sumptuous Bridge of Stone having 16 high Arches'.

The river silted up in the 19th century and maritime trade switched to Bideford. However, Barnstaple prospered as a market town; it's now the largest town in North Devon and the only one to have a railway connection with the rest of the county. And it is that railway that brings visitors to Barnstaple, and the railway that allows them to escape, for the megastored area around the station initially discourages further exploration, although there are suggested walks displayed on a panel outside the station.

"Once you've crossed the bridge the town centre turns out to be agreeably compact."

Once you've crossed the bridge the town centre turns out to be agreeably compact with a pedestrianised town square, a daily market and a very good **museum** which also houses the

TIC. It has the usual displays of local history and Devon life in addition to a display of boldly decorated Barum Ware from the Brannam pottery, and an exceptionally interesting natural history section. I was particularly intrigued by the fossilised fragments of a straight-tusked elephant, found in 1844. It stood 12 feet high and lived around 150,000 years ago when Devon, Britain and its whole vast continent lay close to the equator. The museum is easy to find near the **Albert Clock**. A couple of blocks away off the High Street is the indoor **Pannier Market**, open daily except Sundays, where you can buy everything including a good variety of local produce. The packaging has changed a bit since it was described fondly by S P B Mais: 'Here sit old wives from the country behind stalls covered with trussed chicken, bowls of cream, fruit and vegetables, while their husbands sell calves and pigs in the open market across the way.' Local crafts are sold on Mondays and Thursdays and antiques on Wednesdays.

The **Pannier Market** also stages a one-day **North Devon FoodFest** (⊘ www.northdevonfoodfest.com) in October.

The **Queen's Theatre** (100 Boutport St ⊘ 01271 324242) hosts touring companies year-round.

¶¶ FOOD & DRINK

Claytons & the Glass House 2 Cross St, EX31 1BA ⊘ 01271 323311 ⊘ www. claytonsbarnstaple.co.uk. A classy, modern place offering exceptional food for that special night out.

Everest Gurkha Chef 3 Maiden St, EX31 1HA ⊘ 01271 376863 ⊘ www.everestgurkha. co.uk. And now for something completely different! This tiny, unlicensed, eat-in or take-away restaurant is just what it says: run by Som, a Nepalese Gurkha who learned to cook in his home country and brought his family and his skills to Barnstaple.

Fatbelly Fred's 16 Maiden St, EX31 1HA ⊘ 01271 345700 ⊘ www.fatbellyfreds.co.uk. Seafood is the speciality here, sourced mainly from North Devon and simply cooked to bring out the flavours. Some meat and vegetarian dishes as well. A runner-up in the North Devon Food Awards 2013.

New Inn Goodleigh EX32 7LX ⊘ 01271 342488. The village is a few miles east of Barnstaple and the inn is in a typically rural setting, near the church and with a beer garden. The menu is extensive, the portions large, and the welcome effusive. Very popular so book ahead.

Terra Madre Broomhill Art Hotel, EX31 4EX ⊘ 01271 850262 ⊘ www.broomhillart.co.uk ⊙ daily 11.00–16.00 for bar meals & snacks, restaurant Wed–Sun. Award-winning food in stylish surroundings plus a sculpture garden and displays of art. See page 104.

NORTH OF BARNSTAPLE

The small pocket of countryside between Barnstaple and Ilfracombe has two exceptional **gardens**, close to each other, as well as **Arlington Court**, run by the National Trust, with its famous carriage collection.

2 MARWOOD HILL GARDENS & CHURCH
Marwood, nr Barnstaple EX31 4EB ℘ 01271 342528 ⊘ www.marwoodhillgarden.co.uk
⊙ Mar–Oct daily

On a hillside, stretching down to the valley below, is this delightful garden, with a fresh surprise around every corner. It was the loving creation of a retired GP, Jimmy Smart, who wanted somewhere hidden where his former patients wouldn't find him. He succeeded. Although only four miles from Barnstaple this little hamlet feels untouched by time. Dr Smart started with nothing but 20 acres of overgrown Devon and three lakes, but his enthusiasm and vision created perhaps my favourite North Devon garden which, with its adjacent church, is not to be missed. Late spring is the best time to see the 600 camellias, but at any time of year you can be sure of a blaze of colour. I was there in August, when the hydrangeas were a mass of deep blues. Winding paths meander through flowering shrubs to emerge on sunlit lawns dotted with sculptures including Dr Smart, in rumpled gardening clothes, gazing proudly over his creation. A bog garden provides added interest and variety as do the lakes. Dr Smart died in 2002; the gardens are now owned and maintained by his nephew, Dr John Snowdon. Outside the tea room is a bird list – over 40 species have been recorded here.

The **church** of St Michael and All Angels is equally rewarding. You are immediately struck by the carved bench ends depicting a variety of subjects including what looks like a bagpipe player and what I thought was an elephant, although it's so worm-eaten it's hard to be sure. There are all sorts of grotesque faces and figures doing goodness knows what, as well as an easily recognisable bird and possibly a fox. The intricately carved screen also shows extraordinary detail. A wall plaque from 1828 records that the Reverend Richard Harding gave £100 – a significant amount of money in those days – 'to such poor labourers of this parish as have been exemplary in their good behaviour in life, and have been constant partakers of the blessed sacraments'. In the graveyard is the simple tombstone of James Smart, 'creator of Marwood Hill Gardens'.

3 BROOMHILL SCULPTURE GARDEN

🏠 **Broomhill Art Hotel** Muddiford (page 198)

EX31 4EX, a few miles north of Barnstaple, off the B3230 🖉 01271 850262

🖉 www.broomhillart.co.uk ⊙ daily 11.00–16.00, restaurant Wed–Sun

I found myself walking around this magical place with a smile on my face. The morning sun spotlit sculptures that would be impressive in a gallery setting, but here, chancing upon them as you wander down meandering paths in the woods, past stands of bamboo and giant rhubarb, or alongside the tree-shaded river, you feel that such a garden is the only setting in which to exhibit large sculptures. Not that they are all large. Sometimes you are alerted to their presence by the sign before you see the piece almost hidden in the shrubbery.

Broomhill happened because Rinus and Aniet van de Sande, from the Netherlands, started a gallery to encourage young artists in their home country, but wanted an outdoor venue. Holland was not an option 'because so many galleries and sculpture gardens already existed' so when they found a run-down hotel with a large, overgrown garden on the outskirts of Barnstaple, they knew it was the right place. Broomhill's ten acres are now a mixture of formal garden and natural woodland, and even without the sculptures the steeply terraced and wooded grounds would be a pleasure to stroll in. The combination of the two is stunning, and a must-see for anyone with an interest in art. Or in Slow Food, for its award-winning **Terra Madre restaurant** is exceptional, focusing mainly on Mediterranean cooking (page 102). An awful lot of restaurants claim 'locally sourced food' nowadays, but here the farms supplying the organic/free-range ingredients are listed, and the philosophy of the Slow Food Movement, of which Rinus is a member, is explained. What could be better for this book: nourishment for the body and soul in one place!

4 ARLINGTON COURT

Nr Barnstaple EX31 4LP 🖉 01271 850296 ⊙ Mar–Nov, 11.00–17.00; National Trust

The Chichester family owned the estate from 1384 until 1949 when Miss Rosalie Chichester bequeathed it to the National Trust. She was the only child of Sir Bruce Chichester, who used to take her on long voyages around the Mediterranean on his schooner, *Erminia*. And, yes, Sir Francis Chichester, the round-the-world yachtsman, was a relative: Rosalie's nephew. Her interest in ships is evident throughout

PEDALLING TO INSTOW

The stretch of the Tarka Trail between Barnstaple and Bideford is nine miles. I opted for the six miles to Instow, with lunch at a pub, then back the way I came.

The whole trip couldn't have been easier. I found Tarka Trail Cycle Hire right *in* the station – actually occupying the former gents' toilet. The original owners, John and Margaret Kempson, spent 18 months negotiating with Railtrack for some space, but their persistence paid off. Being able to step off a train and on to a bike with the minimum of fuss has ensured its 20-year success. The new owner, Paul Philips, has a large range of every sort of bicycle including tandems, and a Weehoo double trailer for small children. I asked for 'an old lady's bike' since I didn't want to fuss with lots of gears when the track is level. Maps are provided, but the Tarka Trail is so well waymarked that you mostly don't need them. On a sunny day in May the track was lined with cow parsley and other late spring flowers and fluttering with painted-lady butterflies. Songbirds trilled to my left and water birds lurked in the RSPB Isley Marsh Nature Reserve on my right. There are some hides for proper birdwatching if you want to take a break.

the house in the many exquisite models made from bone and spun glass. Her enthusiasm for animals also appears in the several models and sculptures of questionable beauty, including a truly hideous crystal cat/leopard. The only valuable work of art was found on top of a cupboard in a disused wing of the house: a watercolour by William Blake, painted in 1821. No doubt the mistress of the house didn't like it.

Completed in 1822, the house is described as neo-Greek, and was added to, clumsily, in 1865. More rewarding is the collection of **carriages** in the old stables. It's one of the best in the country with clear labelling and enough variety to retain interest, from the governess cart which can be compared, in its utility design, to the Morris Minor of later years, to the state coaches and even more glamorous state chariots. There are some nice human stories in the inscriptions, such as the footmen who had to stand at the back of the state coach, bolt upright and immobile, even though they only had two straps to hold on to, and the stable boy who lived in a loft above the stables and had to be available at all times.

Behind the house in a dripping cellar you'll find a batcam. Devon's largest population of lesser horseshoe bats spends its summers here in the roof space, and they hibernate in the cellar.

SOUTH OF BARNSTAPLE

Between the rivers Taw and Torridge is Williamson country, with the **Tarka Trail** (pages 99–100) and Tarka Line running close to each river respectively. The Tarka Trail and adjacent attractions dominate the region, but there are some delightful and isolated little churches and the town of Great Torrington with the famous Rosemoor Gardens forming the southern boundary.

INSTOW & TAPELEY PARK

🏠 **Lower Yelland Farm** Fremington (page 199)

Instow

This agreeable village lies at the junction of the Taw and Torridge; it has a little harbour, a broad sandy beach (at low tide) and an award-winning pub, the Instow Arms. Across the water from it, **Appledore** (page 43) is accessible by ferry in the summer. This historic ferry, which runs between the two towns for a few hours either side of high tide, was recently rescued by a lottery grant and is run by volunteers (⊘ www. appledoreinstowferry.com). They will carry bicycles, if there's room, for a small additional charge.

The village failed to impress J L W Page, who hailed a ferry to take him across the river in the late 1800s. 'It is some time before the fluttering handkerchief is noticed. [Instow] is bracing, it is fairly cheap, it has a pretty view and a long stretch of beach, and it is on a railway – that is all that can be said for Instow. Though only six miles from Barnstaple and three more from Bideford, it is neither lively nor picturesque.' Not fair, as you will see.

Instow 'station', on the Tarka Trail, comes as a surprise. The platform is still there, as is the signal box. There are even some milk churns waiting to be loaded on the absent train.

5 Tapeley Park

Instow ✆ 01271 860897 ⊘ www.tapeleygardens.com ⊙ end Mar–end Oct

Tapeley Park has a long, colourful history and an even more colourful current owner. There has been some sort of house here since before the Norman Conquest, but its most notable inhabitants were the Cleveland family who, for 150 years, were in service to the government. Their positions varied: MP, governor in India, and army officer.

Archibald Clevland was one of only three officers to survive the Charge of the Light Brigade – only to be killed a month later. One of his letters describing the campaign is on display in the History Room and on the website.

Archibald's sister married William Langham Christie in 1855, and his daughter-in-law, Lady Rosamund, created the house and gardens that we see today, after removing her husband, Augustus, to Saunton due to his 'childish behaviour' expressed by kicking the furniture with hobnailed boots. Alas, he turned the

"Lady Rosamund created the gardens after removing her husband, Augustus, to Saunton due to his 'childish behaviour'."

tables by dying and leaving the house to a distant cousin, and Lady Rosamund spent the last six years of her life in the law courts proving her rightful ownership. She was successful but died soon after. John Christie, her son, took over, spending part of the year at Tapeley and part at Glyndebourne where he had founded the opera house.

Eccentricity arrived in the form of another Rosamund who, until her death in 1988, ran the house as a visitor attraction, with haphazard cream teas and house tours which she often conducted with a parrot on her head. Hector Christie, the current owner, has left his personality quite gloriously on Tapeley Park. The house (not open to the public) and gardens are run so sustainably that the whole pile could safely be put on the compost heap. Solar panels light and heat the History Room and Hector writes: 'It is my dream that now we could survive off the land … we become off-grid with a mixture of wind, solar, biomass, hydro, anaerobic digesters, and any other new inventions. The idea is to demonstrate to visitors the newest, cheapest, most efficient forms of renewable carbon-neutral energy on the market.'

The garden is a delight, with the view up to the house from the Italian Garden one of the best of its kind in Devon. Garden experts Mary Keen and Carol Klein left their mark on the formal gardens and everywhere there is colour and originality. The teas, taken at tables set out on the lawn, are excellent. Finally don't miss the Permaculture Garden which Hector describes as 'companion planting using predominantly perennial herbs and vegetables, and working with nature as opposed to constantly fighting against it [as in the modern monoculture approach to farming]'. Then there's the attractive straw bale house and some happy poultry. My only disappointment was that the kunekune pigs have gone.

Everything is explained through information boards, and some of the notices themselves are rather special: 'Please do not put doggy indiscretions in the sanitary bins' and, at the bottom of an advertisement for a day-long seminar *Another World is Possible*, with talks on 'How can we stop Fracking?' and 'The Art of Dissent' there was a note: 'This is a loss-making event. It is small enough for the organisers to know who has paid and who has not … Non payers will be approached by unsavoury characters for a quick resolution.' Refreshingly different from the National Trust!

Cyclists can access Tapeley Park from the Tarka Trail; motorists follow the signs from the A39.

SOUTHWEST OF BARNSTAPLE

Between the A386 and the A377 are several places of interest; though somewhat spread out they are all worth the detour. **Tawstock** and **Horwood** have two of the best churches in the region.

6 TAWSTOCK

🏠 **Hollamoor Farm** (page 198)

> The Erle of Bathe hath a right goodly Maner and Place at Tawstoke on the West side of the Haven.
>
> John Leland, travelling during 1534–43

This extraordinary place illustrates the historical position of the local aristocracy in its community better than anywhere I know. The entrance is intimidating enough for a modern visitor, so must have been awe-inspiring for a 17th-century labourer. As you drive or cycle down a narrow lane, you pass between stone pillars topped by faithful hounds. To the left are the huge remains of the manor gatehouse with its vast oak door that would admit a carriage and team of horses. Above it is a coat of arms and the date: 1574. A catastrophic fire in 1787 destroyed the rest of the manor, which was rebuilt in 'Gothick' style by Sir Bourchier Wrey. The original lords of the manor were the Bourchiers, created Earls of Bath in 1536; it passed, through marriage, to the Wreys in the 17th century.

Through the centuries the earls could look down on their little **church**, St Peter's, in its lowly position with a sweep of green hills behind it, and feel they had God just where they wanted Him. The inside of the church is so crammed with Wrey memorials that they compete for holy space; uplifting inscriptions, monuments and memorial stones take over the chancel and much of the side aisle. Nor is it just the memorials that make the church so impressive – and different. Its organ is massive, with pipes almost framing a modern stained-glass window. The additional south aisle was formed by knocking holes into the existing side of the church, and creating arches. The pillars that support them are topped with rather smug carved faces and wreaths of foliage. The eagle lectern is ornithologically worrying: this bird would have been unable to close its splendid beak. The chancel is completely paved with inscribed stones commemorating people who died in the 17th and 18th centuries. You can spend a happy half hour reading these, before moving on to the memorials. The most impressive is to the Earl of Bath who died in 1654. His giant sarcophagus is guarded by 'dogs' that spring from the pages of Harry Potter, with curly manes, menacing claws and oversized canines – another animal that could not have closed its mouth. Only the cropped ears suggest domesticity. Then there are the painted memorials to the third Earl of Bath, William Bourchier, and his wife Elizabeth. Her feet are resting on a goat. At least I think it's a goat. A panel of photos shows how these tombs were restored when the iron holding sections of the stone together started to rust and cause cracking.

"The pillars that support the arches are topped with rather smug carved faces and wreaths of foliage."

Moving on from the Wreys, there are panels listing the charitable actions of the wealthy towards the poor – and the church. In 1677 the Dowager Countess of Bath 'laid out in Land to the benefit of the Poor of this parish for ever' and 'Shee hath also gave the parish a rich embroidered crimson velvet pulpit cloath and cushion and yearly bound out several poor children apprenticed and done many other excellent acts of charity.' Such was the path to the Kingdom of Heaven. Others were less generous – but also certainly less rich; there are several donations of ten shillings. In the side aisle they've also found room for two secular items of rural history: a coffin cart and a plough. Note, too, above the side aisles, the more recent but beautiful plaster ceiling decoration of delicate flowers and tendrils.

If you only see one church in North Devon make it this one. No other is as rich in visual history inside and rural beauty in its setting. It's as English as you can get, and is only about two miles from Barnstaple station down a quiet lane so you can walk or cycle here with relative ease.

7 HORWOOD

Horwood seems little more than a thatched cottage or two and a church, but what a church! Everywhere you look is something old, intriguing or beautiful. When you enter, your attention is immediately caught by the bench ends. These are carved in high relief with a mixture of saints and the initials of the pew owners. Soon you will realise that you are walking on words; almost every inch of the floor is occupied by old memorial slates, finely carved with skulls, angels and inscriptions. Those 17th-century carvers knew how to produce beautiful lettering. Where there is any space between the slates, there are equally old glazed tiles. Once you've finished looking down, look up. The wagon roof is exceptional, particularly above the north aisle, where there are some fine carved bosses. Then take a look at the carvings on the capitals (above the columns). Amongst the foliage are faces, some portraits of distinguished-looking men with beards, but others grotesque death heads. Another has a curious selection of angels and creatures that are part-human, part-beast. Three of them are clasping stones – possibly the 'tablets' presented to Moses. The exception is a rather voluptuous female angel. Then comes a winged figure with a lion's body and human head and hands, and finally there's a mermaid, impractically clad in baggy robes.

> *"Soon you will realise that you are walking on words; almost every inch of the floor is occupied."*

In the lady chapel is the effigy of a woman wearing a horned headdress, with her four children tucked into the folds of her robe. No-one knows for sure who she is, but probably Elizabeth Pollard who died in the 15th century. The stained glass in the lady chapel's east window is very old – 15th century – but the other windows are Victorian. Finally the piscina, near the altar, is unusual: it has a horn-shaped drain. It is nearly a thousand years old.

GREAT TORRINGTON & AREA

⋏ **Woodland Retreat** Langtree (page 199)

Highly praised by residents for its friendliness, Great Torrington (usually just called Torrington) is a market town with some lovely surrounding countryside and the famous **RHS Rosemoor Gardens** nearby as well as the popular **Dartington Crystal**.

8 GREAT TORRINGTON

The town played a prominent part in the **English Civil War** (page 99), 'blown into history by the explosion of eighty barrels of gunpowder' (Arthur Mee). The West Country had been a Royalist stronghold, but in a fierce battle in 1646 the town was captured by the Parliamentarians, and the prisoners were held in the tower of the church which was also being used to store the Royalists' arsenal. What could possibly go wrong? Somehow the gunpowder ignited and the resulting explosion partially destroyed the church and killed 200 men, as well as nearly killing Fairfax on his horse. This marked the end of the Royalist efforts in the region and the battle of 1646 is re-enacted in Torrington each year in February.

"In the Civil War... the prisoners were held in the tower of the church which was also being used to store the Royalists' arsenal. What could possibly go wrong?"

The town has a very good **museum** (✆ 01805 622306 ☼ Mon–Fri 10.30–16.00, Sat 10.30–13.00), enthusiastically run by volunteers, with all sorts of displays: history, agriculture, domestic appliances and a first edition of the *Concise British Flora in Colour* by that industrious churchman, the Reverend William Keble Martin who was vicar of Great Torrington in the 1930s. He had formerly been archpriest of the little church of Haccombe, near Newton Abbot, where I first came across the story that he was urged to find something else to do by his exasperated parishioners after he had visited them all twice in one week. Hence the meticulous botanical illustrations in his celebrated work.

Like many Devon towns, Torrington has a thriving **pannier market**, open daily and under cover, with an assortment of craft and antique shops as well as a range of produce, and the town's concerns nicely emphasised by an advertisement for North Devon Bat Care (protecting the mammals, not helping the county cricketers).

Finally there's the very good **Plough Arts Centre**, where you can watch films or plays, look round an exhibition or do a spot of arty stuff yourself at one of the workshops. It really is a terrific place.

From the car park on Castle Hill, near the helpful **tourist information centre**, you can look down on the river and some narrow strips of land. These are Leper Fields which were once tilled by lepers who lived in the leper village of Taddiport (see page 112), which you can see on the right of the two preserved fields by Little Torrington.

TADDIPORT & FRITHELSTOCK

Both these little villages lie close to the Tarka Trail and make a worthwhile diversion for cyclists – and for drivers. Visit **Taddiport**, with its tiny chapel, to get the feel of what it was like to be a leper in the Middle Ages. Through no fault of their own, they lost their liberty and the right to inherit or bequeath property. However, they seem to have been well looked after at Taddiport, which had a hospital, the little chapel where they could pray for a cure, and the leper fields where they could grow food. Quite a bit of this history is retained: the church, the fields, and even a (privately owned) Leper Cottage.

The tower of the **church of St Mary Magdalene** is only five feet high and five feet square, yet it doesn't look disproportionately small on this little medieval building. The floor space is L-shaped, with an organ taking up much of one side. A touching stained-glass window dedicated to the lepers is the work of a 19-year-old lad in 1972. Here, as in many Devon churches, the Ten Commandments are painted on one of the walls, but what is one to make of the biblical text on the adjacent wall that evidently points an accusing finger? 'Woe to them that devise iniquity and work Evil upon theyr beds … And they covet feilds and take them by violence,

"What is one to make of the biblical text on the adjacent wall that evidently points an accusing finger?"

And howses and take them away: Soe they oppress A man and his howse.' It is assumed that this refers to some ancient misappropriation of land, but no-one knows for sure. Intriguing!

Frithelstock lies a few miles to the northwest, and is a quintessentially English village with a pub, **The Clinton Arms**, set by a large village green and opposite the 13th-century church. A stately line of lime trees lead to the church door, which still has its sanctuary ring which granted protection to all miscreants who could grab it while being pursued by the Law. Abutting the church are the ruined walls of a medieval priory; the west wall is the best preserved, 40 feet high with a fine door and lancet windows remaining.

Inside, it is the carved bench ends that catch your attention. They date from the 15th century and depict a variety of religious symbols from the crucifixion, such as the crown of thorns, a whip, and a reed. More intriguing, however, are secular carvings of two heads, facing each other, with their tongues protruding. It seems that these may represent the Bishop of Exeter and the Prior of Frithelstock, who fell out with one another in the Middle Ages and now insult each other through eternity.

9 RHS GARDEN ROSEMOOR

🏠 **Rosemoor House** (page 199)

Great Torrington EX38 8PH ✆ 0845 265 8072 or 01805 624067 (shop & plant centre)

🖰 www.rhs.org.uk/rosemoor ⏱ year-round, but restaurant closed Oct–Apr

The Royal Horticultural Society's showpiece garden, Rosemoor, has 65 acres with 200 varieties of rose, decorative vegetable planting, and woodland walks. The garden feels surprisingly compact, so even in an hour or so you can see most of it, and there are daily events and exhibitions. Come here on a sunny day, any time of the year, and take your time to breathe in the scents and sights. The knowledge of your fellow visitors can be intimidating: on my last visit a voice boomed out 'Did you tell Daddy about the pelargonium?' The child looked about five.

The Reading Room is open to non-members who can browse the 1,300 reference books, and the restaurant serves good snacks and cream teas. Inside the garden there is self-catering accommodation in the former home of Lady Anne Berry, who donated the garden to the RHS in 1988.

10 DARTINGTON CRYSTAL

Linden Close, Great Torrington EX38 7AN ✆ 01805 626262 🖰 www.dartington.co.uk

⏱ all year, daily, 9.30–17.00 (16.00 Sun)

There's plenty to see and do here as well as buy high-quality glassware. It's not cheap so allow enough time to go to the AV Theatre and round the factory to see glass blowing and engraving in action. You can try glass blowing yourself if you book ahead. The website is exceptionally good, so watch the video of how they create complicated one-off pieces as well as standard hand- and foot-prints.

🍴 FOOD & DRINK

The Black Horse High St, Great Torrington EX38 8HN ✆ 01805 622121. One of the oldest pubs in the area, serving standard pub food with aplomb.

The Clinton Arms Frithelstock EX38 8JH ✆ 01805 623279. A traditional village pub with outside seating on the village green and typical pub food such as fish pie, sausage and mash and steak and ale pie.

Torridge Inn 136 Mill St, Taddiport EX38 8AW ✆ 01805 625042. Surprising to find Thai food served in a classic Devon pub in a small village, but it's done very well and is deservedly popular.

SOUTHEAST OF BARNSTAPLE: BETWEEN THE A377 & A361

Easily accessible from either main road, this green corridor has a scattering of notable churches, a spacious garden and one of Devon's most off-beat and rewarding attractions, the **Quince Honey Farm**.

THE REVEREND JOHN (JACK) RUSSELL

By all accounts the Reverend John Russell most perfectly combined his hobby with making a living. He was a popular minister at St James's church for 46 years, having arrived, with his pack of hounds, in 1833, and indulged his passion for hunting until two years before his death at the age of 87. An estimated 1,000 people attended his funeral. Despite hunting almost daily – he was rumoured to wear his hunting clothes beneath his surplice for a quick getaway – he managed to increase the services at Swimbridge from one each Sunday to four, restored the dilapidated church and its school, and was conscientious in visiting his most needy parishioners. He was also remembered for his charity towards gypsies, who were much persecuted in those days. In return they protected the Rectory from thieves.

Not everyone was happy about his obsession with hunting, however, and eventually he yielded to the pressure to give up his pack of hounds, partly instigated by that scourge of licentious clergymen, Bishop Philpotts of Exeter. For two years Russell was without his own pack, which cast him into such depths of depression that when he was offered the gift of 13 foxhounds his resolve faltered. 'There they stood,' he said,

'the greatest beauties my eye had ever rested on, looking up in my face so winningly, that I mentally determined to keep the lot and go to work again.' His wife told him that he had as much right to enjoy life as other men, and so he kept them.

These days Jack Russell is famous for the terriers which bear his name. The story goes that while he was at Oxford – doing precious little work but a lot of hunting – he was strolling in Magdalen Meadow trying to memorise some Latin, when he met a milkman with a little terrier bitch and bought it on the spot. The terrier's name was Trump, and she became the first of a distinct breed of dog now called the Jack Russell terrier. Russell was a founder member of the Kennel Club and a respected judge of fox terriers so he knew a thing or two about dog breeding.

In his lifetime this larger-than-life character was better known for his hunting than for his sermons, although he managed to combine both in a visit to Sandringham. At the invitation of the Prince of Wales who asked him to 'put a sermon in his pocket' he danced in the new year with the Princess of Wales and preached his sermon in Sandringham's church the following Sunday.

11 SWIMBRIDGE

'No dogs' says a sign on the gate. Unremarkable except that this church is famous because its long-term vicar was the Reverend John Russell, who bred the first Jack Russell terrier (see box, opposite). His plain but conspicuous grave is round the corner in the graveyard – follow the arrows – and the original Jack Russell terrier, Trump, has her portrait on the inn sign for the **Jack Russell pub** opposite the church. The pub is full of Jack Russell memorabilia and less strict than the church about canine visitors.

The **church of St James** is unusual in several ways. It has a lead-coated spire rather than the more familiar tower, and an extraordinary font cover, enclosing the font in a sort of cupboard, with a canopy above, all beautifully carved. The stone pulpit is very fine, as is the intricately carved wooden screen, and don't forget to look up at the impressive roof. All in all, a church worth visiting, even if you don't own a Jack Russell.

The village itself is most attractive, with a skein of white and cream houses climbing up a lane, and some well-tended allotments. It even has a working post office.

UMBERLEIGH

⅄ Vintage Vardos Atherington (page 199)

Umberleigh is one of those places you whizz past on the main road, half registering the name but little more. Set by the River Taw and its arched bridge, it has a quiet sense of community – and pride in dealing with the region's flood problem by dredging the river and clearing the arches so rain water could safely run away. There's an excellent pub, the **Rising Sun**, a post office and a railway station. It has ancient royal connections, too. The Georgian Umberleigh House was once the site of one of those pre-conquest English monarchs that no-one has heard of: King Athelstan. For the visitor, however, it makes a good base to explore the region, being only six miles from Barnstaple, with some good accommodation options and the **Weirmarsh Farm Restaurant** (page 117).

12 CASTLE HILL GARDENS
& CHITTLEHAMPTON CHURCH

Close to **Filleigh**, with its splendid thatched pub, is **Castle Hill Gardens** (EX32 0RQ ✆ 01598 760336 ⌂ www.castlehilldevon.co.uk ☺ year-round from 11.00 except Sat). The formal gardens with colourful herbaceous borders are enjoyable, but really it is the parkland with its extensive views and huge mature trees that is the attraction here. It's an ideal place to exercise lively children and dogs.

Nearby at Chittlehampton is the **church of St Hieritha**, which has some intriguing features, not least its saint who was buried here. St Hieritha, or St Urith, is Devon's very own saint. Converted to Christianity by Glastonbury monks, she was accused of causing a severe drought, and scythed to pieces by the local farmers. A spring gushed forth where her severed head landed and Chittlehampton had not only a reliable source of water but subsequent centuries of wealth from the pilgrims who visited her shrine. A satisfactory outcome for (almost) all concerned.

Donations by pilgrims helped create the imposing church with its high and frilly tower. This is considered to be one of the loveliest in Devon, a view endorsed by a 17th-century writer: 'I observed the tower of the Church to be a work more curious and fair than any in that County'.

"A spring gushed forth where her severed head landed."

Inside, the stone pulpit is unusual and interesting, carved with four glum-faced men with what appear to be log rolls round their heads. They have been described as Latin doctors or leaders from church history. The fifth figure is St Hieritha herself, carrying a palm which symbolised martyrdom. Above the choir the roof is supported by angels, and there's a charming plaque commemorating St Hieritha by her tomb or shrine. The craftsman has made no attempt at fitting the words into the space or even hyphenation, so that 'foundress' becomes 'fo' (next line) 'undress' which is certainly eye-catching.

HEAVY HORSES

Higher Biddacott Farm, Chittlehampton EX37 9PY ℘ 01769 540222 ⊘ www.heavy-horses.net

If you fancy stepping back in time and learning how to work with heavy horses, there's a farm in Chittlehampton which does just that. Jonathan Waterer's horses help him to farm close on 100 acres sustainably. He keeps six Shires for work, weddings, funerals and filmwork, and always has other horses and ponies in from other people for training. Pre-booked wagon rides are available all year-round along with B&B.

Courses are available with Jonathan to learn the intricacies of harnessing and driving these wonderful horses on the land or the road. Depending on the season all sorts of agricultural and forestry tasks can be learned or you can drive a single up to a six-in-hand on the farm or on the road.

¶¶ FOOD & DRINK

The Masons Arms Knowstone EX36 4RY ✆ 01398 41231 ◇ www.masonsarmsdevon. co.uk ⊙ closed Sun eve & all day Mon. From the outside this looks like a typical Devon pub in a small mid-Devon village (Knowstone is just north of the A361 between Tiverton and Barnstaple). But inside it is a Michelin-starred restaurant owned and operated by Mark Dodson, formerly head chef at Michel Roux's Waterside Inn, Bray. That's all you need to know, really. Exquisite food, and lunches are surprisingly affordable.

The Stag's Head Filleigh EX32 0RN ✆ 01598 760250 ◇ www.stagshead.co.uk. A long-established favourite with visitors and locals alike, this thatched pub is within the Castle Hill estate, and is not only a beautiful building but serves excellent local food including pheasant from the estate.

Weirmarsh Farm Restaurant Umberleigh EX37 9BE (check their website directions before relying on sat nav) ✆ 01769 560338 ◇ www.weirmarshfarmrestaurant.co.uk. The place to come for a treat or with a group. This country restaurant was runner-up in the 2013 North Devon Food Awards and serves pre-ordered dinners from a tantalising menu. They email (or post) the menu and you make your choice for the starter and main course of the five-course dinner served on Thursdays, Fridays and Saturdays. Good value for money, and lower-cost lunches are available in the summer.

13 QUINCE HONEY FARM

North Rd, South Molton EX36 3AZ ✆ 01769 572401 ◇ www.quincehoneyfarm.co.uk ⊙ all year, daily except Christmas holidays

You can't judge a book by its cover. This garish building on **South Molton's** main road houses a truly amazing exhibition. If you thought you knew quite a bit about bees you will find that you have only scratched the surface. Here you will learn about the history of bee keeping, going back some 10,000 years; the different species of bees; and where and how they make their homes in other parts of the world. There are observation hives that you can open yourself (by remote control), films, explanatory panels, and bees everywhere, but always behind glass. You can watch the various stages of the commercial aspect of bee keeping, from candle-making to extracting the honey and bottling it, and you can learn a great deal about these remarkable creatures. How does the colony deal with an intruding bumble bee, or mouse, for instance? They sting it to death, and if it is too large to remove from the hive, they bite off all the hairs and mummify it

"If you thought you knew quite a bit about bees you will find that you have only scratched the surface."

in a coating of resin-based propolis so that no bacteria can be released from the decaying body. Extraordinary!

The farm was created more than 65 years ago by George Wallace, who worked as a postman to earn extra income while he was building up his hives, often collecting swarms from one of their favourite places: letter boxes. The farm is still owned by the Wallace family. The commercial hives are in the North Devon countryside and are moved to Exmoor during the heather season.

What I particularly liked about this place is that the information is never dumbed down. While little children can tumble around in the Play Hive, older ones will be fascinated by the bees' behaviour.

The shop, as you might expect, sells every possible product connected with bees, and there is a café.

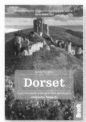
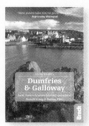
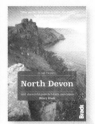

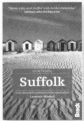

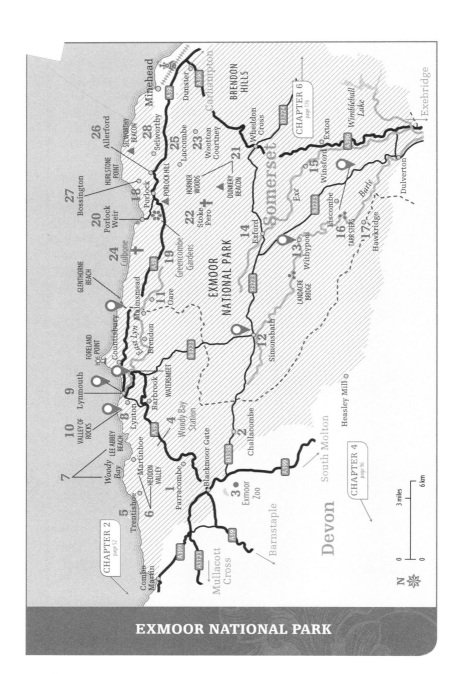

EXMOOR NATIONAL PARK

5
EXMOOR NATIONAL PARK

We came to the great River Exe ... which rises in the hills on this north side of the county ... The country it rises in is called Exmoor. Camden calls it a filthy barren ground, and indeed, so it is; but as soon as the Exe comes off from the moors and hilly country and descends into the lower grounds, we found the alteration; for then we saw Devonshire in its other countenance, cultivated, populous and fruitful.

Daniel Defoe, 1724

This is still an accurate picture of Exmoor if you change 'filthy barren ground' for something more complimentary, for it is the heather-covered moorland as much as the cultivated, populous and fruitful lower ground that draws visitors. This is one of England's smallest national parks, a soft landscape of rounded hills, splashed yellow from gorse and purple in the late summer when the heather blooms, and of deep, wooded valleys. And Exmoor has the coast, adding pebble coves and sea views to its attractions, along with the many rivers that race to the sea from the high ground, slicing into the soft sandstone. With so much of Exmoor managed by the National Trust, clear signposting makes walking or cycling a real pleasure. Astonishingly, for such an utterly delightful region, it's one of England's least visited national parks. You may not believe this on a sunny weekend in Lynmouth or Hunter's Inn when they're buzzing with visitors, but solitude is not hard to find.

The publication of *Lorna Doone* in 1869 gave Exmoor tourism a marketing high from which it's never recovered. I have a theory that not that many people have read *Lorna Doone*, but perhaps I'm making an excuse for my own ignorance. Certainly Blackmore's novel is more identifiably set in a genuine English landscape than most other literary classics, and the number of visitors to Oare church testifies that fiction is as powerful as fact.

Other Exmoor enthusiasts were the Romantic poets who descended on Exmoor a couple of hundred years ago when Samuel Taylor Coleridge and his pal Wordsworth tirelessly walked the hills and coast. Coleridge lived in Nether Stowey in the Quantocks, with William and Dorothy lodging nearby. In the autumn of 1797 they walked the coastal path to Lynton, and are said to have planned Coleridge's most famous poem, *The Rime of the Ancient Mariner*, during that walk, with Watchet (page 190) being the inspiration for the harbour from where the sailor set out. Coleridge was staying near Culbone when an opium-induced flow of poetry was interrupted by 'a person from Porlock'. He never finished *Kubla Khan*. In 1799 Robert Southey, the Poet Laureate, lived in Minehead and penned a sonnet in Porlock, and nine years later Shelley burst in on the tranquillity of Lynmouth, scattering pamphlets and scandal. All in all, anyone who had anything to do with poetry at the turn of the 18th century seems to have ended up on the Exmoor coast.

THE RED DEER OF EXMOOR

The red deer, *Cervus elaphus*, is the largest native British mammal, with stags nearly four feet high at the shoulder and hinds slightly smaller. Red deer have lived on Exmoor since prehistoric times, and the current population – estimated at around 3,000 animals – is thought to be one of the last truly indigenous populations in the British Isles. For most of the year hinds tend to herd together with their calves in certain areas while stags form bachelor groups, but it's common to find young 'prickets' with hinds and not unusual to find older stags in small groups or even by themselves.

Only the stag has antlers (or horns, as they are called locally), which it sheds in the spring every year. As the animal matures so the annual growth of its antlers increases, adding new points each year until 14 or even 16 points are attained, after which he is usually past his prime and starts to 'go back'. Finding horns that have been shed is a local tradition, and they are highly prized. There are often stags' horn competitions at shows during the summer – Exford Show in August, for instance.

All the energy put into growing these antlers is important to achieve supremacy over rival stags during the annual rut from late September until November. The dominant stags round up a harem of hinds, strut around showing off their size, and bellow their challenge to intruders.

Fights often ensue. The calves are generally born in June, and to begin with spend much of their time lying concealed in undergrowth while their mothers graze nearby, returning regularly to let their young suckle. It's very important not to get too close to a calf if you see it, nor touch it, as the hind may abandon it if you do.

You may come upon deer at any time. They are most visible on farmland, where they sometimes congregate in large numbers, but can also be found in woodland and on open moorland (where they are particularly well camouflaged). An organised safari (page 130) will increase your chances as will a guided visit during the rutting season. See *Exmoor Visitor* (page 132) for dates. For an excellent exhibition on red deer visit the Dulverton Heritage Centre (page 185).

There are several places favoured by deer where your chances of seeing them are good. Alderman's Barrow Allotment (⚲ SS836422) is one such place, just off the Exford to Porlock road. Pull off the road and walk south, keeping very quiet and with your eyes peeled. Another area where you may get lucky is along Dicky's Path, which is signed off the road. Park on Stoke Ridge (⚲ SS878426) and follow the path southeast. Prayway Head, between Brendon Common and Simonsbath, and the fields and woodlands around Cloutsham are good places to deer watch from a car, and if you feel like a walk large herds can often be found on Soggy Moor near Molland. Sit quietly with the sun behind you and binoculars at the ready, and you will almost certainly be rewarded.

EXMOOR & THE HAND OF MAN

Exmoor is not a wilderness; from earliest times humans have changed the landscape through their activities. There are a few remnants of Bronze Age barrows, as well as stone circles and standing stones, but nothing like those on Dartmoor where indestructible granite was used.

The climate was warmer and dryer in the Bronze Age (2000–650BC), which encouraged people to settle in the sheltered valleys while hunting and pasturing their animals on the high ground during the summer. In Saxon and medieval times small farming communities became established in high valleys, often with a church, showing the influence of Christianity during this period.

The richer, low-lying areas became market towns and centres for the thriving wool industry, and some of the region's great houses were built for rich merchants or members of the aristocracy. Labourers' houses were traditionally built of cob (a mixture of mud, straw and dung) and thatch.

Although farming had been practised since Neolithic times (preceding the Bronze Age), and much native forest cleared for agriculture, the high moors were never suitable for crops. But they were ideal for hunting, and the Royal Forest was established by William the Conqueror. 'Forest', in this case, did not mean woodland but land reserved for hunting and the red deer were protected for the king's pleasure, with draconian punishments for any who killed or harmed them. It was Henry VII who decided to allow the grazing of ponies, sheep and cattle on the moor, provided that at least a hundred deer were left for hunting.

The Civil War and its aftermath diverted attention from hunting (Oliver Cromwell was not known for his pursuit of pleasure) and in

FARMING ON EXMOOR

Victoria Eveleigh

Even though Exmoor is a national park, three-quarters of it is privately owned and approximately 80% of the land area is farmed. Even the ancient woodlands and open moorland have been shaped by centuries of human activity. The woodlands have been managed for charcoal and wood, as well as cover for game, while the moorland was largely created by deforestation and climate change during the Iron Age, about 2,500 years ago. If the moorland were not grazed regularly, most of it would return to scrub or woodland.

Farming provides food, fuel and fibre for people traditionally, and the farms on Exmoor have produced all three with varying degrees of success depending on the climate and economic conditions of the time. For instance, wool used to be an expensive commodity but it's hardly worth the cost of shearing sheep nowadays.

Exmoor's topography, poor soils, high rainfall and inaccessibility mean that the options for farmers are limited. Most of the land isn't suited to arable crops, especially with modern farming methods, so grassy fields bounded by stockproof hedges are a common sight and most Exmoor farmers specialise in sheep and beef cattle. Some still remain faithful to the local breeds – notably Exmoor horn and Devon closewool sheep and Devon (Red Ruby) cattle – but all sorts of different breeds and cross-breeds have been introduced in an attempt to maximise production and create larger, leaner animals to satisfy market demand. There are also some small specialist farms producing dairy products, pork, poultry, eggs, organic meats and even blueberries.

It is estimated that at the beginning of the 20th century about half of Exmoor was

1652 the Royal Forest was sold to James Boevey who built the first house in the Forest, at Simonsbath, enclosing 100 acres of land for his farm. He seems to have spent most of his energies on lawsuits against his neighbours who were using the common land and, even after the restoration of the monarchy in 1660, when all previous crown land once again reverted to the king, he hung on the farm until his death in 1696.

The greatest change to Exmoor's fortunes came in 1818 when John Knight bought three-quarters of the old Royal Forest and the former Boevey farm at Simonsbath. John and his son Frederic had grand plans for the moor. They aimed to convert some of the heathland to arable pasture and, when this failed, attracted tenants through favourable leases and encouraged them to improve the moorland for the grazing of sheep and ponies. Where arable crops were feasible, they built the

moorland, but by the end of the century the area had shrunk to 27%, much of this being lost in the nine years between 1957 and 1966. This seems ironic, as Exmoor was designated a national park in 1954 in response to the threat posed to its landscape by plans for large-scale conifer plantations. As it turned out, an equally serious threat came from farming due to post-war government subsidies designed to encourage the production of affordable food, together with technological advances that made the reclamation of moorland relatively easy. It's amazing that government grants to drain and improve land continued well into the 1970s even though the loss of moorland was causing alarm.

Concern about the preservation of Exmoor's moorland led to several local grant schemes from the 1980s onwards, as well as later nationwide incentives for farmers to manage their land in a way prescribed by the government under the Common Agricultural Policy (CAP).

Lots of rules and regulations govern what happens on modern farms, and it's a complex job trying to fulfil all the different roles.

Nowadays Exmoor farmers still produce food, fibre and fuel but they also have to think about things like biosecurity (the prevention of diseases such as foot and mouth disease and bovine tuberculosis (TB)), flood mitigation, soil conservation, carbon storage, biodiversity conservation and cultural ecosystem services. That's a lot to worry about!

A good way of learning more about farming on Exmoor is to stay on a farm during your visit. Many of the places selected in the accommodation section of this guide are on working farms. You can also find more on: ⊘ www.devonfarms.co.uk.

beech-hedged walls that are such a distinctive part of the moor today, and embarked on a programme of road building. They also established mining enterprises which employed a large number of local people, but these proved unprofitable and closed one by one.

Thus Exmoor's unique beauty was established more from the failure of ambitions than from their success. When the movement to establish national parks in England's wild areas began in the 1940s, large areas of Exmoor were already owned by the National Trust. It achieved national park status in 1954.

GETTING THERE & AROUND

There is no fast way of getting to Exmoor, only slow. The main route from the south, the A396 from Tiverton, winds its way up the Exe Valley to Wheddon Cross and thence to Dunster and Minehead. Last time I drove it I stopped to view the river in the early morning sun, and caught a flash of blue as a kingfisher zipped over the dark water. The number 398 bus follows the same slow route, going to Dulverton, Wheddon Cross, Dunster and Minehead.

Exmoor really can be enjoyed without a car, at least in the holiday season, thanks to the Moor Rover (see opposite). There's a reasonable bus service, and a steam train as well as the main-line service into Barnstable. It's also relatively cycle-friendly (if you can call 25%-gradient hills friendly) because most of the lanes are wide or across open moor so there's less danger from traffic.

PUBLIC TRANSPORT

Exmoor is poorly served by **railways**, a fact which has contributed to its fortuitous lack of development. The nearest regular railway is the Tarka Line from Exeter to Barnstaple, where you can pick up the 309 or 310 bus to Lynmouth. If you prefer the ease of a **taxi** to take you from the station to your destination, there's a large choice including A1 Taxis, (✐ 01271 322922), Value Taxis (✐ 01271 327777) or Barnstaple Taxi Service (✐ 01271 379455).

Exmoor's bus routes have been reduced recently, and some of the most scenic ones discontinued. The summer-only **Exmoor Coastal bus** (number 300) runs along the A39, providing convenient links for walkers following the South West Coast Path or the East Lyn River trails.

Formerly open-topped in summer, this has now gone, sadly, and even the ordinary service is threatened. For timetables use the very convenient Devon website for this bus, *✆* www.journeydevon.info – even if you're in Somerset.

There are still swathes of Exmoor that have no scheduled bus service, but the most beautiful walks. The Somerset part is served by the excellent **Moor Rover** which will pick up you, your bike, your dog or your luggage – and even your wheelchair – at a prearranged place and time and, for a fee ranging from £10 to £30 per vehicle, drop you anywhere on Exmoor. They will also transport luggage without passengers. It's operated by Atwest (*✆* 01643 709701 *✆* www.atwest.org.uk).

An excellent website for 'car-free days' is *✆* www.exploremoor.co.uk. It has easy-to-follow information on all the Exmoor buses. Also check bus schedules on Traveline (*✆* 0871 200 2233 *✆* www.traveline.info) before you travel.

ACTIVE EXMOOR

A dedicated website (*✆* www.activeexmoor.com) is aimed specifically at the more energetic activities for which Exmoor is so suited, covering walking, mountain biking, horseriding, canoeing and sea kayaking, as well as skilled stuff like coasteering and climbing. **Exmoor Adventures** (*✆* 07976 208279 *✆* www.exmooradventures.co.uk) also runs a variety of courses, from mountain biking to canoeing.

CYCLING

The **West Country Way** (NCN3) traverses the southern part of Exmoor, going through high moorland, and the many quiet lanes on the moor are ideal for cyclists who don't mind hills (of which there are many). Perhaps the most challenging ride is the **Exmoor Cycle Route**, a 56-mile Tour of Britain circuit, or the linear **Culbone Way**, Regional Route 51, which runs from Minehead over Exmoor to llfracombe.

Exmoor is ideal for **mountain biking**. Bikes are allowed on bridle paths and RUPPS (Roads Used as Public Paths) but not on public footpaths or open moorland.

There are bicycle hire places in Porlock (page 159), Minehead (page 178) and at Caffyn's Farm, Lynton (*✆* 01598 753967). Exmoor National Park publishes a number of cycling guides, including *Exmoor for Off-road*

Cyclists and a series of single-sheet *Bike It* guides. See ✆ www.exmoor-nationalpark.gov.uk; click on to 'online shop'.

WALKING & BACKPACKING

Despite its small scale, there are 258 miles of footpaths on Exmoor, including several long-distance paths. The **Two Moors Way** runs from Lynmouth to Ivybridge on the far edge of Dartmoor; the **Macmillan Way West** (102 miles) enters Exmoor at Withycombe and goes to Barnstaple; the 52-mile **Coleridge Way** runs from Nether Stowey in the Quantocks to Porlock and then to Lynmouth. The less well known **Samaritans Way South West** is a 100-mile route linking the Cotswolds, Mendips, Polden Hills, Quantocks, and Exmoor National Park. The Exmoor part is from the Quantocks to the Brendon Hills, across Exmoor to the Doone Valley and Badgworthy Water, from where it follows the East Lyn River and climbs Myrtleberry Cleaves to Lynton. All profits from the guidebook (available from ✆ www.westcountrywalks.co.uk) go to the Samaritans. Finally there's the superlative 35-mile Exmoor section of the **South West Coast Path**, originally created so that the coastguard could keep an eye on smugglers.

Suggested walks are given in each section. If you are planning to do some extensive walking, then it's worth making the most of the best seasons: spring or autumn for woodland or the coast, when the landscape is at its loveliest and the crowds have thinned out, but August or early September for the heather. The eastern moor around Dunkery Beacon, and Winsford Hill, Withypool Common and Trentishoe near the coast, are particularly gorgeous, with a mixture of bell heather and ling so that the landscape glows with different shades of purple.

The Exmoor National Park Association (ENPA) has created a series of 'Ride and Walk' routes which all start with a bus journey. Downloadable leaflets are available from ✆ www.exploremoor.co.uk. Linear self-guided walks are also run by Escape the City Tours (✆ www.escapethecitytours.co.uk); they provide the transport as well as maps, etc.

With so many hotels and B&Bs near the main walking routes, few people will choose to carry a tent out of necessity, but there are some wild spots where camping is permitted. You should be aware, however, that no wild camping is allowed anywhere on Exmoor, although there are organised campsites varying from the comfortable to the very rustic.

JAMES OSMOND/A

ACTIVE NORTH DEVON & EXMOOR

You'll find the best walking in the South West here, above the coast, across moorland or along rivers, as well as a nationally famous cycle path, the Tarka Trail.

1 Hiking on the South West Coast Path on Great Hangman. 2 Kayaking in Combe Martin. 3 Cycling the Tarka Trail. 4 Trotting through the River Barle.

NICK TURNER/A

VE

VISITBRITAIN/BEN SELWAY

CHURCHES, MANORS & WRITERS

The region has an abundance of exceptionally interesting churches. Bench ends provide unique examples of village art, and their monuments often deliver some surprises. The region was favoured by wealthy landowners, and famous writers have made their mark too.

THE BODIES OF THE MERCI FUL ARE BURIED IN PEACE. BUT THEIR NAME LIVETH FOR EVER MORE

IN MEMORY OF SᵗHIERITHA FO UNDRESS OF THIS CHURCH.

1 Culbone church, Exmoor: the smallest and most isolated in England. 2 Abbotsham church. One of the bizarre creatures typical of Devon's bench ends. 3 Chittlehampton church. Why hyphenation matters! 4 Modern carving of a mother and child in the 'chapel' at Greencombe Gardens. 5 Hartland Abbey. 6 Chambercombe Manor – one of the most haunted houses in Britain! 7 The statue of Lady Lorna Dugal, the inspiration for Lorna Doone, in Dulverton. 8 Georgeham's blue plaque commemorating Henry Williamson, author of *Tarka the Otter*.

PETER TURNER PHOTOGRAPHY/S

GARDENS

The mild West Country climate has helped create a variety of beautiful gardens, monuments to the vision and labour of an individual enthusiast.

1 The Italian Garden at Tapeley Park. 2 The RHS Garden at Rosemoor. 3 Broomhill Sculpture Gardens. 4 Marwood Hill Gardens.

HILARY BRADT

HILARY BRADT

CHRISTOPHER NICHOLSON/A

For those who prefer to get to know the moor with a small group accompanied by a knowledgeable guide, the **Exmoor Walking Festival** (⌀ www.exmoorwalkingfestival.co.uk) held each year in May will suit you perfectly.

Walking maps & guides

The incomparable Croydecycle walking **maps** at a scale of 1:12,500 cover a good proportion of Exmoor (page 20). Details are given in the relevant sections. They include all of the coastal area, while Coast Path Map 1, at a scale of 1:15,000, comprises the entire Exmoor stretch from Minehead to Watermouth.

The OS double-sided ❋ Explorer map OL9 covers all of Exmoor at a scale of 1:25,000 but its size makes it unwieldy to use and the area you want always seems to be on the other side. If you're driving or cycling, the ❋ Croydecycle *Exmoor & Taunton* 1:100,000 map gives you just the right level of detail.

Exmoor National Park publishes a number of walking **guides**, including the handy single-sheet Golden Walks.

Shortish Walks on Exmoor by Robert Hesketh and published by Bossiney Books (⌀ www.bosinneybooks.com) are easy to follow, with clear maps, and are ideal for a brief visit. A useful series of self-published walking guides centred round different popular locations is Exmoor Scenic Walks by Shirley and Mike Hesman. The 18 booklets cover all the most popular walking areas of Exmoor; they are cheap, well organised and clearly written, with easy-to-follow maps.

These and other inexpensive guides for Exmoor walks of varying quality are available from local shops and tourist information centres, as are the Croydecycle maps.

By far the best guide for the South West Coast Path is *Exmoor & North Devon Coast Path* published by Trailblazer. It includes suggested accommodation.

HORSERIDING

One of my fondest teenage memories is of pony trekking for a week in the 'Lorna Doone country' of Exmoor with my younger sister. I can remember so vividly the woodland rides and the huge sweep of purple moor, and the exhilaration of being able to gallop without worrying about roads or traffic. We started off gently with a couple of hours of morning and afternoon rides, and culminated in a full day trek with lunch at a pub (so grown up!). I can even remember the name of my cob: Satan.

Not much has changed. You can still go for short or long treks across the heather, you can still have lunch in a pub on the long days, and no doubt there are still bolshy cobs called Satan. If you can ride, there's no better way of seeing the moor, and no better way of getting up those steep hills and across the streams.

For the most authentic riding experience you can ride on the moor on an Exmoor pony (with some age and weight restrictions) at the **Exmoor Pony Centre** in Dulverton. See page 186.

RIDING & TREKKING STABLES

The stables below are listed west to east, in accordance with the sections in this book.
Note: Dulverton is described in the next chapter.

Outovercott Riding Stables Lynton EX35 6JR ✆ 01598 753341 ⌂ www.outovercott.co.uk
Brendon Manor Riding Stables Nr Lynton EX35 6LQ ✆ 01598 741246
⌂ www.ridingonexmoor.co.uk
Dean Riding Stables Trentishoe EX31 4PJ ✆ 01598 763565 ⌂ www.deanridingstables.co.uk
Burrowhays Farm Riding Stables West Luccombe, Porlock TA24 BHT ✆ 01643 862463
⌂ www.burrowhayes.co.uk
Pine Lodge Higher Chilcott Farm, Dulverton TA22 9QQ ✆ 01398 323559
⌂ www.pinelodgeexmoor.co.uk
West Anstey Farm Stables Nr Dulverton TA22 9RY ✆ 01398 341354

INACTIVE EXMOOR

Not everyone can jump on a bicycle and pedal furiously up Porlock Hill, and even reasonably fit walkers can find the hills on Exmoor a challenge. Of course the moor can be enjoyed in your own car; there's good parking at all the well-known places and, out of season, driving here is a real pleasure. In the peak months, however, you'll have to spend a lot of time in reverse on the narrow lanes. The alternative is to let someone else take the wheel.

The following companies offer **safaris in 4x4 vehicles**; these give you not only an overview of Exmoor's scenery but also inside information on its wildlife, traditions and history. Tours last 2½ to three hours, and the route depends on weather and other factors.

EXMOOR PONIES

Victoria Eveleigh

The most obvious thing about Exmoor ponies is that they all look remarkably similar – short and hairy, with brown bodies that are dark on top and lighter underneath, dark legs and hooves and a characteristic 'mealy muzzle' (an oatmeal colour over their muzzles and round their eyes). White markings are not permitted on registered Exmoor ponies.

The distinctive colour of the Exmoor pony has led people to believe that it is a direct descendant of prehistoric wild horses, but neither recent genetic research nor studies of documentary evidence support this view. However, it is still a valuable and rare native pony breed.

During the early 20th century it became fashionable to 'improve' native ponies with Arab and Thoroughbred bloodlines, so in 1921 several local breeders got together and formed the Exmoor Pony Society with the purpose of keeping the breed true to type.

The ponies nearly died out during World War II; most of them were killed for food, leaving only about 46 mares and four stallions, but the local farmers soon re-established their herds with the help of a remarkable lady called Mary Etherington.

Today there are about 300 free-living Exmoor ponies on the moor and about 1,300 worldwide, but only a fraction of these are used for breeding. There are 20 moorland herds on Exmoor, including two owned by the Exmoor National Park Authority.

All the Exmoor pony herds that graze the different areas of moorland are free-living (not truly wild, like red deer) because they are owned by farmers with grazing rights on the moorland. For most of the year the ponies fend for themselves, but in the autumn they are rounded up and the foals are weaned and inspected. Until recently all foals that passed inspection had to be branded, but microchipping is now allowed as an alternative to branding.

Exmoors are well-camouflaged in their natural moorland habitat. However, you will have a good chance of spotting them on Haddon Hill (near Wimbleball Lake), Winsford Hill, Withypool Common, Porlock Common, Dunkery Hill, Countisbury, Ilkerton Ridge and Brendon Common. Please don't try to feed the ponies as it encourages them to associate cars with food, which means they are more likely to be victims of a traffic accident. Also, ponies can be dangerous if they start fighting over food.

Recently a week in August has been set aside for an Exmoor Pony Festival, held throughout the area, and it seems likely to continue (🖱 http://exmoorponyfestival.org.uk).

If you would like to see ponies at close quarters, and perhaps ride one, visit the Exmoor Pony Centre at Ashwick, near Dulverton (page 186). And for more information about the ponies, or if you are interested in buying one, the Exmoor Pony Society website (🖱 www.exmoorponysociety.org.uk) is a useful starting point.

i TOURIST INFORMATION

Tourist information centres

Exmoor National Park Authority Dulverton ✆ 01398 323665
🖱 www.exmoor-nationalpark.gov.uk
Lynton & Lynmouth Town Hall, Lynton ✆ 0845 4583775 & The Pavilion, Lynmouth
🖱 www.lynton-lynmouth-tourism.co.uk
Porlock The Old School, West End, High St, TA24 8QD ✆ 01643 863150
🖱 www.porlock.co.uk

Websites

Everything Exmoor 🖱 www.everythingexmoor.org.uk. An information site that is
extraordinarily comprehensive.
Exmoor Tourism 🖱 www.visit-exmoor.co.uk
Explore Moor 🖱 www.exploremoor.co.uk. Includes suggestions for car-free days on
Exmoor, and bus timetables
Visit Exmoor 🖱 www.visit-exmoor.co.uk

Publications

Exmoor Magazine 🖱 www.exmoormagazine.co.uk. Indepth articles of Exmoor interest.
Exmoor Visitor Published by the national park, this tabloid-sized publication repeats in
newspaper form the information found on the website. It's free, widely available in shops
and tourist information centres, and particularly useful for its detailed list of events.

Because the driver/guides know the moor so well, you have a good
chance of seeing red deer on these trips.

Barle Valley Safaris ✆ 07977 571494 🖱 www.exmoorwildlifesafaris.co.uk. Half- or
full-day excursions from Dulverton are available, with a minimum of four people for
the full day.

Discovery Safaris of Porlock ✆ 01643 863444 🖱 www.discoverysafaris.com. Trips
leave from Porlock in vehicles taking up to six people and last about 2½ hours.
Binoculars provided.

Exmoor Safari ✆ 01643 831229 🖱 www.exmoorsafari.co.uk. The longest-established
company, with a variety of Land Rover safaris on offer lasting 2½ hours. Trips leave
from Exford.

Red Stag Safari ✆ 01643 841831 🖱 www.redstagsafari.co.uk. Various departure points.
Trips last 3½ hours, but all-day safaris can be arranged. Land Rover Discovery vehicle.

WET-WEATHER ACTIVITIES

Allerford Rural Life Museum (page 174)
Dovery Manor Museum Porlock (page 162)
Exmoor Zoo (page 134)
Lynmouth Pavilion (page 144)
Lyn Valley Arts & Crafts Centre (page 142)

WESTERN EXMOOR: TO LYNTON VIA BLACKMOOR GATE

Å Westland Farm Bratton Fleming (page 203)

When you're approaching Exmoor, all roads seem to lead to Blackmoor Gate, and from there most drivers heading east towards Lynton take the relatively uninteresting A39 where they know they will make reasonably good progress. From this route, however, the church at **Parracombe** really shouldn't be missed by anyone who loves old churches. Those approaching (or leaving) Blackmoor Gate via the A399 have two worthwhile diversions: **Challacombe** for its famous pub and its longstone, and **Exmoor Zoo**.

Blackmoor Gate itself has its place in history. It was once an important railway station on the narrow-gauge Barnstaple to Lynton railway, and a livestock market (mainly sheep) is still held here (⬦ www. exmoorfarmers.co.uk). There is now just a preserved two-mile stretch of this railway, down which shiny little steam locomotives puff their way from **Woody Bay Station** to Killington Halt.

1 PARRACOMBE

Cupped within a bulge of the A39, and almost lost in a maze of steep, narrow lanes, is Parracombe, a lovely little village with two churches and a pub. The old church, **St Petrock's**, is rightly the one that draws visitors. It was scheduled for demolition in 1878 when a more conveniently located church had been built, but was saved after a protest led by John Ruskin and is now cared for by the Churches' Conservation Trust.

"The pinnacles look as though they were added by a farmer... like slightly wobbly cairns."

It stands high above the village, overlooking its usurper church and the scatter of white houses, with the fields of North Devon stretching to the horizon. The squat tower is a landmark from the main road, the pinnacles looking as though they were added as an afterthought by a farmer. They're more like slightly wobbly cairns than stone-mason's art, and all the more charming for it. Inside the church is plain and unadorned. No-one has 'improved' it, but it is clearly cared for and cared about. The first thing you notice on entering is the wooden 'tympanum', boldly painted with a royal coat of arms and improving texts: the Ten Commandments and the Creed. The only carving is the screen and even this is less intricate than usually found in Devon churches. The plain box pews are rough with old woodworm, and at the back there's a musicians' area where a hole has been cut in the pew in front to allow free movement for the bow of the double bass. Note, too, the hat pegs by the door.

2 CHALLACOMBE

🏠 **Twitchen Farm** (page 202)

Apart from the famous **Black Venus Inn**, Challacombe is best known for its **longstone**, the most spectacular prehistoric monument on Exmoor, standing nine feet high and remarkably slender. Nearby is the longstone barrow, though there's not much to see there. The longstone is marked on the ❋ OS Explorer map OL9 (♀ SS70514307) and you'll need this map to find it. It's a mile or two from the road (the B3358), northeast of Challacombe, near the source of the River Bray. It used to stand in a hollow that filled with water after rain, and a nearby spring made it even wetter; archaeologists levelled it off with gravel in 2003, but the area around it is still very marshy, so be prepared with the right footwear if you decide to look for it.

3 EXMOOR ZOO

South Stowford, Bratton Fleming EX31 4SG ✆ 01598 763352 ⬦ www.exmoorzoo.co.uk
◔ daily except three days at Christmas 10.00–18.00 (summer) or dusk (winter)

Off the A399 is this well-managed zoo. It well deserves its 2013 award of North Devon's best small attraction. A pair of black leopards, thought to be the Exmoor Beast of local legend, is the most promoted exhibit but there are lots of invertebrates and birds, as well as a good collection of small mammals and of course a regular supply of babies. There's something for everyone and it's family friendly and informative, with invertebrate handling sessions and a 'keeper for a day' experience.

¶¶ FOOD & DRINK

Fox and Goose Parracombe EX31 4PE ☏ 01598 763239 ☉ www.foxandgoose-parracombe.
co.uk. Recommended for its above-average food and wide range of beers. The décor is
genuine Exmoor, with foxes' masks and deer antlers, as well as antiques, and the food is
equally traditional: steak, Guinness and mushroom pie, for instance, and a good range of
seafood dishes and pizza take-aways. As popular with locals for conversation as for food.

The Black Venus Challacombe EX31 4TT ☏ 01598 763251 ☉ www.blackvenusinn.co.uk.
This lovely 16th-century pub is the main reason to visit Challacombe. Hearty meals of
traditional pub food with a few unexpected treats such as Cajun chicken breast, and a
great atmosphere.

The Old Station House Inn Blackmoor Gate EX31 4NW ☏ 01598 763520
☉ www.oldstationhouseinn.co.uk. As the name suggests, a converted railway station,
which makes a convenient stopping place for hungry families.

4 WOODY BAY STATION

EX31 4RA ☏ 01598 763487 ☉ www.lynton-rail.co.uk

Although only two miles long, this narrow-gauge railway is the highest
in England and puffs its way through some of Exmoor's best scenery,
making it a rewarding family excursion or a nostalgic trip for oldies. The
enthusiasm of the volunteers who run this stretch of the original Lynton
& Barnstaple Railway, which operated from 1898 to 1935, is evident in
every detail, from the loving maintenance of the steam locomotives to
the tea room which surely must have been the scene of many a Brief
Encounter. The station was originally planned to serve the actual Woody
Bay (or Woodabay, as it was then called) nearly two miles away with a
branch line. This was never built.

THE COASTAL TRIANGLE

The A399 and A39 roads form the southern edges of a triangular slice
of Exmoor which is quite extraordinary. No serious road builder was
going to give priority to this chaos of moorland, hills and valleys
when a more level highway to the south had served its purpose for
centuries. As you approach the deep **Heddon Valley**, with its popular
inn, driving becomes increasingly challenging, as does walking:
the hills are *very* steep. But the scenery, in all its Exmoor variety, is
sublime: high moor, ancient meadows and hanging woods of sessile
oaks, accessible by lanes so steep and narrow that even devoted drivers

will have second thoughts about taking their cars. The coast, tracked by one of the most scenic stretches of the South West Coast Path, is indented with shingle beaches hidden by high cliffs. And for church – and bat – enthusiasts there is **Trentishoe**.

5 TRENTISHOE

Trentishoe is one of those isolated communities that make Exmoor so special. If you come by car it is best accessed from the west to avoid a near-vertical hill from Heddon Valley. The drive there along a narrow lane from Combe Martin is in the lead for the most dramatically beautiful in Exmoor – particularly if the heather is in bloom, when bursts of purple plus yellow from the gorse alternate with sea views. Chiselled into the hillside is **St Peter's Church**: tiny and, at first glance, pretty ordinary. But

HOLY BATS

Trentishoe church is one of those tiny Exmoor churches which tug at the heartstrings because they look so vulnerable, set alone in the hills, exposed to the wind and rain. And to bats.

There are often piles of droppings on the carpet, especially in the musicians' gallery. Look up and you'll see the culprits: lesser horseshoe bats clinging to the roof, along with, perhaps, a long-eared bat or a pipistrelle. All three species have been identified as roosting here in the summer. I spoke to the local church warden about the bats. 'They weren't a problem until we had the roof repaired in 2006/7 and complied with the regulations to make the church bat-friendly. Since then they're everywhere. I do my best to clean up, but they don't like the hoover and I don't like bats!'

All bats are protected species, but lesser horseshoe bats are particularly rare, surviving only in Wales and the west of England, and churches offer ideal conditions for them. Not only is it against the law to disturb them, they must be actively encouraged to stay in their chosen home. If a church is known to have bats, then before any restoration work can be done a bat expert must visit to assess the situation, identify the species, and set out the requirements. In the case of Trentishoe, special small entrances were created in the roof to allow bats in, though the horseshoe bats enter directly through the slatted vents to the tower. The cost of these alterations falls on the church itself. Think about it: Trentishoe has a congregation in single figures, and a few visitors who generously put coins in the donations box. Complying with the regulations which included paying a fee to DEFRA, paying for the services of the bat expert, and carrying out the required modifications to the church roof cost £1,459.

at first sniff it's not ordinary: it smells. Bats have taken over the interior and the human congregation who attend the occasional service co-exist with them as best they can. Visitors, however, love the bats and the negative comments I used to see in the visitors' book have been replaced by warmly positive ones. This tiny village has supported its church since 1260 and bats are expensive guests so perhaps you can spare a bit more than usual for the upkeep box.

Apart from the bats the church has a unique feature. In its musicians' gallery is a hole cut in the woodwork to allow for the bow of the cello or double bass. There's a similar one at Parracombe, but I believe this is the only one in a gallery – so many such galleries were removed by Victorian 'restorers'. The little organ came from the ocean liner the RMS *Mauretania*, which was scrapped in 1965.

One of the national park's Golden Walks series covers this area: *Trentishoe Down*. It's a five-mile circular walk, taking in a level woodland stretch as well as moorland and a section of the coast path. The Croydecycle map provides all the information you need.

6 HEDDON VALLEY & MARTINHOE

🏠 **The Old Rectory Hotel** Martinhoe (page 200)

This region was scheduled for development at the turn of the 19th century. **Hunter's Inn** (✆ 01598 763230), in the deep fold of **Heddon Valley**, was originally a thatched cottage that served ale to thirsty workers in this isolated place, but it burned down in 1896. Colonel Lake (see below) funded the new design based on a Swiss chalet. It has now morphed into something more in keeping with the scenery and always seems to be swarming with athletic-looking people, either at the beginning or end of their walk or bike ride, or just enjoying a drink or browse in the nearby National Trust shop. Despite being so busy, the staff are always courteous and the food is good. A spacious picnic area surrounded by woodland completes the scene. There's really no point in not stopping here. The inn also has accommodation.

The mile-long walk to **Heddon's Mouth**, down the gorge-like Heddon's Cleave, is deservedly one of the most popular on Exmoor, being blissfully level and ending with the opportunity for a swim. Some of the most glorious stretches of coastal path start or end here, with plenty of opportunities for circular walks. Two Croydecycle maps cover this area so you don't need a detailed description.

On the opposite side of Heddon Valley, up another alarming hill, is **Martinhoe**. This hamlet consists of a few houses, the Old Rectory Hotel, and a peaceful church. Little else apart from height and scenery, and it's none the worse for that.

7 WOODY BAY & LEE ABBEY BEACH

Martinhoe Manor Woody Bay (page 202)

Beyond Martinhoe the road continues east towards **Woody Bay**. As a secluded horseshoe-shaped cove overhung with woods through which a waterfall plunges, this would be perfect for a relaxing day with some wild swimming if it weren't for the very steep descent from the small car park on the road above it (down a lane marked Martinhoe Manor, and then a path). The potential of this now deserted spot was seen at the end of the 19th century. In 1895, J L W Page wrote that the new road to what is now Hunter's Inn 'is the work of a syndicate, who are, it is said, going to do great things at Woodabay – towards the opening up (and probably cockneyfying) of this shady retreat. When I was last there an engineer was already busy taking soundings for a landing stage. As there are only six houses … the enterprise seems, as the Americans would say, a little previous.' Indeed it was, but it was storms that put paid to the plan, not the small population. A pier was indeed built in 1895, the project of a London solicitor, Colonel Benjamin Lake, who had ambitions for Woody Bay to rival Lynmouth as a holiday spot. His plans were for a 100-yard-long pier with a dog-leg extension and landing stage, but eventually he could only afford 80 yards. It was completed for the arrival of the first pleasure steamer in 1897, but the steamers were unable to dock at low tide and the service was sporadic. Three years later storms had all but destroyed the pier and it was finally pulled down in 1902. Colonel Lake had also funded a replacement for the original Hunter's Inn. He ended in bankruptcy and, having used some of his clients' money for his project, prison.

> *"This would be perfect for a relaxing day with some wild swimming if it weren't for the very steep descent."*

Those who don't have the legs or energy to descend (and then ascend) over 1,500 feet to Woody Bay can drive or walk west to **Lee Abbey Beach**. This private shingle cove is the most accessible in the region, with parking nearby. A toll road beyond the bay takes you to the Valley of Rocks (page 145).

LYNTON, LYNMOUTH & AREA

Without doubt this is the most popular part of Exmoor – and de
so. It really does have everything, and all within walking dist.   a
pretty seaside village, a cliff railway, a tumbling river cutting through
forested slopes, the heather-clad moor, and a dollop of recent history.
Painters and poets have rhapsodised about its beauty: Gainsborough
thought it the perfect place to paint, and Shelley (see box, page 143)
lived there for nine weeks with his first wife. S P B Mais, writing in 1928,
felt that: 'Ordinary standards simply won't do to describe this corner of
Devon. One realises dimly and dumbly that no other combe of one's
acquaintance comes quite so obligingly near to the hotel door to show
its beauty of wood or majesty of cliff.'

HIDDEN VALLEY PIGS

East Ilkerton Farm, Barbrook, Lynton EX35 6PH 🖉 01598 753545 ◈ www.hiddenvalleypigs.co.uk

Simon and Debbie Dawson swapped their London lives as estate agent and solicitor for rural Devon, and they and their animals are clearly thriving. Apart from being a self-sustaining smallholding focusing on rare-breed Berkshire pigs, the Dawsons offer a variety of courses from a one-day smallholding taster or two-day animal husbandry course to a pig butchery and processing weekend: learn to butcher a pig; make your own sausages, dry-cured bacon and parma-style air dried ham; and use every bit of the pig. They also offer 'Rear a Pig'. Sadly this doesn't mean you take your piglet home with you, but it remains in the lap of luxury at the farm, growing slowly and naturally without any growth stimulants, and more or less writing progress reports to its mum. (Debbie ensures that you are kept properly informed on its wellbeing; you even have visiting and naming rights if you want.)

When the time comes, the slaughterhouse is only a few miles away and the pigs get a special treat the night before. If, like me, you eat meat but want to ensure that the animal has had a good life, this is as humane as you can get.

Not all the animals at Hidden Valley end up on the table. During my visit I met HoneyBunny, the two hand-reared geese (they are a unit, like their name) which were destined for Christmas dinner until reprieved by soft-hearted Debbie; and Simon – equally soft-hearted – saved a not-so-micro pig called Señorita who has no idea that she is a pig, as well as Curry the once-feral goat who was hand-reared by Simon and Debbie and is now a hand-milking goat adding her milk to their self-sufficient lifestyle.

'I used to be a vegetarian,' says Debbie. 'Now my policy is "If we don't rear it we don't eat it."'

A DARK & STORMY NIGHT

Janice Booth

'Vessel in distress,' reported a message telegraphed from Porlock Weir to Lynmouth Post Office. A force-eight gale had raged all day in the Bristol Channel and by evening Lynmouth's lower streets were awash. Further along the coast, off Gore point near Porlock, the three-masted barque *Forrest Hall* was tossing helplessly, held only by her anchors; she'd been on tow from Bristol to Liverpool when her tug suffered damage and had to abandon her to the storm. The nearest lifeboat, at Watchet, could not launch in the heavy seas, and the telegram requested assistance from the Lynmouth lifeboat. This was in January 1899, when lifeboats were rowed manually and ships could go to their graves in the time that it took for help to arrive. A maroon was fired to summon the lifeboat's crew. The doors of the lifeboat shed were opened but it was clear that the boat – the 3½-ton *Louisa* – had no hope of launching into the churning sea. It was decided to haul her the 13 miles overland to Porlock Weir, and to attempt

a launch from there. Horses were brought – with extra ones for the steep two-mile climb up Countisbury Hill – and ropes were attached to the trailer that bore the lifeboat. Torches and flares were lit. From every home, heedless of weather and darkness, villagers came to help with the preparations, and within an hour of the telegram's arrival all was set. It seemed barely possible, but everyone agreed: 'We'll try'. On her trailer, the *Louisa* weighed ten tons. Slowly and laboriously, men and horses together hauled her up the hill. At the summit some men, exhausted, returned home; 20 remained to see her across the moor in the teeth of the storm. Rain and wind extinguished the torches, which had to be continually re-lit. Ropes were slippery and hard to grip. At one point a wheel came off; the boat had to be lifted manually so it could be replaced. One lane was too narrow for the trailer, so the *Louisa* was lowered on to wooden skids and dragged through while the trailer took a longer route; when they met again the boat

Lynmouth was 'discovered' in the early part of the 19th century when the Napoleonic Wars had closed the continent to English visitors, and the English gentry had to be satisfied with holidaying nearer to home. The Rising Sun Inn was already there to cope with this influx and other inns were hastily built, but it seems that once the war was over, there was fierce competition between the three lodging houses for potential customers. Murray's travel guide of 1856 warns that: 'telescopes are employed at the rival houses for the prompt discovery of the approaching traveller. He had better determine beforehand on his inn, or he may become a bone

was heaved back up. A small group went ahead with picks and spades to widen the narrow lane at Culbone.

Next came the notorious Porlock Hill, a dizzily steep descent needing all available man- and horse-power to prevent the whole thing from hurtling downwards to destruction. At the bottom a garden wall had to be demolished – the lady householder, who had never seen a lifeboat before, enthusiastically joined in the work. Eventually, ten hours after leaving Lynmouth, the *Louisa* was dragged on to the beach at Porlock Weir.

Refusing to rest, the 13 lifeboatmen clambered aboard as helpers pushed the boat into the battering waves. After rowing for about an hour they located the *Forrest Hall*, whose anchors had dragged but held firm. To evacuate her frightened 19-man crew in so wild a sea would have risked lives; she seemed in no immediate danger so the *Louisa* simply stood by. As day broke the barque was drifting alarmingly close

to shore but her tug returned in the nick of time. Some of the lifeboat crew clambered aboard and attached her tow-lines; the *Louisa* then accompanied her – still pounded by the storm – as she was towed to a place of safety on the Welsh coast. There the men had a meal and a hearty sleep before returning to Lynmouth – and a heroes' welcome – the following day.

No human lives were lost but, sadly, four of the horses that had hauled the boat died from their exertions. The cost of the rescue, including repairs to damaged roads and gardens, was £118.17s.6d, of which the *Forrest Hall's* owners paid £75. Members of the *Louisa's* crew each received £5 from local funds and a silver watch from a wealthy local resident. You can find more details of this extraordinary story of courage and determination in the exhibition at Lynmouth and the little museum in Porlock Weir where there's the saying: 'If it's not us, then it's nobody. And it's never not nobody, not in the lifeboat service.'

of contention to a triad of postboys, who wait with additional horses at the bottom of the hill to drag the carriage to its destination.' When you look at the hill they had to climb you can see why additional horses were required. Stage coaches continued to be used here well into the 1900s; the hills were too steep and too rough for the new-fangled charabancs.

The popularity of the village was noted, somewhat sourly, by J L W Page in 1895. 'Lynmouth consists of a single street facing the river. Every other house is a hotel or a lodging house [not much change there, then], but the general appearance of the place is not unpicturesque, and some regard has evidently been had for the romantic surroundings.' He points out that Lynmouth was once the centre of herring fishing until, in 1797, 'they suddenly departed. So Lynmouth had to fish for other fry, and does it pretty successfully. Every year does the shoal of visitors increase, and probably they pay better than herrings.'

"'There's no better place to walk in Britain than this area.'"

The publisher Sir George Newnes lived in Lynton, at Hollerday House, and gave the town its cliff railway in 1890, as well as its town hall. Newnes founded the racy magazine *Tit-Bits* and followed it up with the altogether more serious *Strand Magazine* which was the first to publish Sherlock Holmes stories.

In addition to its other attractions, this area is superb for **walking**, comprising not only cliffs and moorland but a selection of walks, both circular and linear, along the beautiful East Lyn River and its accompanying woodland. Indeed, Croydecycle's Mike Harrison believes 'There's no better place to walk in Britain than this area.' Just two sample walks are described here; buy Mike's ❀ *Lynton, Lynmouth & Doone Valley* map and devise your own.

8 LYNTON

✦ **North Walk House** (page 201), **Coombe Farm** Countisbury (page 201)

Hoskins, in 1954, wrote that Lynton itself has little to commend it. I disagree. Its sturdy Victorian houses and extraordinary town hall are surprising in a place that otherwise feels like a modern holiday centre. The town hall is described in *The Shell Guide* of 1975 as 'a jolly edifice, "15th century" stonework, "Tudor" half timbering, and "Flemish" barge boarding'. There's a church opposite built in a similar style. Lynton's former Methodist Hall is now a cosy 70-seat cinema, and the former Methodist Church now houses the rewarding **Lyn Valley Arts & Crafts Centre**.

The **cliff railway** is a masterpiece of simple engineering and a model of 'green' energy. The two carriages are counter-balanced by water. Fill the tank at the top, and it's heavy enough to pull the other carriage up as it descends. We watched the 'driver' at the bottom judge the amount of water to let out to counterbalance not only the weight of the carriage but the passengers as well. Really neat, and a great way to get to the top of a 500-foot cliff. Before the road was built in 1828, tourists were transported to Lynton on donkeys or Exmoor ponies, as were all the goods arriving in the harbour.

9 LYNMOUTH

If staying in Lynton, most people walk down to Lynmouth and take the railway up. It's a very pleasant, steepish stroll down, the path lit by solar-powered lamps donated by different organisations. Lynmouth is clearly very much older than its partner, with at least one thatched cottage that must surely date from the 15th century, and very pretty with its harbour, cliffs and wooded hillsides.

Near the car park is the **Lynmouth Model Railway** ($\mathscr{O}$ 01598 753330 $\odot$ Easter – Nov), built 'over several years' by Percy Howell from Yorkshire in the 1980s and now run by his son Leslie. It is all wonderfully

PERCY BYSSHE SHELLEY & LYNMOUTH

The poet Shelley was born in 1792. His father, a Whig MP and baronet, had high hopes that his son would follow him into parliament, sending him to Eton and Oxford. He was bullied at the former and expelled from the latter because of his rather too free distribution of a pamphlet he had written, *The Necessity of Atheism*. His next act of rebellion was to marry 16-year-old Harriet Westbrook, not so much because he loved her but because his father had told him that he would support any number of illegitimate children, but would not countenance an unsuitable marriage. He was 19. His father immediately stopped his allowance.

In 1812 the couple came to live in Lynmouth. Shelley described their approach to the village, down Countisbury Hill, as 'a fairy scene – little Lynmouth, then some thirty cottages, rose-clad and myrtle-clad, nestling at the foot of the hills. It was enough.' There is some debate as to where he lived, but most agree that it was at the cottage now named Shelley's Hotel.

Though he explored the area widely, he seems to have written little poetry in his new home, being more interested in disseminating information on radical politics. To this end he would row out from Lynmouth with leaflets sealed into bottles and even suspended from fire balloons. In this endeavour he was joined by a schoolmistress, Elizabeth Hitchener, and also co-opted his manservant Dan Hill to post extracts of Tom Paine's *Rights of Man* in Barnstaple, for which the poor man was arrested and imprisoned.

Life then became a little too hot in Lynmouth and the couple fled to Wales by boat, leaving a mass of unpaid debts and precious little poetry.

Subsequently Shelley fell in love with another 16-year-old, Mary, who went on to write *Frankenstein*. Harriet drowned herself in the Serpentine, and Mary and Percy married and moved to Italy where he was safe from prosecution, and where he started to write his best poetry. He died at sea aged 29 in 1822.

busy and realistic, with the little trains running along a third of a mile of tracks, through tunnels and over bridges, and drawing up at stations. The **Lynmouth Flood Memorial Hall** houses two exhibitions. On the ground floor is the story of the famous **lifeboat rescue** of 1899 (see box, pages 140–1), whilst the upper floor is given over to the story of the great Lynmouth flood of 1952 when, after torrential rain on Exmoor, a wall of water carrying broken trees and boulders washed down the East and West Lyn rivers. It happened in the dead of night, with the electricity supply one of the first casualties, so all the terrified villagers could do was listen to the roar of the approaching torrent. Many houses were destroyed and 34 people lost their lives. As with all major disasters, this has its own conspiracy theory: at that time the government was experimenting with cloud seeding.

Continue on towards the cliff railway and you'll come to the new **Pavilion** and **Exmoor National Park Centre**. Formerly the steamboat

Hollerday Hill & the Valley of Rocks

OS Explorer map OL9, or Croydecycle *Lynton & Lynmouth* map; start: Lynton Town Hall, SS718794; 2.4 miles (or via Lee Abbey, 6 miles); easy (mostly level but some ups & downs; steep ascent from Lee Abbey

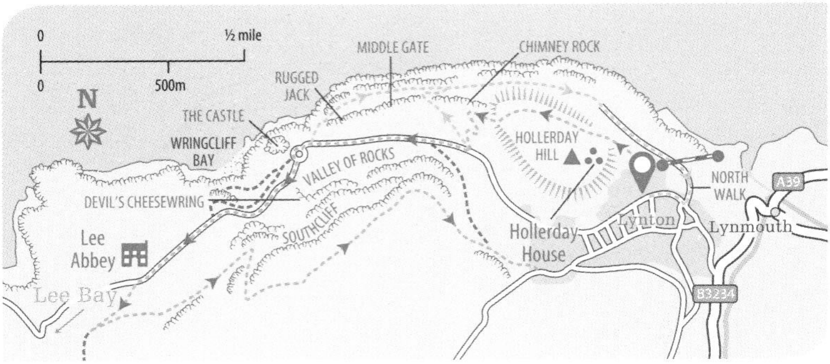

The circular walk here starts at Lynton. A track goes from the town hall and winds up to the site of Hollerday House, over the top of Hollerday Hill and on to the Valley of Rocks. An easier walk is to leave the track earlier and go straight ahead on a level path, parallel to the sea, and you will see the first sign of the rocks, a monolith aptly known as The Castle. Other

terminal, the redevelopment opened in 2013. It has displays of wildlife, webcams, an audiovisual presentation giving an overview of Exmoor, and a microscope with which you can study marine creatures collected from Lynmouth's many tide pools. There are events every day, including guided tide-pooling, so wet or dry there is plenty to occupy you in Lynmouth.

10 VALLEY OF ROCKS

The Valley of Rocks is accessible by car, but it's such a wonderful walk that if you can do it on foot, you should. The valley, which would be unexceptional on Dartmoor, is quite extraordinary on Exmoor where the soft sandstone has left few sharp contours. The most likely explanation for these heaps and castles of rock is that this was once a river valley, the boulders being deposited during the ice age, before the river changed its course. Glaciation and weather erosion did the rest.

rocks, strewn around, have been given names: Rugged Jack, Devil's Cheeswring, Middle Gate and Chimney Rock. The path zigzags down to the flat valley bottom, where feral goats and Exmoor ponies graze. Head towards the roundabout opposite The Castle, and then follow the well-maintained path back to North Walk. This is a most beautiful path, cut into the side of the cliff, with benches where you can sit and admire the view. And what a view! Behind you are the rocks, in all shapes and sizes, and ahead is Lynmouth and the Bristol Channel.

The Castle (Castle Rock) can be climbed by a steadily rising path with superb views to the west and the sheer cliffs to the north bringing home the scale of this striking landscape. Wringcliff Bay, sandy at mid and low tide, is accessible down a steep path.

To make a longer walk, with the goal of an easier swim in Lee Bay or a light lunch or cream tea in a delightful garden, continue heading west until you see the impressive **Lee Abbey** (⬧ http://leeabbey.org.uk), a Christian community centre and retreat. Beyond it, just before Lee Bay, is **Lee Abbey Tea Cottage** (✆ 01598 752621 ⏲ May–Sep, 10.00–17.00), with tables set out in sun or shade in a tranquil garden.

Return to Lynton on the path that zigzags up Southcliff.

Watersmeet & the coastal path

� OS Explorer map OL9, or Croydecycle *Lynton & Lynmouth* map; start: Lynmouth, Tors Rd
⚲ SS7242849460; 4 miles (or 8 if you continue to County Gate and the bus); moderate with
some steep climbs

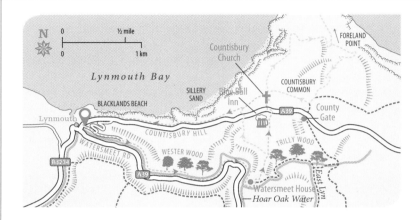

This half-day walk takes in the full spectrum of Exmoor: village, river, tea room, moor, pub and coast. The path from Lynmouth to Watersmeet is both dramatic, up a deep, wooded gorge, and very easy, following the Lyn gently upstream. If it's hot, there are places to paddle. The path is often surfaced, so you can admire the woods and river, and look out for birds, without having to watch where you're going. You could even get a pushchair up the first part. Start walking on the left side of the river; you'll cross to the right for a stretch, and then back again to Watersmeet, where the East Lyn River and Hoar Oak Water

 FOOD & DRINK

The Blue Ball Inn Countisbury EX35 6NE ☏ 01598 741263. A dog- and walker-friendly inn which is open all day, serves large portions of traditional pub food, and has welcoming open fires if there's a hint of chill in the air.

Le Bistro 7 Watersmeet Rd, Lynmouth EX35 6EP ☏ 01598 753302 ☖ www. lebistrolynmouth.co.uk. A small, friendly bistro specialising in locally caught seafood, but with a good varied menu of other dishes. Always popular so book ahead even out of season.

The Esplanade Fish Bar 2 The Esplanade, Lynmouth EX36 6EQ ☏ 01598 753798. A deservedly popular fish and chip shop facing the bay. Huge portions. Eat in or take away: beware seagulls if you eat outside!

come together. The former fishing lodge is now a **National Trust tea room** (◌ daily Easter to Oct, weekends in winter) with excellent snacks in beautiful surroundings, so is very popular.

From the lodge continue upstream, and you'll soon see the sign to Countisbury. Zigzag up the hill through a fairy-tale grove of stunted sessile oaks, all bent and twisted, and emerge on to the moor brightened by clumps of bell heather. Walk over the hill to the A39 and the **Blue Ball Inn** or resist the temptation and cross the road to head for **Countisbury Church**, its pinnacled tower peeping above the horizon. The church is unexceptional inside, but still worth a peep. A rather sad sign identifies the bell clappers which 'were removed from the bell tower in 1964 when the bells were sold to help pay for repairs to this lovely old church'.

Here you have a choice. Ahead is **Foreland Point**, which adds another couple of miles to the walk if you want to stand on Devon's most northerly point, or another four miles if you decide to take the most scenic route along the South West Coast Path to County Gate and catch the bus back to Lynmouth (but check the times before you leave). Or you can take the coast path to the left and walk west back to the town. For Foreland Point set your sights on the radio mast, accessed by a grassy path, and admire the view before dropping down the other side. A path runs round the side of Foreland Point to the lighthouse, but it's precariously narrow, so not very inviting; best to take the lighthouse road there.

A very agreeable variation to this walk is to take the bus up to the top of Countisbury Hill and the Blue Ball Inn and then, using the Croydecycle map, choose one of the paths down through the woods to Lynmouth. Downhill all the way – and beautiful.

The Oak Room Lee Rd, Lynton (opposite the town hall) ✆ 01598 753838 🖱 www. theoakroom.co.uk ◌ winter Wed–Sat 11.30–15.30, summer 18.00–21.00 daily. An award-winning restaurant renowned for its tapas, though the non-tapas menu is pretty good too. Popular with both locals and visitors.

Pavilion Dining Room First floor, Lynmouth Pavilion, The Esplanade (next to the Cliff Railway), Lynmouth EX35 6EQ ✆ 01598 751064. Just the place for a light lunch or tea; uncrowded and with wonderful views over the harbour.

The Rising Sun Harbourside, Lynmouth EX35 6EG ✆ 01598 753223 🖱 www. risingsunlynmouth.co.uk. Has been serving ale to the people of Lynmouth since Shelley's day. A famous and atmospheric thatched pub which is as popular as a bar as it is as a restaurant.

Dishes include freshly caught fish and local game such as pigeon, served in the oak-panelled dining room.

The Vanilla Pod 10 Queen St, Lynton ✐ 01598 753706. A good combination of day-time café, with an excellent selection of coffees and teas during the day, pub-lunch favourites at noon and quality dining, with a Mediterranean bias, in the evening. Order before 19.00 and you qualify for the good-value 'Early Bird' menu.

CENTRAL & SOUTHERN EXMOOR

Inland Exmoor is where you can find the real thing: high heather- and bracken-clad moorland and the patchwork green fields of the lowlands. On a sunny day it's sublime, in rain it can be utterly bleak but at least driving is easier on the high, open-view lanes. The rivers Exe and Barle, and their many tributaries, break up the 'billowy heath' in southern Exmoor with deep wooded valleys giving walkers and mountain bikers that perfect combination of high moor and sheltered combes. And in the wooded valleys that enfold the East Lyn River as it meanders west to Lynmouth, you would scarcely know you were in Exmoor.

THE BRENDON & DOONE VALLEYS

🏠 **Millslade House Hotel** Nr Brendon (page 201), **Rockford Inn** Nr Brendon (page 201)
⛺ **Cloud Farm Camping** Doone Valley (page 203), **Leeford Farm Riverside Camping** (page 203)

From Watersmeet the lovely East Lyn River draws you towards Brendon and on into Somerset where it becomes Oare Water. Walkers from Lynmouth may find it impossible to resist the temptation to keep going to this seductive region of tea shops, pubs and medieval bridges. So why resist? The same equally applies to cyclists and car drivers, although the latter will find the roads alarmingly narrow and parking places limited.

Those on foot have a choice from Watersmeet: take the path that follows the northern bank of the river or follow the stony track on the opposite side which leads through oak and beech woods. Either way, it's 1½ miles to the hamlet of Rockford and the **Rockford Inn** (EX35 6PT ✐ 01598 741 214), a perfectly situated traditional pub with log fires, good food, real ale and accommodation for the weary; all of which proves Oscar Wilde was in good company when he wrote: 'I can resist everything except temptation'.

Further along the road or path is **Brendon**, another small village with an equally welcoming pub, the **Staghunter's Inn** (✆ 01598 741222), highly praised for its excellent food, atmosphere, and as a base for walkers. From here, if you want to keep going, an inviting path runs along the bottom of a steep escarpment into Somerset.

You are now, inescapably, in Lorna Doone country. In **Malmsmead** you will find the **Lorna Doone Inn** (✆ 01598 741450) where, if you sit outside, your cream tea will be shared by bold wild birds, and, near the packhorse bridge, **Lorna Doone Farm** where you can indulge in yet more snacks and cream teas.

11 Oare

Eventually you'll stagger into Oare where you're doomed to get involved in the story because the **church of St Mary** is where, so they tell me, the dastardly Carver Doone shot Lorna on her wedding day. R D Blackmore's grandfather was rector here from 1809 to 1842 so the author of *Lorna Doone* knew the place well. Setting that aside, it's a church with lots of interest. Note the box pews. The one for the squire has seats round three sides so he and his family could be fenced off from his labourers, and in a position to ignore the vicar if so inclined.

Note also the Ten Commandments, painted in the 18th century on wooden boards at the entrance to the inner chancel. Shortening of 'the' to 'ye' is common, but here we have 'yt' for 'that'. It's the first time I've seen this abbreviation. A head held between two hands forms the unusual piscina. This is thought to be St Decuman, who was briefly separated from his head (page 191), but went on to inspire the building of the church dedicated to him in Watchet. What he is doing in Oare is unclear.

"You're doomed to get involved in the story because the church is where the dastardly Carver Doone shot Lorna on her wedding day."

A modern feature of the church is the beautiful carved buzzard lectern created by the sculptor Mike Leach to replace the traditional eagle lectern which was stolen.

At Oare, walkers heading for the A39 and the bus will look in dismay at the steep hill they need to climb. Cyclists and drivers will continue east along a delightfully scenic lane which crosses **Robber's Bridge** before climbing up to the main road in a series of hairpin bends.

Doone Valley walks

Two rivers, Badgworthy Water and Oare Water, meet at Malmsmead to become the East Lyn which makes its way to the sea at Lynmouth. A path runs south along Badgworthy Water through the Doone Valley to, if you are a fan of the novel, the Doone hideout, an abandoned medieval village, mostly hidden in the bracken. Here the path swings right, taking you back over Brendon Common. The round trip is around six miles, and described in *Active Exmoor* (⊘ www.activeexmoor.com), or you can make a pleasant short circuit, described in *Shortish Walks on Exmoor*, of 2½ miles which takes in Oare church and the **Cloud Farm tea rooms**. The Croydecycle map ❋ *Lynton, Lynmouth & Doone Valley* shows other variations.

Some parts of Badgworthy Water have deep pools where you can paddle and (possibly) swim.

River Barle, mine & moor

❋ OS Explorer map 24; start: Simonsbath car park, ♀ SS77383941; 6.7 miles; moderately easy with no steep ups and downs. Option for wild swimming in the river

One of Exmoor's most popular inland walks, this combines a riverside stroll in one direction and a high-level return with good views. The river section is particularly lovely, with ever-changing scenery and bits of history, recent and ancient. The recent history belongs to Wheal Eliza, a copper mine which was originally called Wheal Maria (why its name was changed is not clear). **Wheal Eliza** was one of the projects of the Knight family (page 125). From 1845–54 it mined copper, and when this ran out it switched to iron for three years before being abandoned. A year later the mine was in the news when little Anna Maria Burgess was killed by her father and her body hidden in the one of the mine shafts. He was brought to justice and hanged.

The next landmark is **Cow Castle**, an Iron Age hillfort built around 3,000 years ago; from a high point on the walk you can see the enclosing ramparts. The river here has some lovely deep pools, ideal for wild swimming.

After skirting some conifers, you leave the good bridle path that continues to Withypool and turn back towards Picked Stones Farm (pronounced pickéd) and Simonsbath. The return, I felt, was less rewarding. There are some good views, but over rather bleak, heather-free moorland and conifer plantations. However, the rain and mud probably had quite a bit to do with my disappointment so don't let me put you off. Most people love it, and it does add to the variety of this circular walk.

12 SIMONSBATH & THE RIVER BARLE

⌂ Heasley House Heasley Mill (page 200)

Despite its history of being the place where James Boevey enclosed a hundred acres of moorland for the first Exmoor farm, Simonsbath (pronounced Simmonsbath) is a relatively modern village that grew up at the crossroads of two tracks. It's now popular as a walking base and for the annual **Simonsbath Festival**, (⌂ www.simonsbathfestival.co.uk) which runs for six weeks each year in May and June and offers a daily programme of events varying from walks to music and readings by local authors. For meals there are the **Exmoor Forest Inn** (⌂ 01643 831341) and **Boevey's Tea Room and Restaurant** (⌂ 01643 831622); and there's a convenient car park for the many walks to be enjoyed in the area, most notably along the River Barle.

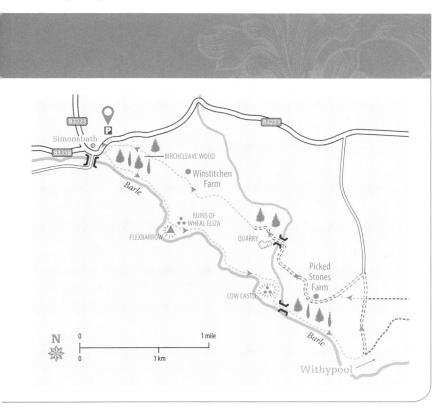

LORNA DOONE: FACT & FICTION

Janice Booth

For a fictional heroine, Lorna Doone has had a surprisingly powerful effect on Exmoor tourism! Little can her creator R D Blackmore have known, as she flowed from his pen, that 21st-century tourists would be seeking out her home and exclaiming over her dramatic life. Her romantic tale is so intertwined with factual places and characters that it's hard to know where imagination takes over from truth. Some of the characters apparently did exist in some form, but not contemporaneously with the story, so Blackmore will have heard of them and woven them into his plot. What is undeniably true is that he caught just the right mixture of love, heroism, villainy and derring-do for his era and the book has remained consistently popular, receiving praise from (among others) Thomas Hardy, Robert Louis Stevenson and Gerard Manley Hopkins. In his preface to the book in 1869, Blackmore writes:

This work is called a 'romance', because the incidents, characters, time, and scenery are alike romantic. And in shaping this old tale, the Writer neither dares, nor desires, to claim for it the dignity, or cumber it with the difficulty, of an historic novel.

13 WITHYPOOL

This village ticks all the boxes. It has a car park, a pub brimming with literary, artistic and historical associations, an excellent post office/village shop that sells everything you might need including maps and walking guides, public loos, tea rooms, benches in the sun, and some historic Shell petrol pumps looking like the remnants of our civilisation in a post-apocalypse movie. The shop is open seven days a week.

The Royal Oak dates from the 17th century and has hosted R D Blackmore, who supposedly wrote part of *Lorna Doone* here – in the bar – and the equestrian artist Sir Alfred Munnings who had a studio in the garret. The owner was the inspiration for Ian Fleming's M, and finally General Eisenhower planned the Normandy Invasion while staying here.

14 EXFORD

🏠 **White Horse Inn** (page 201) **Westermill** (page 203)

The Exe, a mere stream at Simonsbath, has gathered strength from two tributaries and is a proper river by the time it reaches Exford, giving the village much of its charm. It is seriously picturesque with its huge village

The fictional Lorna was kidnapped from a noble family, as a child, by the dastardly Doone outlaws of Exmoor. The Doones seem to have been based in fact: such a family did live in the area around Badgworthy Water and Hoccombe Combe, and terrorised the inhabitants during the 17th century. It's possible they were Scottish miscreants who had fled south to escape the law. Tales of their exploits existed locally and Blackmore, writing *Lorna Doone* in the late 1860s, will have heard them.

Fair Lorna's lover was (true to romantic tradition) honest local farmer John Ridd; a boy of this name existed and went to school in Tiverton, as did Blackmore, but there any record of him ends. In the novel, the Doones murdered his father when he was 12. Later, Blackmore has him stray into Doone country when following a hidden stream in search of loach, and meet the young Lorna. As adults they meet again and fall in love. Naturally, since the paperback version of the book today runs to 627 pages and 75 chapters, the course of their love does not flow smoothly! Lorna doesn't get into her wedding gown until page 613 – and then a shot rings out as the dastardly Carver Doone fires his carbine at her through the window of Oare church, where she and John have just exchanged their marriage vows.

green and 15th-century White Horse Inn dripping with Virginia creeper and is quite a bustling village with a post office, a good range of shops and a few tea rooms (see page 157). It is also the home of Exmoor's blueberry farm, **Sharcott Farm**, which offers pick-your-own **blueberries** in August and September ($\mathcal{O}$ www.exmoorblueberries.co.uk).

The church is only moderately interesting but my attention was taken by a tombstone which was more defiantly unhappy at an early death than is usual in Victorian times. Amos Cann died in 1891 aged 24 and his tombstone reads: 'You that are young behold and see/How quickly death has conquered me./Its fatal stroke it was too strong/It cut me off while I was young;/The God above He knows for why/that in my youth I was to die.'

Held in mid-August is the **Exford Show**, with Exmoor ponies and equestrian events to the fore, along with parades of hounds.

There are classes for Exmoor breeds of sheep and stands selling Exmoor crafts and produce, along with the latest in agricultural machinery. Everything, in fact, to showcase the Exmoor way of life, making it a prestigious event with local farmers.

Withypool to the medieval
Landacre Bridge & Sherdon Hutch

❄ OS Explorer map OL9; start: Withypool car park, ♀ SS845356; 4–6 miles; easy to moderate

If you opt for a there-and-back walk, this is a pleasant, mostly level four-mile stroll at first along the River Barle, and then up on to bleak moorland, to one of Exmoor's oldest bridges, Landacre. It can be extended to about six miles if you come back via the Two Moors Way or opt to go upriver to Sherdon Hutch for a swim.

The path to Landacre is signposted at the Withypool bridge. It follows the river for nearly a mile, sometimes boggy underfoot and crossing several stiles until the path leaves the river and heads uphill to Brightworthy Farm. The public right of way takes you through the farm

15 WINSFORD

Winsford is often described as one of Exmoor's prettiest villages. Its location is idyllic and the Royal Oak pub (see page 158) is chocolate-box charming; indeed, the owners claim that it is the most photographed pub in England. See if you can find all Winsford's eight bridges. Or maybe it's six. Or five – I've read various claims. It needs them because not only the Exe but also the Winn flows through the village.

The **church** also merits a visit. I loved the crooked columns which are a different colour at the bottom, red sandstone, which suggests that these were the originals which were added to later. The pews have been fitted round them. There's a wonderful old oak door, a Norman font, a Jacobean pulpit and the royal arms of James I, dated 1609. A 14th-century stained-glass window depicts, rather strangely, the Virgin Mary

and uphill through open moorland (Withypool Common) from where you can see Landacre Bridge (sometimes called Lanacre which gives a clue to its pronunciation). When you reach a road turn right and the River Barle is a short distance away. The five-arched bridge is impressive, especially when you consider that it has stood here since the 14th century or thereabouts. The riverbanks are a popular picnic spot.

If you have your swim things with you and it's a sunny day, turn left when you reach the road above the bridge, rather than right. You are heading towards Sherdon Hutch ('hutch' is a local word for sluicegate) at the confluence of the Barle and Sherdon Water which the locals know as one of the best places for wild swimming on the moor. After about a quarter mile walking uphill, look for a rough track on your right and follow it for a bit under half a mile, keeping your eye out for a path leading down to the river. Then it's up to you to find the best swimming place – probably by crossing at the ford and casting around for those enticing deep pools. Return the way you came.

To return to Withypool you can either retrace your steps or, energetically, take the lane uphill for a bit under a mile to the junction with the Two Moors Way. Turn right here and follow the broad track until it becomes Kitridge Lane (an old droving road) that brings you back to your car. Watch out for the signposted footpath to Withypool which takes you a more direct route than the lane.

with Jesus astride her shoulder. It's said to be the oldest in Devon, but other churches have made the same claim.

Walkers will find the two Exmoor Scenic Walks books covering Exford and Winsford useful.

16 TARR STEPS

🏠 **Tarr Farm Inn** (page 201)

Perhaps Exmoor's best-known attraction is the beautifully preserved clapper bridge over the River Barle. Some say this bridge is over a thousand years old but it's more likely to date from the 13th century. Either way, the feat of building it out of giant slabs of stone, which were brought in from a considerable distance, is remarkable. Some slabs are over six feet long and weigh more than a ton.

Tarr Steps circular

OS Explorer map OL9; start: Tarr Steps car park, SS872323; 2 miles or 4.5 miles; easy

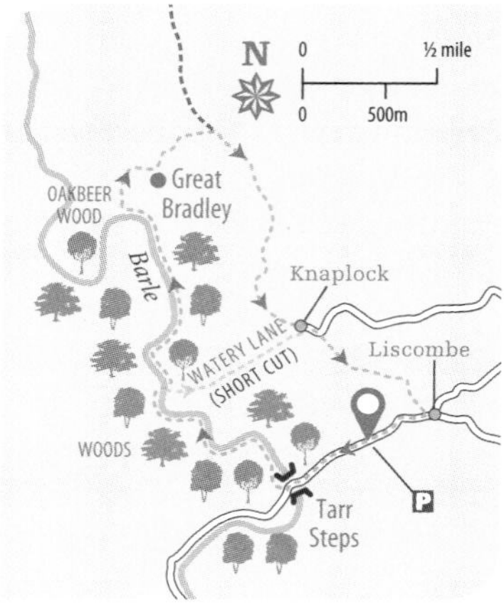

This is such a lovely area for walking, it makes sense to spend some time here. An hour's stroll takes you along the right bank of the Barle, upriver (the car-park side), through ancient woods, then up Watery Lane (more of a path than a lane) to Knaplock where you turn right. Follow the signs to Liscombe, rather than Tarr Steps, and you will join the lane to the car park.

If you want to extend the walk, just keep going upriver to a bridleway signposted Winsford Hill and walk uphill, following the signs, briefly joining the lane that serves the Great Bradley estate. After crossing a cattle grid you leave the lane, bearing right to walk up a grassy track. You are now following signs to Knaplock, and then Tarr Steps via Liscombe which will bring you out above the car park.

There's a spacious and very reasonably priced car park (£2) some way from the river, but disabled parking nearer the steps. This hugely popular place is perfect for a family picnic. Children and dogs love the paddling, and there are several deep pools where you can get fully immersed if you wish. Be cautious about sunbathing on the stones, however – that's the Devil's prerogative. Legend has it that he built the bridge, so was understandably peeved when mere mortals tried to use it. The locals asked the vicar to help; he prudently sent a cat across first to test the waters, so to speak, but it disappeared in a puff of smoke. Undaunted, the reverend set out himself and after a heated argument the Devil agreed to let people use the bridge. Except when he wants to sunbathe.

"Be cautious about sunbathing on the stones, however – that's the Devil's prerogative."

An ice-cream kiosk provides refreshments in the summer and the nearby **Tarr Farm Inn** does huge cream teas and other meals.

17 HAWKRIDGE

Hawkridge is one of those tiny, high (nearly 1,000 feet) and isolated communities that still exist in Exmoor. It has a population of around 40, and there are just ten houses in the village. The **Hawkridge Revel and Gymkhana** has been run on August Bank Holiday for nearly 70 years – indeed, 2015 is the 70th anniversary so expect something special.

> "The most notable feature is the stone coffin lid which was found in the wall in 1877. It has inscriptions in Norman French and Latin."

The squat **church** seems to be hunkered down against the elements, but overlooks a glorious view of the moors. Inside, the visitors' book is full of thanks from tired walkers for keeping the church open (Hawkridge lies on the Two Moors Way). There's a Norman font, but the most notable feature is the stone coffin lid which was found in the wall behind the pulpit in 1877. It has inscriptions in Norman French and Latin, and was probably for William de Plessy, Lord of the Manor, who died in 1274.

Hawkridge is in the same parish as Tarr Steps, and the Devil, who caused so many problems to the early users of his bridge, also wreaked havoc with the masons who built the church of St Giles, cutting their apron strings as they carried the stones for the church across the River Barle.

If you're planning to drive to Tarr Steps from Hawkridge, be warned: the river can be too deep for an ordinary saloon car to cross the ford, and there is no parking on the west side of the river. It's a lovely walk down there from Hawkridge, however, and you can make it a circular walk by taking the Two Moors Way there and coming back via the lane.

FOOD & DRINK

Exford Bridge Tea Room ✆ 01643 831304 🖉 www.exmoortearooms.co.uk. The name is misleading – this excellent place serves breakfast from 08.30, and light lunches as well as teas. It's licensed so you can enjoy a beer or cider with your meal, and also does packed lunches. Sit by a snug fire in the winter or out in the garden in the summer.

Tarr Farm Inn Tarr Steps ✆ 01643 851507 🖉 www.tarrfarm.co.uk. A splendid inn in a lovely location. Its large garden is ideal for a relaxed lunch or cream tea after a long walk; more formal in the evenings for the award-winning à la carte menu. The steak here, from Red Ruby cattle raised and slaughtered on their own farm, was described by a friend as the best he'd ever had, and their menu is accompanied by a choice of over 100 different wines. Rooms available (page 201).

The Royal Oak Winsford ✆ 01643 851455 ⌖ www.royaloakexmoor.co.uk. Once a 12th-century farmhouse, it retains its charm while providing excellent meals. There are at least four internal dining areas here – they can probably seat 120 people – and most seem to be dog-friendly. The menu is weighted towards meat with two simple vegetarian dishes and two fish dishes, cooked traditionally using high-quality ingredients. 'It reminded me of the meals my mother cooked – just good ingredients, simply cooked allowing the natural flavours of the food to come through,' commented a friend. A choice of nine real ales, lagers and ciders (and of course wine) accompanies your meal.

White Horse Inn Exford ✆ 08721 077077 ⌖ www.exmoor-whitehorse.co.uk. Excellent food in cosy surroundings, including an indulgent five-course dinner. Log fires in cold weather and, they claim, the finest single malt whisky collection in the South West. Rooms available (page 201).

Withypool Tea Rooms ✆ 01643 831178 ◷ daily 10.00–17.00 (spring/summer). Cream teas, cakes, savoury pastries, light lunches as well as really good coffee and a variety of teas. And they're open at teatime!

PORLOCK & AREA

Back to the coast and this very agreeable small town, which makes an excellent base for exploring northeast Exmoor. **Walkers** are spoiled for choice. Apart from the coastal walks described later, there are the inland wood and moorland trails through Horner Woods and up Dunkery Beacon, with, in August, the best purple-heather views in Exmoor. The 'Exmoor Scenic Walks' series has several booklets covering this area: *Porlock, Porlock Weir, Webbers Post* and *Horner*; while *Porlock Walks* by Gill and Alistair Campbell, contributors to this book, has detailed descriptions of 12 local walks. ❋Croydecycle's maps *Porlock, Horner & Dunkery*, and *Minehead, Dunster, Selworthy* have the region well covered. All booklets and maps are available from the tourist information centre (page 132).

"Trails run through Horner Woods and up Dunkery Beacon, with, in August, the best purple-heather views in Exmoor."

The long-distance **Coleridge Way** passes through Porlock, so you can follow in the symbolic footsteps of the poet from Wheddon Cross for just under nine miles, and keep going to Lynmouth, as did the poet and his chums the Wordsworths. The icing on the cake here is that the A39 runs close enough to all the best walking areas to allow for a variety of **bus-assisted walks** using

PORLOCK HILL

Gill & Alistair Campbell

In 1794 it was recorded that there was 'no road suitable for carriages' beyond Porlock, and the poet Robert Southey wrote that local people considered it 'the end of the world'.

Eighteen years later the track up the hill was still so poorly kept that the inhabitants of Porlock Parish were summoned to court and fined for failing to maintain a good road. A man was employed to do the work and in 1843 the first stagecoach, from Lynton, made it down to Porlock.

About this time Mr Blaithwaite, a local estate owner, saw an opportunity to build a toll road further west. The 4½-mile Toll Road, with a maximum gradient of just one in 14, is longer and much less steep than the public road, the A39. At first it wasn't popular, drivers preferring to save money by coaxing their horses up the main road.

These days the A39 twists and bends its way up Porlock Hill, climbing 1,300 feet in under two miles. It is the steepest main road in England, so steep that for many years motor cars were not powerful enough to climb the one in four (25%) gradients and negotiate the hairpin bends. The Toll Road was the only alternative and remained popular until long after World War I.

In 1900 a rally driver, Mr S F Edge, was the first to drive a car up Porlock Hill to win a £50 bet – more than £5,000 today. The first motorcycle climbed the hill in 1909 but the first charabanc motor coach did not make it up until 1916.

As a child, I was driven up this hill annually by my father when going on holiday. As we approached, everyone became a little apprehensive and my grandmother handed out barley-sugars to calm our nerves!

Even today, the drive up or down is challenging. Caravans and lorries are told to seek an alternative route and cyclists are advised to dismount. Car drivers are probably not reassured by signs at the top telling of the two escape roads, designed to minimise damage should you lose control.

number 300 bus; it runs twice a day between Minehead and Lynmouth (but only in the summer, and is currently under threat).

The area is quite mouth-wateringly seductive, not just for walkers but for strong **cyclists** – if they can cope with Porlock Hill – and car drivers who try to avoid choking up the roads at the busiest times of the year. Bikes can be hired from **Porlock Cycle Hire** on the High Street (✐ 01643 862535). They do a drop-off service so you can have your bike delivered to wherever you're staying.

And if you end up getting stuck on the moor, there's always **Exmoor Taxis** (✐ 01643 863355).

18 PORLOCK

🏠 **Glen Lodge** (page 201), **New Place** (page 200)

Porlock, along with Lynmouth and Lynton, is one of the three most populated parishes on Exmoor. It combines its villagey feel with wonderful rural surroundings, yet provides all the amenities that visitors need: some delightful cottages and gardens, interesting shops and good restaurants, pubs and tea shops. The poet Robert Southey loved it, writing to his brother: 'If only beauty of landscape were to influence me in choice of residence, I should at once fix on Porlock'.

The town is tightly contained along its High Street where almost every business provides something desirable, whether cream teas, specialist cheeses, antiquarian books, or paintings and crafts. Set back from the main street in Vale Yard is the factory and shop of **D J Miles & Co Ltd** (⊘ www.djmiles.co.uk), a family firm well-known for their specialist teas and coffees; here the coffee is roasted, ground, blended – and sold, together with tea, chocolate and a whole lot of other temptations. Near the church, **The Big Cheese** has a popular café as well as a wide selection of local cheeses, preserves, chutney and cider. The truncated steeple of

BEACHES, PEBBLES & MARSHES

Gill & Alistair Campbell

To the north of Porlock lies its extraordinary tidal saltmarsh. Walk down any lane towards the sea or drive to Porlock Weir and you will discover a marsh that is less than 20 years old.

The Bristol Channel has some of the highest tides in the world and the tidal saltmarsh sits below the mean high-water level. Twice a day, water rushes through a huge breach in the 2½-mile shingle bank, flooding the marsh with salt water. Only plants that are especially suited to this strange environment survive. There are large areas of common glasswort and sea blite, and many rare plants, too, like the everlasting pea, the lovely yellow horned poppy and Babbington's leek.

Until October 1996, this area was hardly affected by salt water; prize-winning barley was grown, there was good grazing and a freshwater lake. But a huge storm, part of Hurricane Lili, changed all that. The storm waters broke through the shingle ridge and salt water flooded the land. The National Trust and other landowners decided that it was time to let nature take its course and the flora and fauna are still adapting. Dotted everywhere are the bleached skeletal remains of old trees.

The storm also moved the remaining ridge inland by as much as 90 yards. Before the storm, the South West Coast Path crossed

the **church** provides a handy landmark; legend has it that the top of the steeple landed up on Culbone, possibly with the help of a giant, but a storm in the 1700s was probably responsible. It is dedicated to St Dubricius, an obscure Welsh saint, and is full of interest. There are two exceptional monuments, one to John, Lord Harington, who fought for Henry V at the Battle of Agincourt, providing 86 archers and 29 lancers. He died a year later, presumably of his wounds. His wife Elizabeth lies by his side, with her feet on a strange, cloven-hoofed animal. The other effigy is a knight, crossed-legged to show that he fought in the Crusades, dating from the end of the 13th century. What strikes the observer of these monuments, first with shock, then with curiosity, is the quantity and age of the graffiti scratched into the soft alabaster. Nothing is sacrosanct – Elizabeth's face is covered in initials. Who would have defaced the tomb in this way back in the 17th century when most of the population was illiterate? We'll never know.

> "Elizabeth's face is covered in carved initials. Who would have defaced the tomb back in the 17th century when most of the population was illiterate?"

the bay along the ridge. Today, that footpath would be well out at sea!

When the ridge moved it exposed the remains of an ancient auroch. These large animals were the precursor of modern cattle but died out around 1500bc. There is also a submerged forest near Porlock Weir, but it is hard to spot except at exceptionally low tides.

There is no memorial to Saxon king Harold, who landed here in 1052 and burned down Porlock before marching to London, but you may come across the memorial commemorating the deaths of 11 US airmen in 1942. Their B24 *Liberator* had been on submarine patrol. Returning in heavy rain and poor visibility, it crashed on the marsh. Only one airman survived.

Indeed, on the marsh's many paths we constantly find remnants of its recent history. Everything is built from huge beach pebbles – lime kilns abandoned around 1860; an ill-fated golf club house abandoned in 1914; pill boxes built during World War II, never used; and a cow shed abandoned in 1996.

The best way to truly appreciate this extraordinary landscape is to walk the marked footpath from Porlock Weir to Porlock or Bossington along the edge of Porlock Marsh. The route is clearly shown on the Croydecycle map.

The clock at the western end of the nave possibly dates from around 1450, but the oldest object in the church is the fragment of a pre-Norman cross set in the wall of the south aisle.

"The oldest secular building in Porlock is the delightful Dovery Manor, at the eastern end of the town."

Beside the church, a stroll up Parsons Street to the area called Hawkcombe brings you to some attractive old cottages; carry on and you'll come to the woods of Hawk Combe. Here the path follows Hawkcombe Water up to Hawkcombe Head, which is open moorland with plenty of walking opportunities.

The oldest secular building in Porlock is the delightful **Dovery Manor**, at the eastern end of the town. This 15th-century house is home to the local museum (○ May–Sep). Its exhibits relate to Porlock and its literary connections, and paintings include one of the launch of the Lynmouth lifeboat which was hauled overland to Porlock Weir (see box, pages 140–1). It also has a small physic garden. Admission is free, but its trustees rely entirely on donations.

Porlock holds an annual **Samphire Festival**, celebrating the region's culinary speciality. The first one was in 2016, and 2017 already is in the planning stage. For more information see ⟨ https://samphirefestival.com.

19 GREENCOMBE GARDENS

West Porlock TA24 8NU ⟨ 01643 862363 ○ Mar–Oct, 14.00–18.00

Although open to the public, this is about as close to a secret garden as you can get. Mossy paths wind through flowering shrubs and dark trees, with surprises around every corner. And you're likely to be alone here, although Greencombe has the country's best collection of erythroniums as well as other unusual plants.

Greencombe was started in 1946 by Horace Stroud but since 1966 it has been the life's work of the late Joan Loraine. All we see in the garden today is there because of her vision and dedication.

Hidden off the road between Porlock and Porlock Weir, Greencombe is set on a hillside with an uninterrupted view of the sea. While the hillside shelters the garden in winter, it also hides the sun for two months of the year. When it returns in late January, Joan used to celebrate with a glass of sherry.

Joan worked in Uganda training teachers and on her return she wanted to indulge her love of horticulture. The garden's steep slope is used to maximise our enjoyment of the planting. Overhead are oaks, conifers, sweet chestnuts and hollies – one holly is said to be the largest and oldest in the country. Amongst the ferns below are camellias and azaleas, roses and clematis, hydrangeas and rhododendrons. The hillside is quite dry, Porlock being sheltered from westerly winds by Exmoor's hills, so more than 25 tons of home-produced compost and leaf-mould are needed each year to keep the soil in good condition. Ruthless pruning is needed all year to stop the garden becoming a jungle.

"Here is the most beautiful woodcarving – almost life size – of a mother and child that I have ever seen."

As I was ready to leave, Joan asked 'Have you seen the chapel?' She left me in no doubt that my visit was incomplete without it, and she was right. Here is the most beautiful woodcarving – almost life size – of a mother and child that I have ever seen. This, and the peaceful, beautiful garden, make Greencombe a very special place.

20 PORLOCK WEIR

Millers at the Anchor (page 200)

The sea left Porlock's working harbour high and dry back in the Middle Ages, but at neighbouring Porlock Weir the shingle bar protected a tidal inlet and kept the harbour open – as it has been now for at least 1,000 years. In the 18th and 19th centuries, Porlock Weir was a busy little port, for coasters carrying timber across to South Wales and returning with coal, and there used to be an oyster fleet. Today yachts come and go from its sheltered marina and fishing boats bring in their catch. In the summer pleasure boats ply their trade. The row of thatched cottages next to the harbour provides a strand of brightness between the grey expanse of shingle and the dark woods above. The village offers a large car park for walkers (with toilets), and a variety of eateries, as well as a little maritime museum with some interesting old photos and relics, a small aquarium, and demonstrations of glassblowing. Those in the know come from far and wide to the classy **Pieces of Eight** boutique (designer fashion), and **No 7 Harbour Studios** (also called Threads of Asia) is a tiny Aladdin's Cave of genuine Kashmiri pashminas in a rainbow of colours, together with hangings, cushions and other exquisite items made from recycled traditional textiles from Rajasthan, Afghanistan and Pakistan.

e Anchor Porlock Weir TA24 8PB ✆ 01643 862753 🖰 www.millersuk.com/
closed Mon & Tue. Snacks and elegant meals in this characterful hotel. Movie and
their private cinema on Wednesday and Sunday and special meals for big events
such as Christmas and New Year.

Piggy in the Middle High St, Porlock TA24 8PS ✆ 01643 862647. Specialise in pies and
take-away fish and chips, although there is a small seating area. Rightly the most popular
restaurant in Porlock, so reservations are essential in the holiday season when they may be
too busy to cope with the demand.

The Café Porlock Weir TA24 8PB ✆ 01643 863300 🖰 www.thecafeporlockweir.co.uk.
Seriously high-quality dinners (🕑 Wed–Sun only , 18.00–20.00). The owners, Andrew and
Sarah Dixon, are passionate about food and cooking, and also have five rooms for foodie guests.

The Culbone On the A39 heading towards Lynmouth some way beyond the top of
Porlock Hill, TA24 8JW ✆ 01643 862259 🖰 www.theculbone.com. Terrific food in relaxed
surroundings (they are proud of their dog-friendly policy). Not cheap but there are plenty
of special deals and imaginative evenings to keep it affordable. The highest restaurant on
Exmoor, so with tremendous views.

The Ship Inn (*'Bottom Ship'*) Porlock Weir TA24 8PB ✆ 01643 863288
🖰 www.thebottomship.co.uk. An attractive long, low, thatched building, with plenty of
indoor and outdoor seating and traditional pub food, the 'Bottom Ship' is popular with
walkers and day visitors as well as locals, and bustles cheerfully on sunny days. It also has a
tea room, with generous cream teas, home baking, and fresh coffee roasted by D J Miles in
Porlock. See box opposite.

The Ship Inn (*'Top Ship'*) High St, Porlock TA24 8QD ✆ 01643 862507
🖰 www.shipinnporlock.co.uk. A lovely whitewashed and thatched pub, serving both
traditional pub food and more classic restaurant choices. There's a 'smaller portion' dinner
menu for those with less hearty appetites. It's deservedly popular locally so does get busy in
the evenings, but they'll squeeze you in if they can (or you can book ahead). The history is
fascinating: see box opposite.

21 HORNER WOODS & DUNKERY BEACON

Of all the places in this section, I think these two – which can be linked
in one long walk – epitomise the pleasures of Exmoor most satisfyingly.
The National Nature Reserve of **Horner Woods** is a magic forest of
gnarled oaks, lichens – 330 species – and mosses, networked with
inviting paths. The stream, Horner Water, adds to the attraction. Like
all places in the Holnicote estate, the paths are well signposted. Aim for
Webber's Post.

TOP SHIP & BOTTOM SHIP

Janice Booth

The distinction is geographical rather than discriminatory: *Top Ship* is the local name for the Ship Inn in Porlock, while the Ship Inn down in Porlock Weir is known as *Bottom Ship*. Between the two of them, they've seen a fair amount of history. Bottom Ship, close to the harbour, is said to have whetted the whistle of the not-so-occasional smuggler in olden times, while Top Ship hosted a far more literary bunch.

The poet Robert Southey wrote a sonnet at Top Ship in 1798 (it starts 'Porlock, thy verdant vale so fair to sight'), and described to his brother a room where he spent the night: 'two long old dark tables with benches and an old chest composed its furniture, but there was an oval looking-glass, a decent pot de chambre and no fleas'. Samuel Taylor Coleridge was another of the Ship's literary customers; he and Southey both developed a taste for the local Porlock speciality, potted laver (seaweed), to the extent that Coleridge even asked a friend for more supplies of it after he'd left. R D Blackmore set some scenes of *Lorna Doone* in the inn, and H G Wells is also thought to have drunk there. More recently, though, the Teletubby Lala dropped in!

Built in 1290, Porlock's Ship is one of the oldest inns in England. Back in those days the sea came further inland than it does today and the inn was close to the shoreline – handy for smuggling, and no doubt the occasional intoxicating barrel found its way from surf to cellar. When stage coaches were the means of transport up wearyingly steep Porlock Hill, spare horses were stabled at the inn to provide extra horsepower when needed. As all good historic inns should, it does have a ghost, but she's a benevolent old lady of unknown origin and doesn't appear often. Less benevolently, it's thought that the infamous press gangs of the 18th century may have drunk there in order to 'persuade' some of the young men of Porlock, when they'd downed a flagon or so too many, to sign up for the navy.

After seven centuries the inn is still very much a part of Porlock life, hosting local functions and welcoming locals and visitors alike. And perhaps, if you indulge in the odd glass there, some ancient literary ghost may be sitting at your side …

Above Horner Woods the moorland stretches in purple swathes towards the high point of **Dunkery Beacon**, at 1,703 feet the highest point in Exmoor. From August to mid-September, when the heather is in bloom, this is the most beautiful heathland. Nowhere else on Exmoor has so much heather, nor such a satisfactory contrast with the green, chequerboard fields in the valleys and the sea beyond. It's exhilaratingly lovely, and makes the climb to the beacon a must-do.

22 STOKE PERO

Stoke Pero is another superlative: Exmoor's highest church at 1,013 feet, and one of the three that were too remote to attract a parson, according to the local ditty: 'Culbone, Oare and Stoke Pero, Parishes three where no parson'll go.' Stoke Pero made do with a curate for much of its history. Not a lot remains of the original church; it was completely rebuilt by Sir Thomas Acland in 1897, with the help of Zulu the donkey who made the journey from Porlock twice a day carrying the timbers for the roof. It's a most appealing and delightful little place, set cosily next to some farm buildings. Inside there's nothing that's centuries old to admire, just a little harmonium and a set of candlesticks because there's no electricity. And a framed drawing of Zulu the donkey on the wall.

23 WOOTTON COURTENAY

A turning to the right when heading for Minehead brings you to this delightful village which is not National Trust, has never seen a chocolate box (except in the village shop), but is as traditional as they come.

The road, or rather lane, itself is full of interest, undulating past woodland and groups of thatched cottages. One such is the unique medieval chapel of ease at **Tivington**. It adjoins the house next door, sharing a thatch, and once you've found the entrance you enter a tiny room dominated by an open fireplace. There is little else inside the simple interior save a couple of religious pictures and a tiny font, but it oozes atmosphere and history. It's not easy to find; as the road rises up, look for a thatched house next to a modern one on the right. The signed entrance is at the side.

The much larger church of Wootton Courtenay dominates the village with its unusual saddleback tower. The oldest part of **All Saints' Church** dates from the mid 13th century and it has an eccentric history. The Norman owner of the manor gave the church to a nearby French priory. This was dissolved by Henry VI who put the proceeds towards the building of Eton College; as a consequence, the college reserved the right to choose the rectors of this church.

I loved the feeling of community and the Englishness of this village; its flourishing shop had a poster advertising Labrador in Need Week.

Wootten Courtenay makes a good base for walking, with a choice of footpaths and Dunkery Beacon (page 165) less than four miles away.

THE WEST SOMERSET COAST: PORLOCK WEIR TO COUNTY GATE

The unpopulated stretch of the South West Coast Path between Porlock Weir and Lynmouth is popular with walkers but the whole stretch is 12 miles, so too long for many people. However, although a strong pair of legs is still necessary for its highlights, **Culbone church** and **Glenthorne Beach**, shorter circular walks and bus-assisted walks make for a less strenuous day.

24 CULBONE CHURCH

The little **church of St Beuno** is utterly enchanting; the smallest working parish church in the country and surely one of the most remote. Although the vicar and some parishioners can bounce and slither to it by Land Rover, for visitors the only access is on foot via the coastal path, a 2½-mile walk uphill from Porlock Weir. It's a lovely tramp though oak and beech forests with glimpses of the sea, and welcome benches, 'donated by the guests of Anchor Hotel'. These woods were one of the favourite haunts of Samuel Taylor Coleridge, who revelled in the local wildlife and views of Wales across the water. He stayed in a farmhouse

LYME DISEASE

Lyme disease is carried by ticks, and is a risk when you're walking in particularly brackeny country where there are also livestock such as deer. The most common early symptom of Lyme disease is a rash of red spots which gradually spreads from the site of the tick bite. It may appear as much as four weeks after the tick has been removed. Occasionally a flu-like illness develops but more commonly there are no further symptoms until some months after the bite, when neurological symptoms may start to develop, including facial palsy, viral-type meningitis and nerve inflammation. Encephalitis (swelling of the brain) is a rare complication.

Lyme disease is treated with antibiotics.

Remember that most tick bites are harmless, and if you don't develop the rash you have little cause to worry. However, it's sensible to protect yourself with insect repellent. Long trousers are usually recommended but ticks can often find their way to your skin undetected. You may be better off wearing shorts and checking yourself at intervals. It takes ticks a while to get established. Carry tweezers with you, and if you do find a tick remove it carefully, ensuring that its mouth parts are not left in the skin to cause infection. If you develop the tell-tale rash, see a doctor as soon as possible.

nearby where he had his opium-induced vision of a 'stately pleasure dome' which became the unfinished poem *Kubla Khan*, interrupted by the arrival of a person from Porlock.

Shortly after leaving the hamlet of Worthy and its thatched toll house, the path passes through two tunnels – intriguing since they seemed to serve no possible purpose. That was before I learned about Ada, Countess of Lovelace, now celebrated as the 'first female computer programmer', who lived in the now-ruined Ashley Combe. The tunnels originally routed tradesmen to the back entrance of the house, so she was spared the unpleasantness of meeting any of the lower orders as she made her way to her bathing hut.

After about an hour of walking, quite suddenly there's the little grey church below you, squatting in a clearing with its spire, set slightly askew, reaching hopefully towards the treetops. Legend has it that this is actually the top of the Porlock church spire which blew off in a gale and landed here. Or maybe was snapped off by a giant and placed here. The church's air of vulnerability brought a lump to my throat and I wanted to savour it before looking inside. An examination of the graveyard is

FAMILY PICNIC PLACES ON EXMOOR

Gill & Alistair Campbell

Whether you are looking for a bench with a view or a grassy meadow with a stream, you can find it on Exmoor. And everyone you talk to has their own favourite. Here are a few that local people have recommended, listed from west to east.

Watersmeet ♀ SS744487. Park in the linear car park on the A39 and walk down to the river or leave your car in Lynmouth and walk up river. There are grassy banks to sit on, even the odd bench. Lots of water to splash about in and a National Trust tea shop, in case you forgot the picnic!

Countisbury ♀ SS750502. Park in the car park by the Blue Ball pub on the A39 and walk seawards past the church. Here there is a long grassy bank and a 180° view. Pick a calm day.

Robber's Bridge ♀ SS820464. A little way south of the A39 and east of Oare, again with a lovely river and views down the Doone Valley.

Allercombe Meadow ♀ SS894430. Set off the road between Webbers Post and Cloutsham, this sheltered meadow is ideal for picnics. There is room enough for a game of French cricket and a lovely stream to dip in, to paddle in, or to dam.

rewarding, with the local family Red being well represented. Look out for the stone of Ethel Red; presumably always unready. And if you've ever wondered what stone carvers do if they make a mistake, there's an example near the path. He put in an extra 'and', tried to change it to … well, it's hard to know what he tried to do, but he obviously thought 'Oh stuff it!' and left it as it is, with a hybrid d and e.

The name Culbone is a corruption of Kil Beun, or church of St Beuno (pronounced Bayno), a Welsh missionary saint. The interior seats 33 at a pinch. There's no room for anything except the pews, including a box pew for the Lovelace family, a tiny harmonium squeezed into a corner, spattered with candle wax, and the Norman font, so roughly carved that the marks of the stonemason's chisel are still visible. There has probably been a church here since Saxon times, and bits have been added through the centuries. One of the oldest features is the twin window on the north side of the chancel which may be a thousand years old, with a strange face carved above it that looks more like a cat than a man. Beyond it is a window where the decorative tracery that holds in the glass is made from wood, not stone. I've never seen this before. And between the two

Webbers Post ♀ SS902439. South of Horner and Luccombe, Webbers Post has easy parking, benches and a huge view over the Holnicote estate. Walk a little way north from the parking to find the Wind and Weather Hut, handy for shelter on a windy day. This is a good place for flying kites.

Horner ♀ SS897454. This small village southeast of Porlock has a good car park with toilets and picnic benches. The village green is a favourite picnic spot with a shallow stream, ideal to play in. For the more adventurous, head into the ancient woods and find your own shady glade.

Bossington ♀ SS897480. This beautiful village east of Porlock has picnic sites by the car park – benches, toilets and even two barbecues. There is a river to play in. It is an easy stroll to the pebble beach or up on to Hurlstone Point – more benches and stunning views.

Bury Castle ♀ SS917471. Slowly climb from Selworthy or walk across from the North Hill road. There is little left of Bury Castle but you can picnic amongst its grassy banks and enjoy spacious views. A great place for hide and seek!

County Gate to Glenthorne Beach

❋ OS Explorer map 0L9 or Croydecycle *Lynton, Lynmouth & Doone* Valley map; start: County Gate car park, ♀ SS793486; about 2 miles; quite strenuous – lots of ups and downs; refreshments and bus stop at County Gate

From the car park cross the main road and turn left for about 100 yards – into Devon – then take the footpath on your right, signed Sister's Fountain and Coast Path. Where the track splits, go straight ahead through the wooden gate signed Coast Path. There are great views ahead across the combe and the Bristol Channel to Wales.

Continue downhill through a second gate at Seven Thorns where you turn right following the sign to Glenthorne Beach and the Coast Path. You may want to make a short diversion to **Sister's Fountain**, a stone cross commemorating the place where, so the legend goes, St Joseph of Arimathea struck his staff into the ground to create a spring to slake his thirst on the way to Glastonbury.

Otherwise keep following the signs to Glenthorne Beach, walking downhill; at the next junction, Coscombe, turn left off the Coast Path, signed Glenthorne Beach, and after 100 yards

is a 'leper squint' – a tiny window at eye level that supposedly allowed the lepers who had been banished to the surrounding woodland to get a glimpse of a church service.

It would be hard not to be moved by this little church. In the booklet telling its story the author writes: 'Its walls are saturated with centuries of worship and it is tended with a care that reveals the devotion of its congregation.' Indeed.

or so turn sharp right at the footpath sign. This can easily be missed. Continue down the combe to a second right turn and cross a small stream – back into Somerset. The path, known as Ben's Path, undulates, keeping the fields and buildings of Glenthorne Home Farm on your left.

Beyond the farm, somewhat hidden in the trees, is **Glenthorne House**, now home to Sir Christopher Ondaatje, the writer and philanthropist. Glenthorne is said to be haunted by its first owner, reclusive clergyman Reverend Walter Halliday. When you meet another track turn left and then, almost immediately, right, signed Glenthorne Beach and then a track left, heading downhill next to the stream, to reach the beach.

This is a real smugglers' beach. The goods were stored at County Gate which, being on the border of Devon and Somerset, was never searched. Out to sea you may spot gannets diving for shoals of fish. When this happens, keep an eye out for the black fins of porpoises.

Leave the beach by retracing your steps up the same track, turning right at the first track junction and then left at the second. Where Ben's Path leaves to your right, continue straight on, gently uphill on the main track. Continue climbing, keeping the stream on your left.

Glenthorne Pinetum was planted by Reverend Walter Halliday between 1840 and 1870 and contains many exotic trees, including Dawn Redwood, Chinese Cow's Tail Pine and Western Hemlock. It was the first time many of these trees had been planted in England. One *Wellingtonia* giant redwood is amongst the tallest in the country, at over 150 feet. On the left are the remains of an ice house and of trout breeding ponds. Further up the slope there is an information board, on the right of the path.

When you reach the Coast Path track, turn right on to it so that you can return to County Gate.

This walk has been adapted from a description by Gill and Alistair Campbell in their book *Porlock Walks*.

To return to Porlock Weir you can either retrace your steps or continue following the coastal path, along and then up the same track that the vicar uses to access the church in the ecclesiastical 4x4, to Silcombe Farm (this is a steep climb), then head east along quiet lanes until you reach the toll road. A footpath runs parallel to this road, alongside Worthy Combe through the lovely twisted oaks of Worthy Wood or, if you have energy to spare, take the bridle path deeper into the woods, to emerge

Porlock Weir. Alternatively, continue along the South West Coast
to **Glenthorne Beach** then head inland to County Gate and catch
us back to Porlock.

EAST OF PORLOCK:
THE NATIONAL TRUST VILLAGES

🏠 **Hindon Organic Farm** Nr Bratton (page 202)

At the edge of Exmoor is the lozenge of glorious countryside between
Porlock, Minehead, the A39 and the sea. It has the coastal path running
over Selworthy Beacon and an infinite choice of woodland trails and
quiet lanes taking you through arguably the prettiest villages of Exmoor:
Luccombe, Allerford, Bossington and Selworthy. These four National
Trust villages are quintessentially rural England with their thatched
cottages strung along narrow lanes. Look out for the lateral chimneys,
set in the side of the cottage rather than the end, and often incorporating
a bulging bread oven. Footpaths and quiet lanes connect all the villages
so it's easy and rewarding to devise a walk that includes them all.

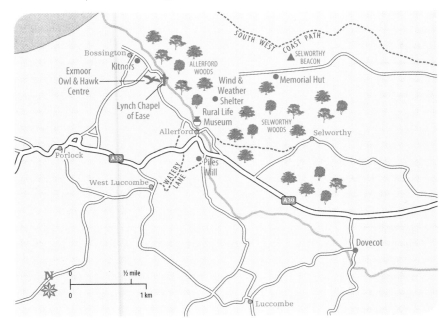

They are part of the **Holnicote estate**, which comprises around 12,000 acres of eastern Exmoor; it was inherited by the Acland family in 1745 and owned by them until donated to the National Trust in 1944 by Sir Richard Dyke Acland, the 15th baronet. It includes four miles of coast, a chunk of the moor including Dunkery and Selworthy beacons, the great Horner Woods – one of the largest National Nature Reserves in Britain – and the villages of Selworthy, Allerford, Bossington, Horner and Luccombe. There are more than 170 cottages and 144 farms on the estate.

The family seem to have been benevolent landowners and the Acland touch is everywhere, from the charming **Lynch Chapel of Ease** between Allerford and Bossington, which was used as a barn until restored by Sir Thomas Acland, to the memorial shelter above Selworthy Woods.

25 LUCCOMBE

The essence of unspoiled Exmoor, Luccombe (not to be confused with the scatter of houses that is West Luccombe) is just far enough off the beaten path to thin the influx of visitors. 'They all go to Selworthy – thank God' said one resident when we complimented him on his village. The **church of St Mary** is lovely inside and out. Lift the rug at the altar end of the nave, and admire the 17th-century brass of William Harrison, resplendent in his ruff and gown. Next to the church is a thatched cottage which surely must once have been a long house, with cattle living at one end.

Before you get to the village, soon after you leave the A39, you'll come to **Blackford House** (the road makes a right-angled turn here). A medieval **dovecot**, circular in shape and owned by the National Trust, makes an interesting visit. It's a curious building, over 20 feet high, with a small door to let you inside. The domed roof has an opening, an oculus, which allowed the birds to fly in and out. Around the walls are 11 rows of nesting holes, more than 300 of them. The dovecot was probably built in Norman times. Wealthy Normans kept domesticated pigeons to provide a luxury food, the tender meat of the young pigeons or squabs. It was illegal for anyone except lords of the manors and parish priests to keep pigeons until the 1800s. A breeding pair produced ten to 12 young birds a year. The keeper would check the dovecot frequently and remove any squabs that were near fledging – about a month old. These birds were nearly as large as adult birds but, as their flight muscles had never been used, their meat was exceptionally tender.

The dovecot can be visited at any time, free of charge.

26 ALLERFORD

🏠 **Cross Lane House** (page 200), **West Lynch Country House** (page 203)

This village is crammed with interest: a 17th-century packhorse bridge and the delightful small **Rural Life Museum** (✎ 01643 862529 ☉ Apr–Oct, Tue–Fri 10.30–16.00, Sun 13.30–16.30) housed in the old village school. The original desks, benches and slates are still there, and there is some Victorian children's clothing for modern-day kids to try on. There is a handy car park for walkers.

"Owls are the main attraction here – six different species – as well as the more familiar hawks."

Nearby is the **Exmoor Owl & Hawk Centre** (West Lynch Farm, TA24 8HJ ✎ 01643 862816 ♂ www.exmoorfalconry.co.uk). Owls are the main attraction here – six different species – as well as the more familiar hawks. There is even a palmnut vulture and a kookaburra. As well as the flying displays, the centre offers riding and horse agility demonstrations. And cream teas.

Just off the A39 is **Piles Mill**, a working mill and study centre which also holds regular activities for children.

27 BOSSINGTON

🏠 **Tudor Cottage** (page 202)

Handy for some relaxation after doing the shore walk from Porlock, this picturesque little village has particularly good examples on many of the cottages of the local lateral chimneys with bread ovens. On a fine day the tables on the lawn of **Kitnors Tea Room** provide a leafy haven of sunshine and birdsong. The thatched house dates from the 15th century.

28 SELWORTHY

This village is probably the best starting point for a walk around the region, giving you a choice of high moorland walking, or valley and village, or a combination of both. It's another chocolate-box village with a spacious green and many thatched cottages. The **church** here is a startling sight when one is used to the usual grey towers that are so typical of England. This is whitewashed – or rather lime-washed – as were most other churches in the region though few are maintained so conscientiously. The interior is full of interest, with a fine wagon roof and bosses, and an hourglass by the pulpit to ensure the sermons ended on time. And there's an absolutely wonderful chest, all worm-eaten

wood and ancient iron, straight out of *Treasure Is...*
over 400 years old. Lunches and cream teas are served
nearby **Periwinkle Cottage**.

From Selworthy you can walk uphill through the woods
South West Coast Path. All paths are well signposted, and the woo...
rewarding mix of mature oak and birch. Near the road at the top you'll
come across a '**wind and weather shelter**' dedicated to Sir Thomas
Dyke Acland who died in 1871. Poems by Heber and Keble are engraved
on each end.

¶¶ FOOD & DRINK

Cross Lane House Allerford TA24 8HW ✐ 01643 863276 ⬧ www.crosslanehouse.com.
This is a boutique hotel (page 200) but its excellent and quite formal restaurant is open to
non-residents. As you'd expect of a restaurant voted by readers of *Somerset Life* as one of
the three best in the county, this is fine dining, with the additional advantage of being in a
beautiful old building in one of Exmoor's prettiest villages.

Kitnors Tea Room Bossington TA24 8HQ ✐ 01643 862643 ⊙ Apr–Oct, daily from 11.00,
otherwise weekends only. This is a super place run by Angie and Cameron Ford, with lots of
delicious home baking, light lunches and teas. Eat inside or in the small garden. On December
weekends they do 'Christmas at Kitnors' cosily by the woodburner with mince pies, etc.

Periwinkle Cottage Selworthy TA24 8TJ ✐ 01823 451587 ⊙ Apr–Oct, 10.30–17.00;
closed Mon. Owned by the National Trust, this picture-perfect thatched tea room is worth a
visit for the setting alone. Light lunches as well as cream teas and a variety of cakes. Try their
whortleberry jam, an Exmoor speciality.

NORTH DEVON & EXMOOR DESTINATION PAGE

For additional online content, accommodation reviews, articles, photos and more on North
Devon and Exmoor, visit ⬧ bradtguides.com/northdevon.

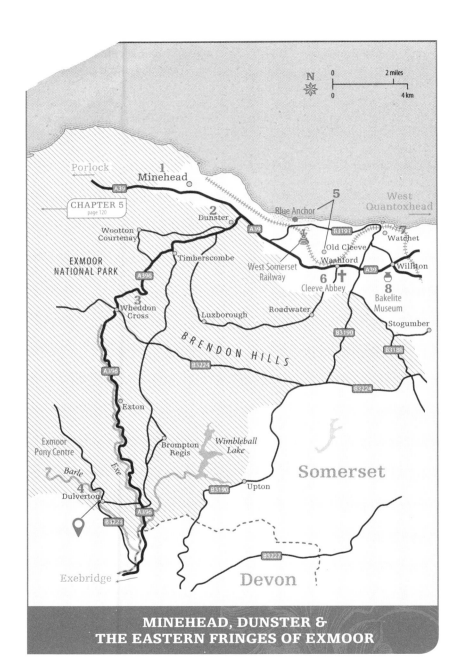

MINEHEAD, DUNSTER &
THE EASTERN FRINGES OF EXMOOR

6
MINEHEAD, DUNSTER &
THE EASTERN FRINGES
OF EXMOOR

The [carriage] drive from Minehead to Porlock is one of the most
beautiful in Somersetshire. On each side of the road rise hills of
varied outline, covered with fern and heather, whilst the rugged
valley charms by its abundant woods, grouped over broken
ground and mingled with cornfields.

A Handbook for Travellers in Somerset, 1899

Between Exmoor National Park and the Quantocks is a snout of land
which, although technically outside the range of this book, deserves
to be included. **Minehead**, after all, is the eastern gateway to Exmoor
and proudly the beginning of the 630-mile South West Coast Path and
Watchet is a most agreeable small town. Then there are the other northern
stations on the **West Somerset Railway**, all deserving their place here,
and one of England's glorious eccentricities: the **Bakelite Museum**.

Within the national park is its most appealing town, **Dunster**, and to
the south is **Wheddon Cross**, which anyone approaching Exmoor from
Tiverton must pass through. **Dulverton**, the national park headquarters,
is a short diversion off the main road. And, by the way, the area of the
national park to the east of the A396 is known as the Brendon Hills, not
to be confused with Brendon Common near Oare.

GETTING THERE & AROUND

In a region where roads are sinuous, and public transport limited,
accessing this part of Exmoor fits well with the ethos of this book: slow
but very scenic. Car drivers usually approach from the south or east,
squiggling up the A396 as it follows the River Exe from Tiverton to
Exton and then to Wheddon Cross, Dunster and Minehead, or by the
faster A358 from Taunton via Watchet.

✻ The Croydecycle 1:100,000 map *Exmoor & Taunton* is useful for drivers and cyclists exploring the region.

PUBLIC TRANSPORT

In the summer, car-free visitors have a choice of two exceptional routes to Minehead: by either the number 300 **bus** from Lynmouth or the **steam train**. Sadly the very popular 300 bus is under threat at the time of writing, so check with ⊘ www.traveline.info or ⊘ www.exploremoor. co.uk. Bus number 28 also runs every half hour from Taunton which is on the main line from Paddington, so Minehead can be reached relatively easily from London.

The **West Somerset Railway** (✆ 01643 704996 ⊘ www.west-somerset-railway.co.uk) is the longest preserved steam railway in the country, running for 30 miles through some of Somerset's loveliest scenery from Bishops Lydeard, four miles from Taunton, to Minehead taking a leisurely 75 minutes. The service runs year-round at weekends and regularly during the summer months, sometimes using diesel engines rather than steam.

There are plenty of **taxi** companies to choose from in Minehead, including: 1st Choice (✆ 01643 702325), AdsCabs (✆ 01643 702719), Ava (✆ 01643 703333), Minehead (✆ 01643 704123 or 705511) and Southwest (✆ 01643 707444).

CYCLING & WALKING

Minehead prides itself on being cycle friendly, and has some dedicated cycle paths to prove it. Pick up the *Minehead and Dunster* cycling and walking map from the TIC by the station. **Bicycles** can be hired from Pompey's (Mart Rd ✆ 01643 704077 ⊘ www.pompyscycles.co.uk) and Exmoor Cycle Hire (6 Parkhouse Rd ✆ 01643 705307 ⊘ www. exmoorcyclehire.co.uk). The latter has the widest range, and will deliver the bike to you.

The town is famous as being the start of the South West Coast Path as it follows the perimeter of Devon and Cornwall, but the 51-mile **Coleridge Way** goes inland through Exmoor's least-visited eastern region and provides a rewarding alternative. From the poet's old home in Nether Stowey, 18 miles from Minehead – and out of the range of this book – it uses bridle paths and lanes to Porlock (38 miles) with an extension to Lynton. Download the route description from ⊘ www.coleridge-way.co.uk.

To access the Way using public transport, your best bet is probably to take the train to Stogumber and join the route a mile or so to the west.

For shorter walks there are plenty of alternatives, particularly the mixture of moor and woodland south of Minehead and Dunster: Alcombe Common, Gallox Hill and Bat Castle. ❋ The Croydecycle *Minehead, Dunster, Selworthy* map covers this area.

 WET-WEATHER ACTIVITIES
Bakelite Museum (page 191)
Dulverton Heritage Centre (page 185)
Dunster Castle (page 183)
Watchet Museum (page 190)
West Somerset Railway (page 178)

1 MINEHEAD

🏠 **Beverleigh B&B** (page 204)

Butlins or the start of the South West Coast Path, amusement arcades or a network of leafy foot and cycle paths high above the town – Minehead has something for everyone, but the Slow traveller will be drawn to the western and upper parts of the town where history and rural pursuits take precedence.

Most shops and restaurants are on The Avenue, while the posh hotels and B&Bs are up the steep hills that lead to Higher Town, with their elegant large houses and tumbling gardens.

St Michael's Church, also in the Higher Town, was ruthlessly restored in 1886, so it is the individual things of interest rather than a harmonious whole that make it worth visiting. A hard-to-see carving on the eastern side of the tower shows St Michael weighing souls (the church guide has a good photo, however). The Virgin Mary, crowned and complacent, is claiming them for heaven although a little monkey-like Devil is doing his utmost to provide a counterbalance by clinging to the scales on the opposite end. Inside are a finely carved 16th-century screen and a pulpit from the 17th century. Of a similar date is the charming figure of Jack Hammer, whose job was to strike the clock although he has long been detached from it. The font is unusual – the lid is raised by a system of pulleys (page 15). The church's most important treasures are a collection of old books including a beautifully illuminated missal.

Minehead is the start/finish point of the **West Somerset Railway** and the TIC is located near the station; it can provide you with plenty of inspiration to keep you busy for a few hours.

Walkers will drift along to the western part of the seafront since, even if you're only planning to walk the seven or so miles into Porlock, it's more or less mandatory to have your photo taken next to the **sculpture**

HUNTING ON EXMOOR

Victoria Eveleigh

Anyone visiting Exmoor is bound to notice that hunting is deeply embedded in its culture. Nearly all the pubs are decorated with hunting memorabilia of one sort or another, and it's likely that the village shop will sell more copies of *Horse & Hound* than of *Hello!* magazine. The history of Exmoor revolves around hunting and farming, and together they've shaped its landscape.

Two of the principal hunts on Exmoor today – the Devon and Somerset Staghounds (D&SSH) and the Exmoor Foxhounds (EFH) – started in the 19th century. Other Exmoor hunts are the Dulverton Farmers Hunt, the Dulverton West Foxhounds, the Minehead Harriers and the North Devon Beagles.

When I moved to our farm on Exmoor 30 years ago, hunting was more or less taken for granted; summer meant tourists and winter meant hunting – and farming benefited from both. The foxhounds were particularly useful to us sheep farmers. Regular meets of the EFH in our area ensured a healthy, fit, well-dispersed and controlled fox population, and meant that we didn't have to control fox numbers by shooting or trapping them ourselves (indeed, it was frowned upon if anyone but the hunt killed a fox).

We tolerated the damage the red deer did to our hedges and crops because we knew the D&SSH would cull a few during the winter, disperse others and maintain a healthy,

that marks the start of the 630-mile South West Coast Path. It depicts a pair of hands holding an Ordnance Survey map.

FOOD & DRINK

Alcombe Fish Bar Brook St, TA24 6BP ℰ 01643 703220. Tucked away in a side street, this is considered by locals to serve the best fish and chips in Minehead. 'Sit on the prom to eat them or drive up to North Hill.'

Cream 20A The Avenue, TA24 5AZ ℰ 01643 708022 ⌖ http://cafecream.co.uk ○ daily 09.00–20.00 & until 21.00 in summer. A crisp, modern – and licensed – place serving excellent breakfasts, light lunches and, in the summer, dinners, with good coffee and cakes at any time. Popular with locals.

Old Ship Aground Harbourside, Quay St, TA24 5UL ℰ 01643 703516 ⌖ www.oldshipaground. com. A very beautiful traditional pub in a lovely location on the harbour, close to the start of the South West Coast Path. Open fires in the winter and outdoor seating in the summer.

Dean's 35 The Avenue, TA24 5AY ℰ 01643 708353 ⌖ www.pipsfish.com. This is a fish restaurant with a difference. Under the same ownership as the Culbone near Porlock (page 164), they really do go the extra mile to provide imaginative meals using locally caught fish as well

---

wild herd. In return for keeping the deer, we were given venison during the hunting season and if we had dead sheep or cattle, a hunt truck would take them away free of charge.

The system worked; it maintained a healthy, controlled population of foxes and deer on Exmoor at a cost to nobody but the hunting people themselves. Farming and hunting worked well together.

Since then several things have changed – including the law. First, new laws about carcass disposal meant an end to the free collection of deadstock, with far-reaching consequences. Then the Hunting Act of 2004 banned traditional hunting. This meant that the hunts had to adapt so that they continued to operate within the law. The D&SSH have maintained their casualty service for sick or injured deer, and they take part in various scientific studies, such as research into bovine TB in red deer.

It's unhelpful to everyone that the law is incredibly complicated, but the hunts still have a vital role to play on Exmoor. Most still meet two or three times a week during the season, and they welcome visitors to their meets (on foot, in a car or on a horse) and at other events – dances, shows, treasure hunts, point-to-points, ferret racing, fun rides and whist drives, to name a few. For further information, see the websites ⌖ www. devonandsomersetstaghounds.net and ⌖ www.exmoorfoxhounds.com.

as standard fish and chips. There are also themed evenings where you might get tapas, or Greek mezze or a Thai menu. Special deals are often available so keep an eye on their website.

The Quantock Belle ✆ 01823 433856 ♨ www.wsra.org.uk. This is food on the move! The West Somerset Railway periodically runs a special dining train that oozes nostalgia for anyone who remembers the 'Good Old Days' when meals on wheels meant being called for the first sitting. A real treat.

2 DUNSTER & AREA

🏠 **Burnells Gardens** (page 204), 🏕 **Willowstream Camping** Timberscombe (page 205)

Dunster sits just within the national park, and is deservedly the most visited small town on east Exmoor. It's utterly charming in a slightly self-conscious way, with its car-harassing narrow streets and backdrop of a splendid castle. In the predecessor of this book, *Slow Devon & Exmoor*, I wrote about 'foot-harassing cobbles' but these were removed in 2011 for health and safety reasons. Lovers of Dunster were outraged, but I have to say that it has been done sensitively, and enough of the cobbles remain to preserve the medieval feeling without the discomfort of walking on them. The shops are tasteful, selling high-quality goods, the traffic is controlled, and there are lots of tea shops and snack bars. Strange to think that in the 12th century Dunster Haven was a busy port. When the shore became land, the town switched its activities to the wool trade so successfully that the local cloth was known as 'Dunsters'. The octagonal **Yarn Market** was built in 1609 to protect the wool traders from the Exmoor weather; it serves a similar purpose for damp tourists today.

Medieval towns like this often feel claustrophobic, but Dunster revels in open spaces and enclosed public gardens. Across one such space, the Village Garden, is the **dovecot**, which probably dates from the 14th century and still has the nest holes. The exceptionally informative leaflet explains that it originally belonged to the priory but after the Dissolution of the Monasteries was sold to the Luttrells at Dunster Castle. Young pigeon, squab, was a luxury food, and until the 17th century only lords of the manor and parish priests were allowed to keep pigeons.

Near the dovecot is a lovely little church garden, and the red sandstone **church of St George**. First impressions are of a gloriously intricate wagon roof, some good bosses, and a font with a complicated cover. And the famous screen. Now, most old churches have screens, and many have screens as beautifully carved as this one, with fan vaulting to support the weight of the rood. But none, anywhere, has a screen this length, stretching across the full 54-foot width of the church. The reason it was made had nothing to do with the worship of God but everything to do with sour relations. The Benedictine monks from the priory had used the church since its founding in about 1090, whilst the townspeople, with their vicar, carried out the usual church duties of services, marriages, baptisms and burials in the same church. The dispute arose about who did what, where and when. Nasty tricks were played, such as tying up the bells out of the reach of the monks, and even imprisoning them for a time at the east end of the church.

"The dispute arose about who did what, where and when."

Things got so heated that the matter went to arbitration at Glastonbury in 1498, and the verdict was that a screen should be built to separate the parishioners and their vicar from the monks. The nave belonged to the town and the chancel to the priory. This seems to have left everyone relatively happy – at least until the Dissolution of the Monasteries some 40 years later.

A rural lane running alongside a stream leads to the **Water Mill**. Dating from the 17th century and grinding wheat daily to produce flour for its shop and local bakeries, it's an interesting place to visit and the tea room serves very tasty light meals. Continue past the mill and you enter the spacious gardens of **Dunster Castle**. This is the perfect approach to the castle: peaceful and uncrowded with, when I was there, only the sound of birdsong and the river. A path winds round to the main, steep entrance to the castle, past a sign near a doorway saying 'Ghosts' (I wasn't sure if this was an instruction or a warning) and into the very grand castle itself.

Dunster Castle is mentioned in the Domesday Book and was home to 18 generations of the Luttrell family from 1405. And the house, now in the care of the National Trust, is gorgeous. The ornate plasterwork on the ceilings and fireplaces, and the intricately carved grand-scale wooden staircase are particularly impressive, but so are the paintings, and the furniture, and even the bath. I would rank it with Hartland Abbey as my favourites among the stately homes I visited for this book. And don't miss the Dream Garden at the bottom of the hill, created by or for Alys Luttrell. Even in early October it was a riot of flowers – chrysanthemums – penned in by little box hedges, with paths winding between them and a backdrop of the church tower.

In early December, the **Dunster by Candlelight Festival** ($\oslash$ www.dunsterbycandlelight.co.uk) plunges the town into darkness save for lanterns. A procession, led by stilt-walkers, wends its way through the streets which are banned to cars, and cafés and shops that are normally closed in the winter open for business.

¶¶ FOOD & DRINK

Cobblestones 24a High St, TA24 6SG $\oslash$ 01643 821595 $\oslash$ www.cobblestonesofdunster. co.uk ⊙ year-round, Sun–Tue 10.30–16.00, Wed–Sat 10.30–20.00. A terrific café; meals include a lunchtime Sunday roast, and cream teas in comfortable surroundings. And there's a sunny walled garden for the summer. Can get busy, therefore slow, in the holiday season.
Luttrell Arms Restaurant 32–36 High St, TA24 6SG $\oslash$ 01643 821555 $\oslash$ www.luttrellarms. co.uk. A dog-friendly pub with a gorgeous garden for summer and open fires in winter, with a choice of two places to eat, the bar and the more fancy (though still informal) Psalter restaurant.
Reeves Restaurant 20–22 High St, TA24 6SG $\oslash$ 01643 821414
$\oslash$ www.reevesrestaurantdunster.co.uk. An upmarket restaurant that is not cheap, but as the best one in Dunster, you wouldn't expect it to be. An imaginative menu, beautifully cooked.

3 WHEDDON CROSS

⌂ **Cutthorne** (page 203)

After Dunster, Wheddon Cross comes as a bit of an anti-climax. It gained importance as a major crossroads and now consists almost entirely of inns and B&Bs.

The place comes into its own each February when a woodland valley is carpeted with snowdrops. **Snowdrop Valley** is owned by the Badgworthy Land Company and is an ESA (Environmentally Sensitive Area). It's a gentle 45-minute circular walk, easily accessed from Wheddon Cross car park from where a Park & Ride scheme operates if you don't want to take the footpath through woodland from the village.

The area is anyway predisposed to snowdrops, and you'll see bursts of them beside the road as you drive to Wheddon Cross. Make a day of it and have a meal in the village.

¶¶ FOOD & DRINK

Exmoor House TA24 7DU $\oslash$ 01643 841432 $\oslash$ www.exmoorhouse.com. This B&B is open to non-residents for evening meals (reservations essential) and light lunch and tea during the Snowdrop Festival. The meals are the essence of home cooking, with a small menu carefully created with truly local ingredients, and good vegetarian options.

The Rest and Be Thankful TA24 7DR ✆ 01643 841222 ⌕ www.restandbethankful.co.uk. Deserves its popularity; the food and service are very good and the menu varied. Ideal for a lunch-time warm-up after Snowdrop Valley, or something more substantial in the evening.

4 DULVERTON & AREA

⌂ ⚿ **Streamcombe Farm**, Dulverton (page 204) ⌂ **Town Mills**, Dulverton (page 204), **Riverside Cottage** Brompton Regis (page 205), **West Withy Farm** Upton (page 205)

Dulverton seems to have everything going for it: lovely surroundings, plenty to see and do, yet avoiding any suggestion of being a tourist hotspot. No wonder the national park chose to have its headquarters here at Exmoor House.

Like so many places in Exmoor, Dulverton has its Lorna Doone association. Jan Ridd met the heroine here, and there's a small statue of the young woman outside Exmoor House. It's actually of Lady Lorna Dugal 'who, in the seventeenth century, was kidnapped in childhood by the outlaw Doones of Badgworthy.'

The town's attractions include plenty of car parking on the edge of town, a 17th-century bridge over the River Barle, a variety of independent shops, and the excellent Heritage Centre. There is also such a good selection of top-class restaurants that deciding where to dine out here becomes quite problematic.

Art lovers old and young, or anyone searching for quality crafts, should take a look at **Number Seven** (7 High St ✆ 01398 324457 ⌕ www.numbersevendulverton.co.uk) which, as well as its cards and arty items, hosts the outstanding illustrator Jackie Morris and other artists.

Also not to be missed is **Tantivy** (✆ 01398 323465 ⌕ www.tantivyexmoor.so.uk ⊙ daily from 06.00, café from 09.00), a super delicatessen and general store selling a good selection of maps and books as well as picnic supplies so you'll be all set to head for the moor. But not before you've visited **The Guildhall Heritage and Arts Centre** (✆ 01398 323818 ⌕ www.dulvertonheritagecentre.org.uk). Admission is free but donations are appreciated. There are fixed and shifting exhibits here with lots of variety and surprises, like Granny Baker's Kitchen where, at the touch of a button, the good lady will chat to you about her life and times. The red deer exhibit tells you everything you need to know about Exmoor's iconic animal and also shows what can be done with those antlers they so wastefully cast every year. Local artist Tom Lock makes chairs (among other things) out of them – and has been doing so for 70 years. His grandson is following in his footsteps.

In a separate building is a **model railway**, beautifully made and correct to the last detail. It's Dulverton as it was before the railway was closed, and the little trains purr their way through tunnels and the familiar landscape before drawing to a halt at the station.

The Heritage Centre is linked to the **National Park Centre** with information about Exmoor and a good range of books and maps.

Each year Dulverton celebrates a Sunday festival, **Dulverton by Starlight**, in early December; the town is decorated, the shops stay open, there's an evening fireworks display from the church tower, and other events are held to help get people into the Christmas spirit. More information on ⥁ www.dulvertonbystarlight.co.uk.

¶¶ FOOD & DRINK

The Bridge Inn 20 Bridge St, TA22 9HJ ⌀ 01398 324130 ⥁ www.thebridgeinndulverton. com. Pies, pies and more pies. Wonderful and varied pies! This is what The Bridge does best, and it also has an impressive selection of craft beers and ciders, as well as single malt whiskies.

Longdam Thai 26 High St, TA22 9DJ ⌀ 01398 323397 ⥁ www.longdamthai.co.uk. My 'man on the spot' reports: 'I rate this very highly. Great food, great staff. Can appreciate that visitors do not come to Exmoor for Thai food – but it is a real treat for locals.'

Mortimer's 13 High St, TA22 9HB ⌀ 01398 323850 ⊙ closed Wed. Good, hearty lunches and an impressive array of specialist teas.

Woods 4 Bank Sq, TA22 9BU ⌀ 01398 324007 ⥁ www.woodsdulverton.co.uk. What's special here is that the owner, Paddy Grove, has a farm which supplies many of the ingredients that end up on the table. The restaurant is in a good location and described by a friend as 'shabby chic' outside and Exmoor rustic inside. The same friend described the home-reared Gloucester Old Spot pork as 'up to Mason's Arms' (see page 117) standard'. They also have a very extensive wine list. Check ⥁ www.bradtupdates.com/northdevon for regular eating recommendations from the **Upton Supper Club**.

THINGS TO SEE & DO NEAR DULVERTON

About four miles west of Dulverton is the hamlet of Ashwick and the **Exmoor Pony Centre** (⌀ 01398 323093 ⥁ www.exmoorponycentre.org. uk), home of the Moorland Mousie Trust (named after one of the most popular pony books of all time, published in 1929). This charity was set up to give the surplus foals from moorland-bred herds a future by training them to be useful family ponies, so lovers of this distinctive native breed (page 131) get a chance to meet them face to face and perhaps 'adopt' a pony to help with its upkeep. Best of all you may be able to go for a two-hour ride on Exmoor, on an Exmoor pony (see the website for further details).

In the opposite direction, east of Dulverton, is the huge expanse of water that is **Wimbleball Lake** (TA22 9NU ✎ 01398 371460). This reservoir has been developed into a country park with all sorts of water and land activities in pleasant surroundings. It's the place to learn how to kayak, canoe, sail or windsurf and even try your hand at angling.

On the way to Wimbleball Lake, in a deep valley beyond Brompton Regis, is the idyllic **Pulham's Mill Craft Centre and Tea Rooms** (✎ 01398 371366). On a fine day you can eat lunch or drink your tea outside accompanied by the sound of the river. As well as light lunches and teas they do a Sunday roast (advance booking essential).

River Barle circuit

❊ OS Explorer map OL9; start: Exmoor House car park, ♀ SS9123327830; 3.8 miles; fairly easy (some steep inclines)

Cross the bridge and turn immediately right along a lane which soon turns into a track leading uphill (do not take the road to the left). You are heading for Marsh Bridge along a footpath, signposted Tarr Steps, which curves around the end of Burridge Woods with the river below you on the right.

You will soon see signposts to Marsh Bridge, before joining a lane at Kennel Farm which will take you to the road bridge across the Barle. More excitingly you cross the old packhorse bridge, then trudge uphill, up Looseall Lane, following signs to Court Down. This track passes through woodland,

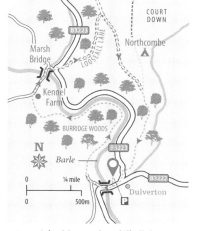

eventually levelling out at a T-junction where you turn right. It's now downhill all the way to Dulverton, with signposts to keep you on track.

WALKS IN THE DULVERTON AREA

With the River Barle on Dulverton's doorstep, making its gentle way to Tarr Steps, there is a good selection of walks. The National Park Centre has maps and walking guides to inspire you. With a footpath running almost all the way along the Barle to Tarr Steps, this is the most attractive option, but be warned: there is no longer a bus linking the two places and a circular walk, though rewarding, is 12 miles. However, you could use the Moor Rover (page 127) to return to Dulverton, thus reducing the walk to a little over five miles. The route on page 187 gives you a taste of the local scenery in just over three miles.

¶¶ FOOD & DRINK

The Anchor Inn Exebridge TA22 9AZ ✆ 01398 323433 ⌂ www.theanchorinnexbridge. co.uk. Exebridge is near Dulverton but outside the national park. However, it's worth the diversion to the Anchor Inn for its lovely riverside beer garden and good, local food. Rooms available.
The George Brompton Regis TA22 9NL ✆ 01398 371273. A friendly local pub in this small, high village. Whopping helpings of traditional fare.
Pulham's Mill See page 187.

OUTSIDE THE NATIONAL PARK: BLUE ANCHOR, WATCHET & AREA

The West Somerset Railway gives access to a scattered selection of interesting places, described here in the order that you would come to them after Minehead. Of course you can drive to them as well.

5 BLUE ANCHOR & OLD CLEEVE

A place for families and a stop on the railway line, this resort has a huge stretch of sand and shallow sea so is safe for children. At low tide there's enough beach to build a life-sized sand castle.

Up the hill is something altogether more curious – the church in **Old Cleeve** which has an effigy of a young man with his feet resting not on a lion but on a cat. And the cat has been busy – it has its paws on a rat. The figure may be Sir John Golafre, husband of Phillipa Mohun, heiress of Dunster Castle.

Old Cleeve can also be accessed from Washford railway station, up the steep Monk's Path.

6 CLEEVE ABBEY

Washford TA23 0PS ✆ 0870 333 1181 ◷ Mar–Nov; English Heritage

A 15-minute walk from the railway station of Washford, but with a large adjacent car park, this 800-year-old ruined Cistercian abbey has much to commend it. English Heritage has done an excellent job with its exhibitions and labelling. I particularly liked the Monk's Trail signs aimed at children which describe, in simple language, how the monks lived and worked in the abbey until it was dissolved by Henry VIII in 1536. Somewhat alarmingly, given the history of deliberate wrecking along the nearby coast, the monks were granted 'Right of Wreck' in their area. There is also a charming quote from an account of their land labours in 1589 indicating that they wore gardening gloves and pulled up 'broome', probably gorse, 'until their new gloves were well worn and their hands sore with drawing of broomes'. Several of these labouring monks were over 80.

Most of the abbey is too ruined to be of great interest, but the refectory is absolutely splendid. Here is a Great Hall, remodelled in the 15th century by the increasingly prosperous community. It imitated the Great Halls found in manor houses, and has a wonderful wagon roof. As with many churches, there are carved angels and bosses, but these angels are different. Instead of supporting the buttresses, they sit astride them, and at first glance seem to be wearing safety belts to prevent them tumbling to the floor. In fact these are scrolls and if you look carefully you'll see that some angels are pointing to words (now lost) with one finger ('Thou shalt not') and some with two fingers ('Thou shalt'). When the refectory was restored recently a green man was discovered among the carved bosses, decorated with flowers and foliage.

Another marvel is the refectory floor, which will move to a permanent home in 2015 (it is currently displayed under canvas). The beautiful glazed tiles, in subtle earth colours – ochre, terracotta and black – decorated with heraldic designs including two-headed eagles and coats of arms, were made in the late 13th century. Though each title is painted in great detail, together they make a harmonious whole. When the abbey was destroyed the floor, or pavement, was covered in earth and thus protected until it was excavated in 1876.

All this, with spacious grounds where children can play or picnic, means that Cleeve Abbey is worth making an effort to see. To walk there from Washford, avoiding the main road, turn left out of the station and walk to the bus shelter. From there follow the signs to the abbey.

7 WATCHET

⌂ Langtry Country House Washford (page 204), **Railway Cottage** Williton (page 205),
Swain House Boutique B&B (page 204)

Whether or not it's true that Watchet was the inspiration for *The Ancient Mariner* – or at least matched the harbour of Coleridge's imagination where 'merrily did we drop/Below the kirk, below the hill, below the lighthouse top' – it has certainly stood this delightful little town in good stead. On the seafront stands a fine statue of the mariner with the albatross round his neck, and the commercial implications are not lost on the town's business community. The Esplanade Club boasts that it is 'recommended by the Ancient Mariner' and you'll find Albatross Antiques on Swain Street. Coleridge supposedly stayed in The Bell Inn, penning the first few lines of his poem there. Well, who knows?

I first visited Watchet during Open Studios (page 17) and it seemed that every other shop was a craft shop, gallery or temporary gallery. Clearly this is an arty place, and is satisfactory in so many ways: small enough to walk around, with an excellent museum, a good (and level) ramble along a disused railway line, and an interesting church (though some way from town).

The **museum** (⊘ www.watchetmuseum.co.uk), housed in the old market by the harbour, is particularly interesting, with a fine 'Chronicles of Watchet' at the back of the building where you can trace the history of the town from prehistoric times to the present day through illustrations and photos. I particularly liked the elephants strolling through Watchet after a dip in the sea. They'd arrived with a travelling circus. There is also the story of Florence Wyndham who was laid in her coffin wearing a precious ring. Temptation overcame the sexton and he sneaked into the church at night, broke open the coffin and started to cut off the ring finger of the corpse. Whereupon she screamed and sat up. The screams of the would-be thief were even louder and he was never seen again. The good lady made a complete recovery and went on to give birth to a son. Or perhaps twins – accounts differ.

Watchet was the terminus of the **Mineral Railway**, built in the mid 19th century to carry iron ore from the Brendon Hills to Watchet harbour; the museum has photos and explanations.

Some of the old railway track is now a popular two-mile walk to Washford, a station on the West Somerset Railway, or part of a shorter circular walk that takes in the **church of St Decuman**. One of those colourful saints that crop up in churches from time to time, Decuman arrived in Somerset from Wales in the seventh century, having sailed across the Bristol Channel on his cloak with a cow for company and sustenance. He and his cow settled in Watchet but this pastoral life didn't last; he made the wrong sort of enemies and was beheaded. Whereupon the saint picked up his head, washed it and put it back where it came from. The local people, much impressed, helped him build the church which is dedicated to him.

There's an impressive memorial to William Wyndham, dated 1683, who 'having Heroically trod in the steps of his ancestors in theire Faithfull and Important Services to the Crowne and in particular having with bless'd successe... devoted himself, and his very weighty Interest to the closeing the dreadful breach of the late monstrous Divisions, Betooke himself on nine and twentieth day of October in ye one and fiftieth year of his age to the Enjoyment of his more Glorious Immortality.' It makes it sound as though death, for this Civil War hero, was a fairly casual decision.

¶¶ FOOD & DRINK

The Bell Inn 3 Market St, TA23 0AN ✆ 01984 631279. A historic old pub (16th century), family run, serving good food and a wide range of local beers in pleasant surroundings. Open fires in the winter. Dog-friendly.

Peebles Tavern 24 Market St, TA23 0AN ✆ 01984 634737 ⏥ www.peeblestavern.co.uk. Not a restaurant but a bar specialising in cider — around 20 varieties! Friendly, distinctive, and well worth a tipple before or instead of eating.

The Spice Merchant 14A Market St, TA23 0AN ✆ 01984 633010. A good Indian restaurant for eat in or take away.

Star Inn Mill Lane, TA23 0BZ ✆ 01984 631367. A quiet pub tucked behind a traffic-free street. A varied menu, well cooked, along with a wide selection of real ales.

8 THE BAKELITE MUSEUM

Orchard Mill, Williton TA4 4NS ✆ 01984 632133 ⏥ www.bakelitemuseum.co.uk
🕑 Mar–Oct, 10.30–18.00; daily in main school holidays & Thu–Sun in term time

In a corner of a Somerset village, crammed into every possible space in a 17th-century mill, is this higgledy-piggledy collection of plastic objects. Once you start collecting plastic where do you stop? You don't, you just run out of room. It's utterly delightful because it's so different: rows and rows of hairdryers, typewriters, Barbie dolls, telephones, irons, kettles, sewing machines, games, clocks, fridges, radios – lots of radios

EXMOOR INTERNATIONAL DARK SKY RESERVE

Exmoor is rightly proud of being Europe's first such reserve. It has taken a combined effort to achieve this, with the two county councils and Exmoor land owners working together to reduce light pollution.

We can all look up on a moonless night at the thousands of stars visible to the naked eye and say 'Wow!' but, like all things in the natural world, you need an expert to show you what you're seeing and explain its significance, and you need a telescope.

I achieved both on a wonderfully clear (and cold!) night in September when I went to West Withy Farm which has become the centre for stargazing in southern Exmoor. Seb Jay, Mr Telescope himself, was there with his Dobsonian reflector telescope and his infinite knowledge of infinity. My own knowledge was limited to recognising the Plough, or Big Dipper, and that was about it. The first *eureka* moment was identifying the North Star and then the nearby constellation of Cassiopeia. It helps when stars form recognisable patterns (such as a saucepan or dipper for the Plough and a W for Cassiopeia). I shall remember those and they're visible to the naked eye. Seb explained that Saturn had just set below the southwestern horizon, which was a shame because its rings definitely have the wow factor, but we were soon transported a brain-numbing distance to two galaxies called Messier 81 and Messier 82, which Seb told me were 11.8 million light years away. In comparison the Andromeda galaxy was a baby at 2½ million light years. Remember that light travels at close to 200,000 miles per second, and do the maths. If distance wasn't enough to cause brain shut-down, the oldest cluster of stars we looked at was the Hercules globular cluster, which is a whopping 12.7 billion years old.

– and televisions. Because, for us oldies, that's what Bakelite is all about. If we didn't own a Bakelite radio ourselves, our parents or grandparents certainly did. And, let's face it, compared with most museums the objects here are not intrinsically beautiful or old; that's the whole appeal. It was while I was contemplating the advantages and disadvantages of the plastic coffin that I heard an excited 'Wow!' from a youngster at some discovery. Kids who are bored out of their minds at conventional museums love this place, as do their grandparents. 'Thank you for letting Grandad and me relive our memories' I heard as they left, but it sounded as though the pleasure had been mutual.

Bakelite goes back a surprisingly long way – to 1907, when a Belgium-born chemist, Leo Hendrik Baekeland, working in New York, discovered the potential of phenol-formaldehyde. Light-weight, a poor conductor

Is there any other word but mind-boggling? Here's the huge sweep of Exmoor sky, and Seb can not only identify but give the vital statistics of everything up there! I asked him how he got into it. 'I grew up in North Wales which was pretty dark, so when Mum heard that there was to be a total eclipse of the moon she let me stay up late to see it. We looked at it through binoculars – and I was hooked! I bought a cheap telescope and a wobbly tripod and saw Saturn. Wow! That led to a better telescope, while I was still a teenager, and my doing careful drawings of what I saw so I could learn about it.' Seb studied geology at university, and in 2009 decided to set up his own star-related business which eventually led him to become one of the few companies in England to hire out telescopes – and knowledge.

I know I'll only retain a tiny proportion of what I was told that night, but I will look at the night sky with a new appreciation and a little bit more understanding. It's a start.

Seb Jay's *Exmoor Dark Skies: Our Window into a Universe of Fragile Starlight*, published in 2014, is the definitive book for Exmoor stargazers.

WHERE TO GO STARGAZING

Exmoor Dark Skies Safari run by Exmoor Safari (page 132). ☺ Oct–Mar. Powerful binoculars and star chart supplied.

Exmoor National Park Centres Dulverton, Dunster and Lynmouth. Enquire about hiring a telescope and perhaps Seb Jay himself for a special event.

West Withy Farm (page 205). This is the complete package with accommodation, Seb Jay and a big white telescope.

of heat and easily moulded, it changed the world. The museum's founder, Patrick Cook, bought his first Bakelite radio in 1969 and just keeps adding to the collection.

The museum is still run by Patrick and his wife who served me a delicious toasted tea cake in the little tea room. Long may they continue.

¶¶ FOOD & DRINK

Stable Cottage Triscombe TA4 3HG ✆ 01984 618239 ⊘ www.stable-cottage.co.uk ☺ Easter–end Oct, Tue–Sun 14.00–17.30, Nov–Easter Sun 14.00–17.00. Not in the area covered by this book but such a lovely stopping-off place when heading for Exmoor on the A358 from Taunton – or when going home – that I couldn't resist including it. The cream teas are great and the view from the tea garden across the Quantocks terrific. While there take a look at nearby Crowcombe: the church, by Crowcombe Court, has the most fabulous carved bench ends.

ACCOMMODATION

The places to stay included here have been listed either with an eye to their location, because they are special or unusual in some way, because they encapsulate some aspect of Slow – or because they're just wonderful and readers should know about them. The list is certainly not exhaustive, and inclusion doesn't necessarily mean they are the best in the area – just places I came across or had recommended to me. I steer clear of prices, but most accommodation is cheaper off season or if you stay several nights; most self-catering places can only be let for four days or more. Campsites run the gamut of possibilities from a meadow that's only open in July, to glamping in such luxury it hardly counts as camping. In Devon and Exmoor, by far the most popular holiday accommodation for families is self-catering.

Two good websites for the area are ⟨ http://exmoor-holidays.co.uk and ⟨ www.devonfarms.co.uk. Others include Classic Cottages (⟨ www.classic.co.uk) which specialise in the southwest, as do Helpful Holidays (⟨ www.helpfulholidays.com). English Country Cottages (⟨ www.english-country-cottages.co.uk) also cover this region, and the luxury 'private home custodians', Unique Homestays (⟨ www.uniquehomestays.com) have a few places in the area. Trip Advisor is always worth checking, if only for some evocative phrases such as 'Woke up watching sheep grazing in the most comfortable bed ever.' Note that sat nav is often unreliable in North Devon and Exmoor (and in Exmoor there's rarely a mobile phone signal), so always check the accommodation provider's directions. Go to ⟨ www.bradtguides.com/ndevonsleeps for further reviews and additional listings.

1 NORTHWEST DEVON: THE CORNISH BORDER TO THE RIVER TORRIDGE

Hotels

New Inn Hotel High St, Clovelly EX39 5TQ ⟨ 01237 431303 ⟨ www.clovelly.co.uk. You don't stay here because you want a perfect hotel, you stay here because the New Inn *is* Clovelly. It's been here a very long time (since the 17th century), and has hosted, among others, Charles Dickens. The hotel is very comfortable, with eight en-suite rooms decorated in Arts & Crafts style. Across the road in New House is budget **B&B** accommodation, with a shared bathroom.

Yeoldon House Durrant Lane, Northam EX39 2RL ⟨ 01237 474400 ⟨ www.yeoldonhouse.co.uk. A Victorian house converted to an elegant hotel with just ten individually furnished rooms.

There is a lovely garden with spacious views, and the restaurant is outstanding, so this is the place for that special holiday treat when you are looking for more than just **B&B**. Note that because of the age of the building there is no lift to the bedrooms.

Self-catering

Beara Farmhouse Buckland Brewer, Bideford EX39 5EH ✆ 01237 451666 ⬧ www.bearafarmhouse.co.uk. Buckland Brewer is a quiet, inland village with an excellent pub and this delightful whitewashed farmhouse with two self-catering places: Shippon, which sleeps four, and the larger Sparrows which accommodates six. Ann and Richard Dorsett also do B&B (two rooms, and a private lounge with an open fire) and their artistic flair is evident throughout the buildings.

Blegberry Farm Hartland EX39 6AY ✆ 01237 441713 ⬧ www.blegberry.co.uk. This 700-acre working farm is in a terrific position just three miles from Hartland and the nearby beaches and walks, so its large (sleeps eight) Puffin House plus two smaller self-catering cottages are understandably popular. They range from complete luxury, with their own hot tubs, to a rather superior static caravan, Little Puffins, which sleeps four at a very economical rate.

Bridge Cottage Peppercombe ✆ 01628 825925 ⬧ www.landmarktrust.org.uk. A tiny, pink thatched cottage half-concealed in the combe that leads to a pebble beach: this is cliché-typical Devon. It sleeps three, is dog-friendly, and has an orchard and garden. Some of the best walks in northwest Devon are on the doorstep, including the classic stroll down Hobby Drive to Clovelly (page 36).

Poacher's Cottage Appledore. Book through South Yeo (below) ✆ 01237 451218 ⬧ www.southyeo.com. A charming two-roomed former fisherman's cottage in a courtyard setting close to the quayside. There is no private parking (guests use the public car park) but this is a town where you can happily do without a car.

South Yeo Yeo Vale EX39 5ES ✆ 01237 451218 ⬧ www.southyeo.com. In the Yeo Valley south of Fairy Cross is this beautiful country estate, its 15 acres including two walled gardens and the River Yeo. Owned by Jo and Mike Wade, this is truly intimate, with just one room for B&B guests and a small self-catering cottage sleeping four. B&B in the main house is in a lovely double bedroom with its own sitting room. This is a working farm with cattle and sheep – and chickens to provide the free-range eggs for breakfast.

Camping & glamping

Koa Tree Camp Hollacombe Farm, Welcombe EX39 6HE ✆ 01225 858038 ⬧ www.koatreecamp.com. Welcombe is west of the A39, close to the Cornish border. This luxury site has five Mongolian yurts and five bell tents, all beautifully furnished and with an eye to comfort and sustainability. The yurts are supplied with electricity, but heated by wood-burning stoves. There are also extensive activities available.

Loveland Farm Hartland EX39 6AT ℘ 01237 441894 ⬧ www.lovelandfarmcamping.co.uk ☺ Mar–Oct. Loveland Farm is, on first appearance, a small campsite within a stone's throw of the gorgeous scenery of Hartland Point. But it has a *pièce de résistance*: the **Loveland Pod**. This is a space-age geo-dome, with all the comforts of glamping: very comfy beds, a lounge and a wood-burning stove. It's set on a high wooden deck, which deals with the sloping land, beside the kitchenette and eco-loo. In addition to the pod there are, at present, 16 simple camping pitches where dogs are allowed (they are not allowed inside the pod) and there are plans for yurts and other glamping structures.

2 NORTH DEVON'S SEASIDE

Hotel
Pack o' Cards High St, Combe Martin EX34 0ET ℘ 01271 882300 ⬧ www.packocards.co.uk. This world-famous folly has six rooms of various sizes and prices (one with a four-poster bed) and a good restaurant. Although built as a private residence it has been a pub since the 1800s. The rooms have a separate entrance from the pub and restaurant, and are quiet and comfortable. The hotel is frequently used by walkers doing the South West Coast Path so owners Chris and Debbie are used to arranging luggage transfers.

B&Bs
Langleigh Guest House Berrynarbor EX34 9SG ℘ 01271 883410 ⬧ www. langleighguesthouse.co.uk. Berrynarbor is a quintessential Devon village, set high above Combe Martin, so a stay here sets you apart from the main tourist traffic. The guest house has five well-furnished en-suite bedrooms and a family room. The garden is gorgeous, with plenty of outdoor seating; breakfast can be taken on the terrace if the sun is shining. Guests are greeted with a cream tea or homemade cakes by the very hospitable owners, Gill and Andy. Berrynarbor's flowerpot men like it here, so that's a good start.

Self-catering
Mill Cottage Braunton EX33 2EU ℘ 01271 812671 ⬧ www.millcottagebraunton.com. A 17th-century mill by the River Caen in the old part of this surfing town. Two double bedrooms, a small kitchen, a garden – everything you need for a cosy stay – and it's dog-friendly. An added bonus is that Emma, next door, does beauty treatments including massage. A nice indulgence after being bashed by surf or walking the coastal path.
West Challacombe Manor Nr Combe Martin ℘ 0844 335 1287 ⬧ www. nationaltrustcottages.co.uk. This 15th-century manor house is of national historical importance, with a fabulous oak hammer-beam ceiling in what is now an upstairs living room, but was once the Great Hall (page 77), as well as a splendid porch bearing a 16th-century coat of arms. It sits in a wild garden with picnic benches and splendid views,

a stone's throw from the South West Coast Path. Inside there is a Rayburn cooker, a farmhouse-style dining room, an open fire and three bedrooms (sleeping five people). Guests need to co-exist with the protected bat colony! No dogs allowed.

Camping & glamping

Little Meadow Watermouth, Ilfracombe EX34 9SJ ✆ 01271 866862 🖱 www.littlemeadow. co.uk. Fifty pitches on a 100-acre organic farm in an excellent location for local walks. The well-supplied shop sells their own produce.

Longlands Farm Coulsworthy, Combe Martin EX34 0PD ✆ 01271 882004 🖱 www. longlandsdevon.co.uk. Longlands has five luxury safari lodges, each sleeping six people, which give you a semblance of camping – nature all around, sitting in the sun on the deck in front of the lodge with views to the sea, a private barbecue platform – without any of the cramped discomfort. Inside there are very comfortable beds, wonderful showers and a separate loo. A wood-burning stove heats the lodge and doubles as a cooker, although there is also a gas ring, whilst a separate wood burner heats the water. There's even a private boating lake. Dog-friendly. The farm is practically opposite the junction between the A3123 and the A399. See advert in fourth colour section.

North Morte Farm Caravan & Camping Park Mortehoe EX34 7EG ✆ 01271 870381 🖱 www.northmortefarm.co.uk. The position's the thing, here. You are within a stone's throw of Rockham Beach as well as the sandy bays of Barricane and Grunta, and the huge sweep of Woolacombe Sands. Not to mention one of the best stretches of the South West Coast Path. Perfect for families with kids willing to do some walking.

Under the Milky Way Combe Martin ✆ 07851 246876 🖱 www.underthemilkyway. co.uk. Four pre-pitched luxury bell tents, well separated in ten acres of gently sloping fields and wooded valleys. The tents are furnished with rugs, futon/airbeds, wood-burning stove, tables and chairs, with light provided by solar-powered lanterns. Each has its own private shower with under-floor heating and toilet. A communal washing area, with electricity, deals with laundry and phone-charging requirements. It's a quiet, peaceful area with, as the name suggests, wonderfully dark skies. You might want to consider hiring a telescope at the Lynmouth National Park Centre for proper star-gazing (page 193).

3 LUNDY ISLAND

The Landmark Trust is responsible for all the Lundy accommodation options, and they are listed on its websites with full descriptions and photos; or you can ask for an illustrated brochure by post. All bookings are made through the Landmark Trust: ✆ 01628 825925 🖱 www. landmarktrust.org.uk or 🖱 www.lundyisland.co.uk. There are 23 **self-catering properties** of various sizes available for short breaks and weekly holiday lets; these may be fully booked up to a year ahead. Lengths of stay available for each property are shown on the website, and in winter are dictated by the days (Monday and Friday) that the helicopter operates. There's also a **campsite** near the village with space for 40 people, and a **hostel** (The Barn) with two rooms with eight and six single beds. See page 85 for details of equipment, etc. Here is a taster of the variety of properties available. For just one person there are two places: **Old Light Cottage** next to the Old Light, and the **Radio Room** behind the Tavern. Old Light Cottage was the lighthouse keepers' store, solidly built of granite to the usual Trinity House standard; while the Radio Room is a small, granite-built cottage which once housed the island radio used to communicate with the mainland. In fact the old radio is still in there at the foot of the bed! For two people there's a wider choice, including the popular **Old School**, the island's former Sunday school, a small building of corrugated iron with a snug matchboard-lined interior. A great place to stay, serenaded in June by the haunting sounds of the Manx shearwaters as they return to their nesting burrows during the night. The largest property on the island (sleeping 12) is **Millcombe House**, a large classical villa built for the Heaven family which looks down a wooded valley below the village and out to sea. It has a curious concave copper roof which caught rainwater for great tanks in the cellars. The most remote place is **Tibbetts**, which sleeps four; it's on one of the highest points of the island, nearly two miles from the village.

4 BARNSTAPLE & INLAND NORTH DEVON

Hotel

Broomhill Art Hotel Muddiford EX31 4EX ✆ 01271 850262 ⬧ www.broomhillart. co.uk. The building is late Victorian, set on a hill, with sculptures not only in the gardens but in the galleries which double as sitting rooms. The award-winning restaurant is one of the attractions and guests and non-residents can enjoy a variety of meal options detailed on the website.

B&B

Hollamoor Farm Tawstock EX31 3NY ✆ 01271 373466 ⬧ www.devonhorsebedbreakfast. co.uk. A 300-year-old farmhouse in a lovely area for gentle sightseeing, owned by Sir Bourchier and Lady Caroline Wrey. Three rooms in the house and one in a separate barn. Delicious, organic evening meals on request. It's dog- and horse-friendly.

Lower Yelland Farm Fremington EX31 3EN ☏ 01271 860101 🖝 www.loweryellandfarm. co.uk. Award-winning, dog-friendly accommodation in a 350-year-old farmhouse located between Bideford and Barnstaple, close to the Tarka Trail, with seven rooms including two singles. Breakfasts are a treat, with homemade bread and marmalade served in the splendid oak-beamed lounge. Two self-catering lodges, with hot tubs, are also available.

Self-catering

Anderton House Goodleigh (east of Barnstaple) ☏ 01628 825925 🖝 www.landmarktrust. org.uk. This 'uncompromisingly modern' house is a departure for the Landmark Trust which usually rescues old buildings. Designed in the 1970s by architect Peter Aldington who described it as 'perhaps the nearest we came to an integration of inside and outside spaces', it is open-plan with lots of glass allowing an unhindered view of the Devon countryside. Three rooms, sleeping five. Dogs allowed.

Rosemoor House Great Torrington EX38 8PH ☏ 01805 626810 🖝 www.rhs.org.uk/gardens/ rosemoor (click on 'About Rosemoor' and then 'Holidays'). Three self-catering apartments in the gardens, sleeping two and four, giving a unique opportunity to wander in tranquillity outside Rosemoor's normal opening hours. Three-, four- and seven-night bookings are available, with arrivals and departures on Mondays and Fridays. Booked up well ahead during the spring and summer.

Camping & glamping

Vintage Vardos Higher Fisherton Farm, nr Atherington, Umberleigh EX37 9JA ☏ 07977 535233 🖝 www.fishertonfarm.com. A vardo is an old-fashioned gypsy caravan with a bow top. The three vardos are beautifully and individually decorated, and sleep two in comfort. There's a hot outdoor shower and a loo-with-a-view. The vardos can only be rented together, so you need to be a group of six minimum. The owners, Gavin and Gemma, farm rare-breed sheep and cattle for their exceptional meat, and grow their own vegetables. They provide guests with a welcome basket of homemade bread, free-range eggs and milk, and other farm produce can be purchased. The cooking is done outside on an open fire.

Woodland Retreat Langtree, Great Torrington EX38 8NP ☏ 01805 601532 🖝 www. summerdazecamping.co.uk. The name describes this place perfectly – a rustic 'treehouse' (more of a wooden building on stilts), it sits in an isolated four acres of woodland, and provides a double bed and a couple of bunks for children, and a wood-burning stove. Everything else is outside, though covered, including the compost loo at the end of a solar-lit woodland path. Cooking is done on an open fire with a tripod stove for outdoor cooking and firewood is there for the collecting – and for the cutting: a bow saw and axe are provided. This is camping as it used to be, but with a lot more comfort and sustainability, run by Lynda (an artist) and Alex (a musician) Duncan who want to share their rural dream.

5 EXMOOR NATIONAL PARK
Hotels

Cross Lane House Allerford TA24 8HW ℘ 01643 863276 ⌂ www.crosslanehouse.com. It's impossible to fault this boutique hotel which combines the charm of the 16th-century house in one of Exmoor's prettiest villages with expert management from the two owners, Max Lawrence and Andrew Stinson. Four seriously comfortable rooms, individually furnished with lovely views, an excellent restaurant, and the best of Exmoor just outside the door. No, it's not cheap, but would you expect it to be?

Heasley House Heasley Mill EX36 3LE ℘ 01598 740213 ⌂ www.heasley-house.co.uk ⊙ closed Mon & Tue (after breakfast), & Sep–Apr when it becomes a shooting lodge. Heasley Mill is a very small, very compact village just inside Exmoor National Park. Miles and Mandy Platt worked in brand marketing before buying this Georgian house in 2014, and they've got it absolutely right. Comfort and good food (including evening meals) are priorities here, so it's a dog- and child-friendly place where you wouldn't feel guilty tramping a bit of mud indoors, but when it comes to eating and sleeping – and chatting – it couldn't be better. There are eight individually styled rooms with super-king-sized beds, and guests are encouraged to stay for a minimum of two nights.

Millers at the Anchor Porlock Weir TA24 8PB ℘ 01643 862753 ⌂ www.millersuk.com/anchor. The inn has been providing rooms and hospitality for over two centuries, and is an extraordinary place, crammed with books, paintings and antiquities. It even has a billiards room. Tariffs are per person, so it can work out quite expensive for couples, but prices vary according to the size of the room and the view. Note that the restaurant is closed on Mondays and Tuesdays.

New Place Bossington Lane, Porlock TA24 8ET ℘ 01643 862321 ⌂ www.newplace-exmoor.com. This is accommodation with a difference. Heather Elmhirst specialises in offering 'rest and recuperation, with an opportunity to give yourself space and to nourish your spirit'. The large Victorian house is hidden from the road amid peaceful grounds. The vegetable garden provides the home-cooked vegetarian or vegan meals which are available on request, and resident chickens supply eggs.

The Old Rectory Hotel Martinhoe EX31 4QT ℘ 01598 763368 ⌂ www.oldrectoryhotel. co.uk ⊙ closed Oct–Apr. The owners, Huw Rees and Sam Prosser, have created the ultimate in country house ambience. Awarded the accolade 'The Best Small Hotel in England' by Visit England in 2014, the Old Rectory is set in three acres of gardens with its own river (otters visit in April). There is every inducement to spend all day there if it weren't for beautiful, hilly Exmoor on the doorstep. 'Guests pay for the exclusivity', Sam told me. The excellent home-cooked meals are at a set time and for guests only. Full- or half-board is the only option and no under-14s are allowed. There are 11 rooms in total, eight in the main house and three in the coach house; some rooms have both bath and shower. The hotel generally has full occupancy in the summer so book well in advance.

Rockford Inn Nr Brendon EX35 6PT ℘ 01598 741214 ⊘ www.therockfordinn.co.uk. An irresistible place for walkers, allowing you to take the footpath along the East Lyn River from Lynmouth, have a comfortable stay in this delightful rural inn hidden among the trees in a deep valley, and then continue to Oare and beyond. It has the advantage of having one single room, as well as the usual doubles. Special off-season rates available.

Tarr Farm Inn TA22 9QA ℘ 01643 851507 ⊘ www.tarrfarm.co.uk. You don't expect such a rewarding place so close to Exmoor's most popular attraction. They manage to cater for the large number of families that amble in during the day, whilst converting to a classy hotel with award-winning dining and very pleasant rooms come the evening. Dogs are allowed in some rooms (for an extra charge), but no children under the age of ten. This is one of Exmoor's most popular shooting hotels.

White Horse Inn Exford TA24 7PY ℘ 01643 831229 ⊘ www.exmoor-whitehorse.co.uk. Exford makes an excellent base for exploring central Exmoor, and the White Horse Inn is set up to help visitors get the most out of the moor. They even employ their own guide and the Exmoor Safari company operates from here. There are 28 comfortable en-suite rooms, some of which allow dogs (for an extra charge).

B&Bs

Coombe Farm Countisbury EX35 6NF ℘ 01598 741236 ⊘ www.brendonvalley.co.uk/coombe_farm ⊙ Mar – end Nov. Coombe Farm rears Ruby Red Devon cattle and Exmoor horn sheep and the 17th-century stone-built farmhouse is as authentically Devon as the animals. The location is about as good as you can get as a base for exploring the coast and rivers of west Exmoor. Four affordable rooms of different sizes including single; no dogs allowed inside the house.

Glen Lodge Hawkcombe, Porlock TA24 8LN ℘ 01643 863371 ⊘ www.glenlodge.net. A splendid Victorian country house set in 21 acres of beautiful gardens high on a hill overlooking Porlock. Hosts David and Meryl Slater bring both elegance and hominess to this lovely place, the five stylishly decorated rooms are comfortable, breakfasts are sumptuous and multi-talented Meryl's evening meals (by request and with local ingredients) are an extra treat. For the energetic, there are also Fitness Weekends with a professional instructor.

Millslade House Hotel Brendon EX35 6PS ℘ 01598 741322 ⊘ www.millslade.co.uk. An unpretentious country hotel in this lovely valley abounding in good pubs and tea gardens – and footpaths. Five reasonably priced double rooms, dog-friendly, bed and breakfast (no main meals). They also have a self-catering cottage.

North Walk House North Walk, Lynton EX35 6HJ ℘ 01598 753372 ⊘ www.northwalkhouse.co.uk. The little lane that calls itself North Walk is one of the joys of Lynton; it leads to the cliff path which in turn leads to the Valley of Rocks. The very hospitable Ian and Sarah Downing greet arriving visitors with delicious cakes served in the cosy lounge or on the sun terrace, and the excellent breakfasts and optional dinners are cooked on the Aga.

Ian and Sarah are members of Slow Food UK, so ingredients are organic and locally sourced, and guests are seated around one large table, which is what I like: I have never had a dull conversation while staying at North Walk House! Dinner is always available if booked in advance and is generally provided on Mondays, Wednesdays, Fridays and Saturdays. There are six rooms (one is dog-friendly) and a **self-catering**, dog-friendly studio apartment for two people. See advert in fourth colour section.

Tudor Cottage Bossington TA24 8HQ ✐ 01643 862255 ✆ www.tudorcottage.net. West Country villages don't come more charming than Bossington, with its squat thatched cottages, nor accommodation as cosy as the 15th-century Tudor Cottage. There are three modern rooms – two double, one twin/super king – and the village is a perfect base for a peaceful getaway. The cottage has a comfortable (small) lounge for guests, breakfasts are cooked on the Aga, and local knowledge is dispensed by the hospitable owners Ash and Anne Shaw. Evening meals are available on request (and they are licensed); and, for those walking the South West Coast Path which passes through the village, luggage transfers can be arranged.

Twitchen Farm Challacombe EX31 4TT ✐ 01598 763568 ✆ www.twitchen.co.uk. Economically priced accommodation on this family-run farm with a good choice of rooms (eight) in the farmhouse and stone barn, including one that is wheelchair accessible and others that are dog-friendly. And if you want to bring your horse, there is stabling. Sisters Helen and Jaye provide delicious breakfasts with mostly organic produce, and for meals the Black Venus pub is just a short walk across the fields.

Self-catering

Cloud Farm Doone Valley EX35 6NU ✐ 01598 741278 ✆ www.cloudfarmcamping.co.uk. The farm owns three self-catering cottages in the Doone Valley overlooking Badgeworthy Water, and one at the Lorna Doone Farm at Malmsmead. This sleeps six, whilst the others at Cloud Farm vary from two to six.

Hindon Organic Farm Nr Bratton TA24 8SH ✐ 01643 705244 ✆ www.hindonfarm.co.uk. This 500-acre organic farm in a peaceful location between Minehead and Porlock has one self-catering cottage, and three bedrooms in the main house for **B&B** guests, who can indulge in the home-cooked breakfasts derived from the farm's Gloucester Old Spot pigs and fruit from the garden. Dogs may stay for an extra charge. There is a hot tub in the garden, and it's just a short walk to Selworthy or the South West Coast Path.

Martinhoe Manor Woody Bay EX31 4QX ✐ 01598 763424 ✆ www.martinhoemanor.co.uk. The former manor was converted to a hotel in 1885 by Colonel Benjamin Lake, who had grand plans for the area (page 138). It has been reconverted into eight two-room apartments, set in one of the most stunning locations imaginable: 26 private acres and access to the beach (though it's a steep descent) with both rock pools and sand, plus a waterfall and a part natural, part manmade swimming pool. Guests provide their own linen.

Camping & glamping

Cloud Farm Camping Doone Valley EX35 6NU ✆ 01598 741278 🖥 www.
cloudfarmcamping.co.uk. Three riverside fields in an absolutely beautiful location. The
facilities are fairly basic however. A camper's tip: the closer you are to the river, the less sun
you'll have in this shady valley.

Leeford Farm Riverside Camping Brendon EX35 6PS ✆ 01598 741231. A peaceful
location next to the East Lyn River and within easy reach of Brendon with its pub and tea
garden. No-frills camping, but there are hot showers, camp fires are allowed, and the farmer
(Ray) supplies firewood and conversation on a daily basis.

Westermill Exford TA24 7NJ ✆ 01643 831238 🖥 www.westermill.com. A large but
secluded riverside campsite in the heart of Exmoor, on a working farm which primarily rears
Aberdeen Angus cattle as well as sheep. There is stabling for your own horse, plenty of room
for your dog, and you can fish in the river. The site is run sustainably with solar-powered hot
water and a wood-chip biomass boiler. The farm shop stocks essential supplies plus their
own high-quality meat products and free-range eggs.

West Lynch Country House Lynch, Allerford TA24 8HJ ✆ 01643 862800
🖥 www.lynchcountryhouse.co.uk. This is an amazing former country estate, built at the turn
of the century in Arts & Crafts style, in spacious grounds within the National Trust area. The
gardens are a joy in themselves, seven acres of unusual plants and shrubs with the extra bonus
of a lake. The six apartments sleep between two and eight people. Electricity, including heat,
is charged extra.

Westland Farm Bratton Fleming, Barnstaple EX31 4SH ✆ 01598 763301
🖥 www.westlandfarm.co.uk. Despite its address this small farm is close to
Blackmoor Gate, so really handy for west Exmoor. They have a terrific variety of
glamping possibilities: a Mongolian yurt, which sleeps six, a shepherd's hut (appropriate,
on this sheep farm) which sleeps two, and a Drover's Hut to accommodate five or six
which is roomy enough to cook inside. There are also conventional tent pitches if you
want to bring your own or **B&B** in the farmhouse. Guests can collect their own breakfast
eggs from the hen coop, and there's a nearby shop selling fresh produce that's open
seven days a week.

6 MINEHEAD, DUNSTER & THE EASTERN FRINGES OF EXMOOR
Hotels

Cutthorne Luckwell Bridge, Wheddon Cross TA24 7EW ✆ 01643 831255
🖥 www.cutthorne.co.uk. An all-inclusive retreat for those wanting to get away from it all,
with three en-suite rooms in the house, and two separate cottages with meals (including
home-grown vegetables) taken in the house. Dogs and horses welcome for an additional
charge. Special deals for longer stays.

Swain House Boutique B&B 48 Swain St, Watchet TA23 0AG ✆ 01984 631038
🖱 www.swain-house.com. More hotel than B&B despite its name, this was once a shop, so you mustn't mind being on view as you eat your breakfast – though you should be too busy chatting, since guests sit at one big table. In every way this is a hotel with a difference, with stylish modern furnishings in the four double rooms and amazing bathrooms with deep, luxurious baths. Located right in the middle of Watchet, it is convenient for the town and railway, so you could happily stay here without a car.

B&Bs

Beverleigh B&B Beacon Rd, Minehead TA24 5SE ✆ 01643 708450 🖱 www.beverleigh. co.uk. An Edwardian house set in a gorgeous garden in the North Hill area, away from the razzmatazz of seaside Minehead. Lovely rooms – one has a four-poster bed – with views over Minehead and the sea. There are miles of North Hill footpaths on the doorstep and if you're about to embark on the South West Coast Path, it's an encouraging downhill walk to the 'Hands Sculpture'. Leo and Janna will do luggage (and people) transfers, too.
Burnells Gardens Knowle Lane, nr Dunster TA24 6TX ✆ 01643 822045 or 07796 833183 🖱 www.burnellsgardens.moonfruit.com. This homely and welcoming farm has just two rooms (not en-suite but the smart bathroom is nearby and bathrobes are provided). Though the rooms are small they are beautifully equipped and decorated. It's very much a working farm with animals part of the scenery and breakfast conversation. This place specialises in welcoming dogs: Libby will dog-sit or dog-walk on request for a small extra charge, and you can also bring your own horse. The farm is very near Dunster and Minehead but hidden away down a narrow lane (an ability to drive in reverse is a definite advantage!).
Langtry Country House Washford, Watchet TA23 0NT ✆ 01984 641200
🖱 www.langtrycountryhouse.co.uk. The owner, Susan, is a Cordon Bleu cook so the book-in-advance dinners should be part of the treat of staying here (bring your own wine since they are unlicensed). The house is as elegant inside as out, as are the three large bedrooms which have lovely views over the Quantocks. Cream teas and homemade cakes are on offer daily for residents and Thursday to Sunday for non-residents.
Streamcombe Farm Dulverton TA22 9SA ✆ 01398 323775 🖱 www.streamcombefarm. co.uk. It's all happening here! Karen and Ian Jarmarkier not only own a notable B&B, but Ian runs weekly one-day cookery workshops and provides delectable evening meals (not on Sunday or Wednesday) for guests. The three luxury bedrooms are in a converted barn, which has its own entrance and a cosy lounge with wood-burning stove. Meals, which include Ian's home-baked sourdough bread, are taken in the conservatory.
Town Mills 1 High St, Dulverton TA22 9HB ✆ 01398 323124 🖱 www.townmillsdulverton. co.uk. This converted mill house, next to the river yet right in Dulverton, has six spacious rooms and hosts are Charles and Alison, whose care extends to a carafe of white port in each bedroom!

Self-catering

Railway Cottage Williton TA4 4LW ✆ 01823 431622 ⊘ www.lavenderhillholidays.
co.uk. Do modern children still want to be engine drivers? If so this is for them or their
grandfathers, but anyone fascinated by the whole heritage of steam will relish staying
so close to the West Somerset Steam Railway in this former ganger's cottage. It has been
refurbished with an eye on luxury, and even has its own hot tub. The Railway Cottage sleeps
six in three bedrooms, has two bathrooms, a large garden and can accommodate dogs.
Riverside Cottage Brompton Regis TA22 9NT ✆ 01398 371366 ⊘ www.pulhamsmill.co.uk.
Set deep in a valley is this old mill, whose buildings have been converted into a café, craft shop
and self-catering cottage. Riverside Cottage is a former shippon (cowhouse) and has been
carefully converted by its owners Ian Mawby and Pauline Clements. It has one double and two
twin bedrooms; many of the items here were made by Ian, a furniture maker.
West Withy Farm Upton TA4 2JH ✆ 01398 371322 ⊘ www.exmoor-cottages.com. Ian
and Lorena Mabbutt offer far more than self-catering in their two barn conversions (which
sleep a total of nine). Their organic vegetable garden produces enough, in season, for each
guest to receive a veg box; the welcome pack includes homemade jam, eggs and anything
else that the farm has produced. Children can collect eggs from the free-range chickens, pick
their own vegetables, or give the pigs a special scratch behind the ear. But what makes West
Withy Farm unique is that it is the Exmoor telescope hire base for Dark Sky Telescope Hire and
where Seb Jay bases himself when he's in Exmoor.

Camping

Streamcombe Farm Dulverton TA22 9SA ✆ 01398 323775 ⊘ www.exmoorgreenandwild.
co.uk. There's a wide choice of sites here. Nearest the farmhouse is the Paddock, properly set
up with good loos and hot showers; the Woodland Combe has more simple tent pitches next
to the stream; and if you're a group wanting to hang out together you can hire the whole
four-acre Wild Flower Meadow. No cars are allowed here – to reach it you cross the stream
over stepping stones. Finally there's a shepherd's hut, sleeping two, with a double bed and
wood-burning stove. The private wet room (in a stone barn) and chemical toilet are nearby,
or there's a characterful compost loo for the eco-conscious.
Willowstream Camping Timberscombe TA24 7TR ✆ 01643 841467
⊘ www.willowstreamcamping.co.uk ☉ Jul only. Somewhat eccentrically, this idyllic place
is only open for 28 days in July, but if that's when you're exploring eastern Exmoor and
looking for a quiet spot for your tent, then it's a perfect choice. Portaloo-style toilets, hot
showers and wood available to buy for campfires; no music allowed on site.

INDEX

Entries in **bold** refer to major entries; those in *italic* indicate maps.

INDEX OF ADVERTISERS

Speke's Mill Mouth Waterfall was described by J L W Page as, 'perhaps the finest cascade on the coast.'

On the western border of Exmoor, overlooking the spectacular North Devon coast, lie five fully equipped beautifully furnished luxury Safari lodges. Each lodge sleeps six, with ensuite shower and separate wash room.

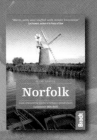